The Passion in Mark

The
PASSION
in MARK

Studies on Mark 14–16

Edited by Werner H. Kelber

---

with contributions by

John R. Donahue, S. J. Norman Perrin

Vernon K. Robbins Kim E. Dewey

Werner H. Kelber Theodore J. Weeden, Sr.

John Dominic Crossan

FORTRESS PRESS Philadelphia

Library of Congress Catalog Card Number 75-36453

ISBN 0-8006-0439-3

5407L75   Printed in U.S.A.   1-439

Bible, N.T. Mark XIV-XVI — Criticism, interpretation etc. — Addresses, essays, lectures

Contents

Abbreviations

PERIODICALS AND SERIALS

AER	*American Ecclesiastical Review*
AnBib	Analecta Biblica
AnGreg	Analecta Gregoriana
ASTI	*Annual of the Swedish Theological Institute*
Bib	*Biblica*
BibTB	*Biblical Theology Bulletin*
BiKi	*Bibel und Kirche*
BiLe	*Bibel und Leben*
BJRL	*Bulletin of the John Rylands Library*
BR	*Biblical Research*
BT	*The Bible Translator*
BZ	*Biblische Zeitschrift*
BZAW	Beihefte zur Zeitschrift für die Alttestamentliche Wissenschaft
BZNW	Beihefte zur Zeitschrift für die Neutestamentliche Wissenschaft
CBQ	*Catholic Biblical Quarterly*
CBQMS	Catholic Biblical Quarterly—Monograph Series
ChrTo	*Christianity Today*
Conc	Concilium
CTM	*Concordia Theological Monthly*
CV	*Communio Viatorum*
EKKNT	*Evangelisch-Katholischer Kommentar zum Neuen Testament*
ÉtHistPhilRel	Études d'Histoire et de Philosophie Religieuses
EvT	*Evangelische Theologie*

ExpT	*Expository Times*
FBBS	Facet Books, Biblical Series
FRLANT	Forschungen zur Religion und Literatur des Alten und Neuen Testaments
Greg	*Gregorianum*
HTR	*Harvard Theological Review*
Interpr	*Interpretation*
JBL	*Journal of Biblical Literature*
JFI	*Journal of the Folklore Institute*
JR	*Journal of Religion*
JTS	*Journal of Theological Studies*
LiMö	*Liturgie und Mönchtum*
LingBibl	*Linguistica Biblica*
NovTest	*Novum Testamentum*
NRT	*Nouvelle Revue Théologique*
NTAbh	Neutestamentliche Abhandlungen
NTS	*New Testament Studies*
NTSMS	New Testament Studies—Monograph Series
NTSup	Supplements to Novum Testamentum
OrBibLov	*Orientalia et Biblica Lovaniensia*
RB	*Revue Biblique*
RBíb	*Revista Bíblica* (Buenos Aires)
RBibIt	*Revista Biblica* (Italiana)
RHPhilRel	*Revue d'Histoire et de Philosophie Religieuses*
RHR	*Revue de l'Histoire des Religions*
RivB	*Rivista Biblica*
RocTChAT	*Roczniki Teologiczne Chrześcijańskiej Akademii Teologicznej*
RTL	*Revue Théologique de Louvain*
SBT	Studies in Biblical Theology
ScuolC	*La Scuola Cattolica*
SE	*Studia Evangelica* I, II, III (= TU 73 [1959], 87 [1964], 88 [1964])
ST	Studia Theologica
StANT	Studien zum Alten und Neuen Testament
TDig	*Theology Digest*
TDNT	Theological Dictionary of the New Testament

TS	*Theological Studies*
TU	*Texte und Untersuchungen*
TZ	*Theologische Zeitschrift*
UNT	Untersuchungen zum Neuen Testament
USQR	*Union Seminary Quarterly Review*
VD	*Verbum Domini*
VigChr	*Vigiliae Christianae*
VT	*Vetus Testamentum*
WoWa	*Wort und Wahrheit*
ZKT	*Zeitschrift für Katholische Theologie*
ZNW	*Zeitschrift für die Neutestamentliche Wissenschaft*
ZTK	*Zeitschrift für Theologie und Kirche*

KEY BOOKS AND ARTICLES

BERTRAM
Bertram, Georg. *Die Leidensgeschichte Jesu und der Christuskult.* FRLANT NF 22. Göttingen: Vandenhoeck & Ruprecht, 1922.

BEST
Best, Ernest. *The Temptation and the Passion: The Markan Soteriology.* NTSMS 2. Cambridge: Cambridge University Press, 1965.

BLASS-DEBRUNNER
Blass, Friedrich and Debrunner, Albert. *A Greek Grammar of the New Testament.* Translated and revised from 19th German ed. by Robert W. Funk. Chicago: University of Chicago Press, 1961.

BULTMANN
Bultmann, Rudolf. *The History of the Synoptic Tradition.* Translated from 3d German ed. by John Marsh. New York: Harper & Row, 1963.

DIBELIUS
Dibelius, Martin. *Botschaft und Geschichte.* Edited by Günther Bornkamm. Vol. 1: *Zur Evangelienforschung.* Tübingen: J. C. B. Mohr [P. Siebeck], 1953.

DONAHUE
Donahue, John R. *Are You the Christ? The Trial Narrative in the Gospel of Mark.* SBL Dissertation Series 10. Missoula, Mont.: University of Montana, 1973.

DORMEYER   Dormeyer, Detlev. *Die Passion Jesu als Verhal-*
                 tensmodell. NTAbh NF 11. Münster: Aschen-
                 dorff, 1974.

DOUDNA   Doudna, John C. *The Greek of the Gospel of*
                 Mark. JBL MS 12. Philadelphia: Society of
                 Biblical Literature, 1961.

HAWKINS   Hawkins, John C. *Horae Synopticae. Contribu-*
                 tions to the Study of the Synoptic Problem. 3d
                 ed. Grand Rapids, Mich.: Baker Book House,
                 1968.

KELBER   Kelber, Werner H. *The Kingdom in Mark. A*
                 New Place and a New Time. Philadelphia:
                 Fortress Press, 1974.

LINNEMANN   Linnemann, Eta. *Studien zur Passionsgeschichte.*
                 FRLANT 102. Göttingen: Vandenhoeck &
                 Ruprecht, 1970.

MARXSEN   Marxsen, Willi. *Mark the Evangelist.* Translated
                 by Roy A. Harrisville et al. Nashville, Tenn.:
                 Abingdon Press, 1969.

NEIRYNCK   Neirynck, Frans. *Duality in Mark. Contributions*
                 to the Study of the Markan Redaction. Biblio-
                 theca Ephemeridum Theologicarum Lovanien-
                 sium 31. Leuven/Louvain: Leuven University
                 Press, 1972.

PERRIN   Perrin, Norman. "Towards an Interpretation of the
                 Gospel of Mark." *Christology and a Modern*
                 Pilgrimage. Edited by Hans Dieter Betz. Clare-
                 mont, Calif.: New Testament Colloquium,
                 1971. Pp. 1–78.

SCHENK   Schenk, Wolfgang. *Der Passionsbericht nach*
                 Markus. Gütersloh: Gerd Mohn, 1974.

SCHENKE   Schenke, Ludger. *Studien zur Passionsgeschichte*
                 des Markus. Tradition und Redaktion in
                 Markus 14, 1–42. Forschung zur Bibel 4.
                 Würzburg: Echter Verlag, 1971.

TAYLOR   Taylor, Vincent. *The Gospel According to St.*
                 Mark. 2d ed. London: Macmillan, 1966.

TURNER Turner, Cuthbert H. "Marcan Usage: Notes, Critical and Exegetical, on the Second Gospel." *JTS* 25 (1924), 377–86; 26 (1925), 12–20, 145–56, 225–40; 27 (1926), 58–62; 28 (1927), 9–30, 349–62; 29 (1928), 275–89, 346–61.

WEEDEN Weeden, Theodore J. *Mark—Traditions in Conflict.* Philadelphia: Fortress Press, 1971.

WREDE Wrede, William. *The Messianic Secret.* Translated by J. C. G. Greig. Greenwood, S.C.: The Attic Press, 1971.

CONTRIBUTORS

John R. Donahue, S.J., associate professor of New Testament, Vanderbilt University, Nashville, Tennessee

Vernon K. Robbins, associate professor of Religious Studies and the Classics, University of Illinois, Urbana-Champaign

Werner H. Kelber, assistant professor of Biblical Studies, Rice University, Houston, Texas

Norman Perrin, professor of New Testament and Biblical Theology, University of Chicago

Kim E. Dewey, doctoral candidate, Divinity School, University of Chicago

Theodore J. Weeden, Sr., professor of New Testament, St. Bernard's Seminary, Rochester, New York

John Dominic Crossan, professor of Biblical Studies, DePaul University, Chicago

PREFACE

The seven authors of this collection of essays on the Mkan Passion Narrative share the conviction that the key to Mk 14–16 lies in a theological interpretation of the text. This marks a distinct departure from a long-standing tradition of reading the Passion Narrative as a prime source for the political and legal history of the time of Jesus.

While the essays vary in their utilization of pre-Mkan and non-Mkan material, they belong methodologically in the broad area of redaction, composition, and literary criticism.

Although different authors are bound to express at times differing views on a subject as controversial as the Passion Narrative, it will not escape the reader that there emerges from these essays a remarkably coherent view of the theology of Mk's Passion Narrative.

I wish to express my appreciation to Rice University for a research grant which enabled me to carry out my duties as editor. I owe a special word of gratitude to Professor Niels C. Nielsen, chairman of the Department of Religious Studies, Rice University, who encouraged this project throughout and supported my work in every way possible. I am very grateful to Mrs. Josephine Monaghan for her extremely competent typing of a difficult manuscript. Finally, I wish to thank my wife, Mary Ann, for her assistance at every stage of this work.

Rice University
September 1975   WERNER H. KELBER

I.

Introduction:
From Passion Traditions
to Passion Narrative

John R. Donahue, S.J.

Since the advent of source, form, and redaction criticism, the Synoptic Gospels have been an arena for investigation into the sayings and deeds of Jesus, the transmission and alteration of the Jesus tradition by the early Church, and the theological concerns of the individual Evangelists. Although the Passion Narratives form the climax of the Gospels and occupy roughly fifteen per cent of the Gospel tradition, Gospel research has been directed mainly toward the pre-passion parts of the Gospels. Varied reasons explain this situation. At the end of the last century M. Kähler enunciated what became a dogma in Gospel research, that the Gospels are Passion Narratives with extended introductions.[1] Later, M. Dibelius, one of the founders of form criticism, held that the story of the passion was the longest extended block of tradition, prior to the formation of the Gospels.[2] The categories developed by the form critics such as apophthegm, dominical saying, miracle story, and legend were not easily applied to the Passion Narrative, and form criticism increasingly focused on the *teaching* of Jesus. Finally,

---

1. M. Kähler, *The So-Called Historical Jesus and the Historic, Biblical Christ*, trans. and ed. C. E. Braaten (Philadelphia: Fortress Press, 1964; 1st German ed. 1892), 80 n. 11.
2. M. Dibelius, *From Tradition to Gospel*, trans. B. L. Woolf, rev. 2d ed. (New York: Scribner's, n.d.), 180.

not only was the Passion Narrative seen as the most traditional and the most extended block of pre-Synoptic material, but it was also viewed as the most historical part of the Gospel.[3] By and large the Passion Narrative was not regarded as being theologically influenced by the early Church or the Evangelists.

In contrast to earlier neglect, the last decade has witnessed an explosion in studies on the growth of the passion traditions. Mk's Passion Narrative is now seen as much a product of his literary and theological creativity as the first thirteen chapters of the Gospel. The present introductory essay seeks to describe the major contributions to the study of the Mkan Passion Narrative. However, since cross and resurrection were a subject of early Christian preaching and were re-presented in ritual even prior to Mk, studies on these pre-Mkan settings for the Passion Narrative will also have to be surveyed. Finally, we will indicate some ways in which redaction criticism offers a valuable key for unlocking the theological riches of the Mkan Passion Narrative.

1. THE PASSION IN PREACHING AND WORSHIP

Dibelius, who wrote on the Passion Narratives over a period of thirty-five years, was a pioneer in the discovery of the use of Old Testament allusions as a creative matrix in constructing the Passion Narrative. In line with his conviction that preaching was at the basis of New Testament traditions, Dibelius wrote:

> Long before the existence of the books of the Gospels, and long before any connected account of the Passion, the teachers of the community had access to these sources [the Old Testament] and the preachers dealt with these "texts."[4]

Old Testament texts served a double function. On the one hand, they helped to show that Jesus died "in accordance with the scriptures" (1 Cor 15:3); on the other hand, they exerted a formative influence on the

---

3. For extra-biblical references to Jesus' crucifixion, see Josephus, *Ant* 18, 63–64; Tacitus, *Annales* 15, 44; *The Babylonian Talmud*, trans. I. Epstein (London: Soncino Press, 1935), V, 281. For an evaluation of extra-biblical data, see J. Klausner, *Jesus of Nazareth*, trans. H. Danby (New York: Macmillan, 1925), 17–60; X. Léon-Dufour, "Passion [Récits de la]," *Dictionnaire de la Bible, Supplement* VI, 1421–1424.

4. DIBELIUS, "Die alttestamentlichen Motive in der Leidensgeschichte des Petrus- und des Johannes-Evangeliums," 223 (my own translation).

tradition since stories were composed to illustrate Old Testament allusions.[5]

Subsequent to Dibelius, C H. Dodd proposed the theory that collections of early Christian *testimonia*, mainly citations of Ps 22 and Isa 52:13–53:12, served as an apology for the passion and also provided a substructure for Christian theology.[6] J. Jeremias and C. Maurer noted the many allusions to Isa 52:13–53:12 in the Passion Narrative and argued that the figure of the suffering Servant depicted in Isaiah was applied to Jesus.[7] The most complete examination of the use of the Old Testament in the passion apologetic is found in the often overlooked work of B. Lindars, *New Testament Apologetic*.[8]

While admitting that the kernel of the Christian kerygma was the resurrection (Acts 3:13b–15a; 4:10–11; 5:30; 10:39–40; 13:27–30), Lindars states that it was impossible to speak of the resurrection without attaching some positive significance to the death.[9] The earliest passion apologetic developed from a reflection on Isa 53:12 (LXX), "His soul was 'delivered up' (*paredothē*) to death." The use of *paradidonai* in Mk (9:31; 10:33; 14:21) reflects this use of Isa 53:12. The early Church had not only to cope with a suffering Messiah, it had to find a warrant for Jesus' shameful death (cf. Deut 21:22–23) and for the rejection by his own people.[10] Lindars further observes that Isa 53:3 (LXX), "He was despised and rejected by men" (*ētimasthē*, but in some versions *exoudenōmenos*), has influenced the saying on the rejection (*exoudenēthē*) of the Son of Man in Mk 9:12. The terms

5. Ibid., 224–47. According to Dibelius, the Passion Narrative does not rest on eyewitnesses who took careful note of the passion events, but on teachers who read the psalms and prophets as sources for an understanding of the passion of Jesus.

6. C. H. Dodd, *According to the Scriptures* (New York: Scribner's, 1953), 72, 92–93, 127.

7. J. Jeremias and W. Zimmerli, *The Servant of God*, SBT 20 (London: SCM Press, 1965); J. Jeremias, *"pais theou,"* TDNT V, 654–717; C. Maurer, "Knecht Gottes und Sohn Gottes im Passionsbericht des Markusevangeliums," *ZTK* 50 (1953), 1–38. The debate subsequent to these publications is not whether Isa 53 influenced the Passion Narrative, but whether the *figure* of the suffering Servant did and whether Jesus conceived of himself as the Servant.

8. B. Lindars, *New Testament Apologetic* (Philadelphia: Westminster Press, 1961). Neither LINNEMANN, SCHENKE, SCHENK, nor DORMEYER cites this study.

9. Ibid., 75.

10. Ibid., 76: "It must be remembered that the rejection of the Lord's Messiah by *his own people* was a wholly new constituent in the picture, even where the death of the Messiah was visualized."

exoudeneisthai and *exoutheneisthai* then suggested reference to other Old Testament texts by equating Jesus with the rejected stone of Ps 118:22.[11] Lindars thus shows that it was not simply *the* figure of the Servant in Isa 53 which influenced the formation of the passion traditions, but that reflection on specific texts and on other texts linked through word association enabled the early Christians to develop a whole textual network of Old Testament reflections on the passion. Early Christian exegesis appears much like the *pesher* mode of interpretation practiced by the Qumran community.[12]

The second major body of texts discussed by Lindars are the psalms. In the Mkan Passion Narrative clear references to psalms are found in the following places:

14:18	Ps 41:9	15:24	Ps 22:18
14:34	Ps 42:6, 11;	15:29	Ps 22:7; 109:25
	43:5	15:34	Ps 22:1
15:23	Ps 69:21	15:36	Ps 69:21

References to Ps 22 show a marked concentration in the crucifixion account (Mk 15:20b–41), so much so that Lindars has called this psalm "a quarry for pictorial details in writing the story of the Passion."[13] Other psalms explain different aspects of the passion: crucifixion as the method of death (Ps 34), Jesus' table fellowship with a betrayer (Pss 41, 69, and 109), and "above all the need to account for the collapse of the whole final demonstration of Jesus, from the cleansing of the temple to the death on the cross (Ps 69)."[14]

In addition to Lindars's work on explicit allusions to the Old Testament, L. Ruppert's studies present a comprehensive analysis of the motif of the suffering Just One in the Old Testament and its influence in the

---

11. Ibid., 81–84. Cf. also N. Perrin, "The Use of *(para)didonai* in Connection with the Passion of Jesus in the New Testament," *Der Ruf Jesu und die Antwort der Gemeinde*, ed. E. Lohse et al. (Göttingen: Vandenhoeck & Ruprecht, 1970), 204–12; reprinted in *A Modern Pilgrimage in New Testament Christology* (Philadelphia: Fortress Press, 1974), 94–103. Perrin proposes a different picture of the use of Isa 53:12 than Lindars.

12. Elements of the *pesher* mode of exegesis are: (a) freedom with the text, (b) the actualization of the text in terms of the interpreter's own experience, and (c) the tendency to make a historic narrative of the text. See Lindars, *Apologetic*, 15–17, and H. Ringgren, *The Faith of Qumran* (Philadelphia: Fortress Press, 1963), 7–11.

13. Lindars, *Apologetic*, 90.

14. Ibid., 110.

New.[15] This motif, found mainly in the psalms of lamentation, portrays a figure in much the same situation as Jesus in the passion. Enemies conspire to kill him (Mk 14:1; Pss 31:4; 35:4; 38:12; 71:10), friends betray him (Mk 14:18, 43; Ps 55:14–21), false witnesses arise (Mk 14:56, 57, 59; Pss 27:12; 35:11; 109:2), the Just One remains silent (Mk 14:61; 15:5; Pss 38:14–16; 39:9), and enemies mock him (Mk 15:20, 29; Pss 22:7; 31:11; 35:19–25; 69:20; 109:25).[16] Ruppert's emphasis on the motif of the suffering Just One is not unique. What is new in his work is the description of the various transformations of the motif. The fourth Servant Song (Isa 52:13–53:12) portrays the suffering prophet. The suffering of the pious in Daniel (11:33–35; 12:1–3), persecutions of the Qumran community (1QH 2:20–30; 3:37–4:4; 15:14–17), and, close to the New Testament period, the sufferings of the Righteous One in the Wisdom of Solomon (2:12–20; 5:1–7)—all represent adaptations and appropriations of the motif, under the influence of historical circumstance and eschatological urgency.[17] In casting many of the details of the passion of Jesus in the mold of the suffering Just One, early Christian "scribes" and preachers were adapting the motif to their own experience as various other groups had done before.

Just as Dibelius was the forerunner of those who studied the influence of the Old Testament on the Passion Narrative, so too, did he stress the eschatological dimension of the account. He writes:

> It was not in the healings, or in the parables, . . . but in the Passion that the eschatological event manifested itself which was to point immediately toward the turning of the ages (*Weltenwende*). The Passion is the beginning of the end time.[18]

Eschatological urgency was a force in the development of a Passion Narrative, for in the passion the events themselves were the message of

15. L. Ruppert, *Der leidende Gerechte. Eine motivgeschichtliche Untersuchung zum Alten Testament und zwischentestamentlichen Judentum,* Forschung zur Bibel 5 (Würzburg: Echter Verlag, 1972), and *Der leidende Gerechte und seine Feinde. Eine Wortfelduntersuchung,* Forschung zur Bibel 6 (Würzburg: Echter Verlag, 1973), and *Jesus als der leidende Gerechte,* Stuttgarter Bibelstudien 59 (Stuttgart: Katholisches Bibelwerk, 1972). The last work is henceforth cited as *Jesus.*

16. Ruppert, *Jesus,* 16–18; DORMEYER, 249.

17. Ruppert, *Jesus,* 16–22.

18. DIBELIUS, "Das historische Problem der Leidensgeschichte," 249 (my own translation).

salvation, while in other parts of the Gospels the events were illustrative of the kerygma.[19]

Eschatology and the influence of the Old Testament merge in the use of Zechariah in the passion traditions. Just as Isa 53 and the psalms of the suffering Just One provided a storehouse for reflection on the suffering of Jesus, so were the Messianic and apocalyptic texts of Zechariah considered suitable for viewing the passion as the prelude to a new age. Jesus' entry into Jerusalem (Mk 11:1–10) alludes to the coming of the Prince of Peace (Zech 9:9–10). The blood of the covenant (Mk 14:24) and the betrayal for money (Mk 14:11) refer to Zech 9:11 and 11:12. The explicit citation of Zech 13:7 as scripture in Mk 14:27 shows that Zechariah not only influenced the pre-Mkan tradition, but also its final redaction.[20]

The Old Testament, therefore, was a creative agent in the formation of passion traditions. In turning to the Old Testament text as their sacred text and the source of their understanding of their salvation history, the early Christians were in effect creating a new sacred text and writing their own account of salvation history—a history which they saw as both fulfillment of the past salvation history and the beginning of a new stage in this same history.

Not only was the death of Jesus preached by early Christians, it was celebrated in the worship of the community. Prime evidence in the New Testament for such a setting is the Lord's Supper *paradosis* of 1 Cor 11:23–26, as well as the hymnic fragments[21] of Phil 2:6–11, Col 1:15–20, 1 Tim 3:16, and the evocation of Jesus as a paradigm for confession in 1 Tim 6:13. G. Bertram suggested that the Passion Narrative was formed as a cult legend to celebrate the victory of the hero whom the community worshiped and with whom they were to identify.[22] In the trial before Pilate, for example, the "wonder" (*thaumazein*) of Pilate (15:5) does not recount history but expresses the religious awe the believer should have before the Lord.[23] The use of *egō*

19. Ibid., 250.
20. For DORMEYER, 112, Mk 14:27a is tradition and 14:27b redaction. SCHENKE, 388, likewise considers 14:27b redactional.
21. Cf. J. T. Sanders, *The New Testament Christological Hymns*, NTSMS 15 (Cambridge: Cambridge University Press, 1971), 58–87, 94–95.
22. BERTRAM, 5–6.
23. Ibid., 65–71.

eimi in Mk 14:62 makes the trial into the narration of an epiphany of the Lord to the worshiping community.[24]

G. Schille[25] refined and revised the insights of Bertram. He suggests that the earliest form of the passion traditions arose from the baptismal liturgy (cf. Rom 6:3–6) reflecting a structure of descent, death, and exaltation. Crucial to his reconstruction is the indication in 1 Cor 11:23–26 that the *agape* was a night celebration, commemorating "the night when he was betrayed." By analogy, the Mkan "night" of 14:17–15:1 was formed as a narrative of the passion events from a cultic perspective.[26] Schille then turns to the time designations of the crucifixion account (15:1, 25, 33, 34) and argues that they reflect a liturgical practice of three-hour periods of watching and prayer (14:38) on a day following the commemoration of the supper which ended with a cockcrow (14:72). A final block of pre-Mkan cultic tradition is found in the "grave legends" of 15:42–47 and 16:1–6. Time and place references (15:42; 16:1–2) reflect an early Christian Easter celebration. Mk's redaction of these traditions consists in the insertion of connecting phrases and in the addition of the Anointing (14:3–9), the preparations for the Supper (14:12–16) and the Sanhedrin trial (14:53–65). While Schille's insights call attention to possible cultic references within the Passion Narrative, the uniformity of style which permeates the narrative as well as the relationship of the narrative to the rest of the Gospel militate against the picture of Mk as simply a collector of cultic traditions.[27]

While the examination of the setting of the passion traditions in preaching and worship does not explain the final form of the narrative, it does open a window on important developments of early Christianity. The growth of the passion traditions is a miniature of the growth of early Christianity as a self-conscious religious group. New texts are formed, symbols (e.g., the suffering Just One) are transformed. Sacred

24. Ibid., 55–61.

25. G. Schille, "Das Leiden des Herren. Die evangelische Passionstradition und ihr 'Sitz im Leben,' " *ZTK* 52 (1955), 161–205.

26. Ibid., 177–81.

27. DORMEYER, 15–16; R. Scroggs and K. I. Groff ("Baptism in Mark: Dying and Rising with Christ," *JBL* 92 [1973], 531–48) suggest that 14:51–52, the young man leaving the linen cloth, and 16:5, a young man dressed in a white robe, reflect the baptismal practice of stripping off old garments and putting on new garments symbolic of identification with the suffering and rising Jesus.

stories are created which speak to the present experience of a group, but root this experience in the time of the beginnings. A world of meaning is created to express the community's consciousness that it belongs to a new time.[28]

2. A PRE-MARKAN PASSION NARRATIVE?

In addition to the recognition of the influence of the Old Testament and liturgical traditions, there has been a general consensus concerning the existence of a connected narrative behind Mk's passion section.[29] This thesis has sometimes been asserted almost in the face of evidence to the contrary. Dibelius, for example, observed a thematically imbalanced Passion Narrative: there are insertions and expansions (14:2–10, 12–16, 32–42, 55–65); Jesus was arrested before the feast, which conflicts with the tradition of a passover meal with the disciples; 14:28 presupposes a resurrection appearance and is in tension with the Empty Tomb narration in 16:1–8. Still, Dibelius affirms the existence of a connected pre-Mkan Passion Narrative.[30] R. Bultmann postulated a four-stage growth of the tradition: (a) a kerygmatic tradition of Jesus' suffering and death, (b) a short historical narrative of the arrest, condemnation, and execution, (c) the addition of originally unconnected stories such as the Anointing and Gethsemane and (d) supplementary embellishments (e.g., the Sanhedrin trial).[31] From an analysis of the frequency of Semitisms and the presence of pericopes which interrupt the flow of the narrative (14:3–9, 22–25, 32–42; 47–52, 54, 66–72; 15:2, 6–14, 16–20, 25, 27, 31–32, 40–41) V. Taylor concluded that there was an A source and a B source. The former (not listed here) represents a straightforward account written for the Roman community and the latter (the verses above) is based on recollections of Peter.[32]

28. This suggestion of the sociological context of the growth of early Christian traditions is developed by J. G. Gager, *Kingdom and Community: The Social World of Early Christianity* (Englewood Cliffs, N.J.: Prentice-Hall, 1975), esp. 11.

29. By way of example, see R. E. Brown, *The Gospel According to John*, Anchor Bible 29A (Garden City, N.Y.: Doubleday, 1970), 787 and 789: "Critical scholars of diverse tendencies (Bultmann, Jeremias, and Taylor, to name a few) agree that the Marcan Passion Narrative is composite and that one of Mark's chief sources was an earlier consecutive account of the passion." Cf. also G. Schneider, "Das Problem einer vorkanonischen Passionserzählung," *BZ* 2 (1972), 222–44.

30. DIBELIUS, "Leidensgeschichte," 249–51, and *Tradition*, 178–217.

31. BULTMANN, 275–84.

32. TAYLOR, 653–71.

The chief arguments for a pre-Mkan account have been carefully stated by J. Jeremias.[33] He observes a resemblance between the Synoptics and Jn in their depiction of Jesus' final week in Jerusalem and an even greater agreement between Jn and Mk in the events which follow Jesus' arrest. Jeremias then postulates a four-stage development of the Passion Narrative: (1) an early kerygma much like 1 Cor 15:3b–5 and drawn up in Semitic language; (2) the *short account* beginning with the arrest; (3) the *long account* which contained in close succession such stories as the triumphal entry, the Temple cleansing, the Last Supper, Gethsemane, arrest, trial before the Sanhedrin, denial by Peter, condemnation by Pilate, crucifixion, and empty grave; (4) an expansion of the then existant narrative into the form as we now have it in our Gospels.[34]

However persuasive the agreements between Jn and Mk are for postulating a pre-Mkan Passion Narrative, certain issues must be considered which raise the question as to whether Jn may not have known the Mkan account. There are a number of places where only Mk and Jn are in verbal agreement: the ointment of pure nard (Mk 14:3; Jn 12:3); the 300 denarii Mk 14:5; Jn 12:5); Peter warming (*thermainomenos*) himself (Mk 14:54, 67; Jn 18:18, 25); Peter's going "into" the courtyard (Mk 14:54; Jn 18:15); the cry "crucify him" in the imperative (Mk 15:14; Jn 19:15); the purple robe (Mk 15:17; Jn 19:2, 5); the mention of the preparation day (Mk 15:42; Jn 19:31).[35] Secondly, it is significant that when Jn diverges from the Mkan order and presentation of material, he does so in function of his own theology. For example, Jn pictures Jesus during the arrest as possessing foreknowledge and in control of the situation (Jn 18:4–9). Furthermore, the Fourth Evangelist heightens the guilt of the Jewish officials (Jn 18:14) and dramatizes the Pilate trial (Jn 18:28–19:16) into an elaborate scenario illustrating the *krisis* or judgment which Jesus came to pronounce on the world.[36] Finally it is significant that like Mk Jn intercalates the Jewish trial (Jn 18:19–24) within the story of Peter's

33. J. Jeremias, *The Eucharistic Words of Jesus*, trans. N. Perrin, 3d ed. rev. (New York: Scribner's, 1966), 89–96.
34. Ibid., 96. Jeremias concludes, "It goes without saying that these four stages are only milestones in a much more colourful and complicated development."
35. Léon-Dufour, "Passion," 1441–1442.
36. Concerning the theology of these Johannine scenes, see Brown, *John*, 817–18, 835–36, 862–65.

denial (Jn 18:15–18, 25–27)—a technique which is characteristic of Mkan composition.[37]

With the publication in 1970 of E. Linnemann's *Studien zur Passionsgeschichte* a new stage in the study of the Mkan Passion Narrative was reached. She is the first scholar who rejects the thesis of a pre-Mkan Passion Narrative on the basis of a detailed form critical analysis of the Mkan composition. She draws a distinction between a report (*Bericht*) and an account (*Erzählung*).[38] A report consists of disconnected items, while an internal and smooth connection is essential to an account. Linnemann examines each pericope carefully for logical tensions and thematic incongruities. The arrest of Jesus (14:43–52), an exegetical bulwark for those who hold a pre-Mkan connected Passion Narrative, is selected as a test case.[39] The tension between the bystanders (14:47) and Jesus' followers described as the twelve (14:43) or the disciples (14:32) seems to presuppose differing traditions of who accompanied Jesus. The armed crowd in 14:43 does not react to the attack reported in 14:47. Jesus' saying that the crowd came to arrest him as a robber (14:48) should logically follow 14:43. Jesus is seized in 14:46, yet allowed to speak freely according to 14:48–49. In addressing these problems Linnemann suggests three distinct strata which underlie the arrest pericope: (1) a biographical apophthegm (14:43, 48, 49b), (2) a report about Judas the betrayer (14:44–46), and (3) a fragmentary note concerning the role of the disciples during passion (14:47, 50–52).[40] Since, according to Linnemann, each pericope reveals similar difficulties she concludes that the so-called Passion Narrative is a collection of independent reports (*Berichte*) rather than the rewording of a connected account (*Erzählung*). Mk, in effect, is a collector and not an author.

While Linnemann's study of the Mkan Passion Narrative began with the Gethsemane story, the massive work of L. Schenke covers 14:1–42.[41] The work represents an advance vis-à-vis Linnemann because

---

37. E. von Dobschütz, "Zur Erzählerkunst des Markus," *ZNW* 27 (1928), 193–98; DONAHUE, 58–63.
38. LINNEMANN, 45.
39. Ibid., 41–42.
40. Ibid., 68–69.
41. See SCHENKE. The author has also published a smaller work which covers 14:53–15:47: *Der gekreuzigte Christus*, Stuttgarter Bibelstudien 69 (Stuttgart: Katholisches Bibelwerk, 1974).

Schenke distinguishes tradition from redaction on the basis of a careful analysis of Mkan language. He also suggests a definite setting in life for the pre-Mkan traditions and relates the Passion Narrative to theological themes found throughout the Gospel. The pre-Mkan tradition consists of 14:3b–8, 12a, 13–16, 21b, 22b–24, 32, 33b, 34, 35a, 36–37, 38b, 40b, 42. Mkan redaction explains the remaining verses, although Schenke does not equate redaction with composition since in redactional sections Mk often brings in older material (e.g. 14:25).[42]

Like Ruppert, Schenke suggests that the suffering Just One provided the model for the oldest passion traditions.[43] The second level of tradition reflects the theology of a Hellenistic community which conceived of Jesus as a divine man and which Mk counters in his redaction. Mk 14:3–9, for example, stresses the miraculous foreknowledge of Jesus; Mk's redaction plays down this aspect of Jesus by attributing equal foreknowledge to the woman and making her association with Jesus in suffering a model of how the Gospel is to be proclaimed.[44] The addition of 14:17–21 (the prediction of betrayal) to the foreknowledge of Jesus in 14:13–16 shows that mere association with Jesus is insufficient for discipleship. If the disciple is to avoid condemnation (14:21), he must follow the way of the cross.[45] The eucharistic tradition (14:22b–24) originated in a Palestinian community but was quickly taken up by Hellenistic enthusiasm in which communion with the divinity was achieved through a ritual meal. Mk adds 14:22a and 14:25 to make the meal into a paschal meal which points to the future Kingdom and thereby counters the realized eschatology of the enthusiasts.[46] The prediction of Peter's fall (14:27, 29–31) is mostly Mkan redaction and represents simultaneously the high point of the disciples' misunderstanding and a promise of a new mode of discipleship after the resurrection (14:28).[47] Mk's redaction of the Gethsemane pericope stresses the continued "coming" of Jesus to his sleeping disciples (14:39, 41) who are meant to symbolize the Christian community to

42. SCHENKE, 302–306.
43. Ibid., 550.
44. Ibid., 110–18.
45. Ibid., 275–84.
46. Ibid., 332–47.
47. Ibid., 388–423.

whom Jesus comes as suffering Lord.[48]   Schenke thus sees extensive Mkan redaction of previous passion traditions.   He further recognizes that the Mkan redaction is designed to correct a false Christology and to encourage a particular view of true discipleship.[49]

The opinion that Mk's redaction takes place in dialogue with theologies of Hellenistic communities characterizes the work of J. Schreiber and W. Schenk.[50]   In his study of the crucifixion account (15:20b–41) Schreiber distinguishes two pre-Mkan traditions.   The first (15:20b–22a, 24, 27) characterized by the use of the historical present is closest to a historical report.[51]   The second (15:25, 26, 29a, 32c, 33, 34a, 37–38) is influenced by Jewish apocalyptic.   The darkness which covers the earth (15:33) is the pre-creational darkness (Gen 1:2).   Jesus' cry from the cross (15:37), like the voice of God in Gen 1:3, ends the rule of darkness and inaugurates the new age.   Though using motifs from Jewish apocalyptic, this tradition is anti-Jewish (the implied destruction of the Temple in 15:38) and mirrors a Christology of the hidden and revealed redeemer.   Schreiber locates this second tradition in a Hellenistic-Jewish community which has been influenced by Gnosticism.[52]   Mk builds on the second tradition and, by his additions (esp. 15:39–41), portrays the crucifixion of Jesus as an enthronement.[53]

Like Schreiber, W. Schenk devotes much space to the crucifixion narrative.   Behind it he finds a "Simon tradition" (15:20b–22a, 23a, 24, 27, 29b) and a "seven hour" apocalypse (15:25, 26, 29ac, 30, 33, 34a, 37, 38, 39).[54]   On the basis of these two strata Schenk then divides the whole Passion Narrative and postulates two traditions prior to Mk: (1) a simple narrative which has an apologetic purpose of proving the innocence of Jesus and which uses frequent Old Testament allusions, and (2) an apocalyptic tradition which represents the theology of Mk's opponents.[55]   The adherents of the apocalyptic tradition

---

48. Ibid., 525–40.
49. SCHENKE, 564, calls Mk a *Seelsorger*, i.e., a pastoral counselor.
50. See SCHENK; J. Schreiber, *Theologie des Vertrauens* (Hamburg: Furche-Verlag, 1967).
51. Schreiber, *Theologie*, 32–33, 62–66.
52. Ibid., 34–41, 66–82.
53. Ibid., 41–49, 218–43.
54. SCHENK, 24.
55. Ibid., 272–74.

held that the end time had come with the destruction of the Temple and they were living in the fullness of the new age. Mk responds to them by making 10:45 the leitmotif of his whole Gospel, by spacing portions of the apologetic tradition in such a way that it counters the apocalyptic tradition, and by adding 14:24, "my blood . . . poured out for many," as a hermeneutical key to the passion account.[56] Thus the Passion Narrative composed by Mk constitutes a call to belief in a suffering Jesus, and the centurion and the women (15:39–41) are symbols of proper discipleship and confession.

The most recent and most massive study of the Passion Narrative has been undertaken by D. Dormeyer. Due to the care with which the analysis is done and the impressive control of secondary literature, his book will become a standard reference tool for work on the Passion Narrative. Building on the work of previous authors who attempted to separate tradition and redaction in the first thirteen chapters, Dormeyer tries to construct a "redactional vocabulary" of the Passion Narrative on the basis of a statistical relationship between terms in the Passion Narrative and their frequency in tradition or redaction.[57] He then correlates word studies with analysis of style (e.g., Semitizing versus more literary Greek), and insights from form criticism and a study of different genres.[58]

After an investigation of each pericope Dormeyer concludes that the Passion Narrative is made up of three levels: T, a primitive Christian Acts of a Martyr; Rs, a secondary redaction of T, characterized by the addition of dialogue and sayings of Jesus (paschal meal, prophecy of Peter's denial); and Rmk, the final redaction by Mk.[59] T is itself a combination of influences from Jewish stories of martyrdom (e.g. 2 Mac 6:18–31; 2 Mac 7) which emphasize the *death* of the martyr and from Hellenistic Acts of martyrs which stress the conduct of the martyr before his accusers.[60] T also shows the influence of the suffering Just One motif. The redaction of T by Rs is mainly in the direction of Christology which identifies Jesus of Nazareth as the crucified and risen

56. Ibid., 275.
57. DORMEYER, 26–30.
58. Ibid., 30–56.
59. Ibid., 238–87; 288–90 present a summary of the work.
60. Ibid., 243–44.

One and states that it is in this sense that Jesus is "Messiah," the pro-claimer of the coming Kingdom.[61]   In the final redaction, Rmk uses the Son of Man title to reinterpret the Christology of Rs and to portray Jesus as judge of the end time and a model to be imitated in the interim. Rmk also introduces the anti-Temple saying of 14:58 and the splitting of the veil in 15:38.   It therefore represents a community which has separated from Judaism.[62]

Summary: The survey of different settings and traditions underlying the Mkan Passion Narrative yields a number of crucial results.   The very discovery of a complex tradition history behind the Mkan Passion Narrative casts some doubt on the validity of postulating an independent and coherent Passion Narrative prior to Mk.   The hypothesis of a pre-Mkan connected narrative, if not completely abandoned, is somewhat shaken.   There is almost universal agreement that the Anointing (14:3–9), substantial elements of the passover meal tradition (14:12–25), the prediction of denial (14:26–31), the Sanhedrin trial (14:53–65), and major elements of the crucifixion tradition (15:20b–41) have been brought to the narrative by Mk.   In addition, each pericope—whatever its original status—shows considerable Mkan redaction, and Mk is seen as responsible for the connection of pericopes, the very temporal and geographical references which transform isolated reports into a coherent narrative.

Major themes which permeate the Gospel culminate in the Passion Narrative.   The proclamation of the Kingdom (1:14–15; 14:25; 15:43), the meaning of discipleship (8:34–38; 14:8–9, 17–21, 27–31, 32–51, 54, 66–72), the relation of Jesus to Jerusalem and the Temple (11:1–20; 14:58; 15:29–30, 38), the christological question concerning the identity of Jesus (8:27–30; 14:62), the conjunction of the sufferings of Christians with that of Jesus (13:9–13; 14:32–42), the orientation toward Galilee (1:14–15; 14:28; 16:7–8), the mean-ing of "Gospel" itself (1:14–15; 14:9)—all are themes which Mk weaves into the Passion Narrative. [63]

---

61. Ibid., 262–65.
62. Ibid., 276–78, 286–87.
63. In addition to the highly technical works discussed, the following studies on the Mkan Passion Narrative should be mentioned: BEST; H. Conzelmann, "History and Theology in the Passion Narratives of the Synoptic Gospels," *Interpr* 24 (1970), 178–97; R. H. Lightfoot, *The Gospel Message of St. Mark* (Oxford: Oxford Univer-

The continuous attempts to see the pre-Mkan traditions as leaving their linguistic imprint on the present text of Mk, which can then be parceled out into half and quarter verses, are problematic. Studies of the Greek style of Mk, especially the recent work of F. Neirynck, show that the text in its final form is the product of one creative hand.[64] Analysis of language, style, and forms in Mk can show places where Mk may be working with tradition, but it may not always reveal the exact language and form of the tradition.

The suggested divisions of the Passion Narrative surveyed above not only reveal wide disagreement about almost every verse, but encourage a fragmentation of the text which rivals the attempts early in this century to divide the Pentateuchal narrative into a multitude of J's, E's, and P's. While the works surveyed are a witness to the care and thoroughness of German scholarship, they also betray a very particular understanding of redaction criticism. Since redaction criticism originated in the works of G. Bornkamm and H. Conzelmann who found the theology of Mt and Lk by studying the alterations they made in the Mkan *Vorlage*, German redaction criticism has been dominated by a desire to find pre-Mkan traditions and to see Mk's theology primarily in his editorial or redactional comments on the tradition.[65] Mk thus becomes an occasional commentator on tradition rather than master of his work.

In the following section we will make some remarks about a different conception of redaction criticism and about the emerging structuralist

sity Press, 1950); E. Lohse, *History of the Suffering and Death of Jesus Christ*, trans. M. O. Dietrich (Philadelphia: Fortress Press, 1967); M. A. Ramsey, *The Narratives of the Passion* (London: Mowbray, 1962), and "The Narratives of the Passion," *SE* II, ed. F. L. Cross, *TU* 87 (1964), 122–34; G. Schneider, *Die Passion Jesu nach den drei älteren Evangelien* (Munich: Kösel, 1973); A. Vanhoye, *Structure and Theology of the Accounts of the Passion in the Synoptic Gospels*, trans. H. Giblin (Collegeville, Minn.: Liturgical Press, 1967); G. S. Sloyan, *Jesus on Trial* (Philadelphia: Fortress Press, 1973). This last volume contains an excellent bibliography, 134–49.

64. NEIRYNCK, 37, observes that "there is a sort of homogeneity in Mark, from the wording of sentences to the composition of the gospel." See also the linguistic studies of DOUDNA, TURNER, and ZERWICK.

65. G. Bornkamm, G. Barth, and H. J. Held, *Tradition and Interpretation in Matthew*, trans. P. Scott (Philadelphia: Westminster Press, 1963); H. Conzelmann, *The Theology of St. Luke*, trans. G. Buswell (New York: Harper & Row, 1960); MARXSEN. Marxsen also finds Mkan theology by reconstructing a pre-Mkan tradition. For a survey of this type of redaction criticism, see J. Rohde, *Rediscovering the Teaching of the Evangelists*, trans. D. Barton (Philadelphia: Westminster Press, 1968).

(or semiotic) exegesis which suggest a way out of the *cul-de-sac* of finding the author's purpose only on the basis of the distinction between tradition and redaction.

3. MARK AS AUTHOR AND THEOLOGIAN

In what has now become a standard definition, N. Perrin describes redaction criticism as an effort to uncover "the theological motivation of an author as this is revealed in the collection, arrangement, editing, and modification of traditional material, and in the composition of new material or the creation of new forms within the traditions of early Christianity."[66] With this definition Perrin points out two major aspects of redaction criticism: editorial criticism, the author over against the tradition he inherits, and composition criticism: the author as master of the material whose purpose is found in the composition of material and creation of new forms. In substance, however, this definition is still weighted in favor of the earlier understanding of redaction criticism as a study of the alterations an author makes in traditional material.[67] In the years since penning this definition, Perrin himself has moved in the direction of taking the author on his own terms and has called for a study of the composition and structure of a whole work, an examination of the Gospel's using such categories as "protagonist" and "plot," the description of themes particular to each Evangelist, and contact with secular literary critics especially with regard to their insights into the nature of symbolic language.[68] Perrin illustrates this type of redaction criticism when he shows that Son of Man in Mk is used in strategic places to reinterpret Son of God.[69] In his most recent statement on the Gospel as a whole, Perrin describes Mk as "an apocalyptic drama" in

66. N. Perrin, *What is Redaction Criticism?* (Philadelphia: Fortress Press, 1969), 1.
67. Cf. R. H. Stein, "What is Redaktionsgeschichte?" *JBL* 88 (1969), 45–56; and "The Proper Methodology for Ascertaining a Markan Redaction History," *NovTest* 13 (1971), 181–98.
68. N. Perrin, "The Evangelist as Author: Reflections on Method in the Study and Interpretation of the Synoptic Gospels and Acts," *BR* 17 (1972), 5–18, and "Eschatology and Hermeneutics: Reflections on Method in the Interpretation of the New Testament," *JBL* 93 (1974), 3–14.
69. N. Perrin, "The Creative Use of the Son of Man Traditions by Mark," *USQR* 23 (1968), 237–65 (reprinted in *Pilgrimage,* 84–93); and "The Christology of Mark: A Study in Methodology," *JR* 51 (1971), 173–87 (reprinted in *Pilgrimage,* 104–21).

which Mk and his Church are self-consciously caught up in events they view as the end of history. The Gospel portrays this drama in three acts: John the Baptist preaches and is "delivered up" (*paradidonai*, 1:14); Jesus preaches and is "delivered up" (9:31; 10:33; 14:41); the Christians preach and are "delivered up" (13:9–13). The Gospel looks to the return of Jesus as the victorious Son of Man (13:26; 14:62; 16:8).[70] Not only in his discussion of Mk, but also in his treatment of Mt and Lk-Acts, Perrin shows how an analysis of the relationship of parts of the author's work, the significance of material peculiar to each Evangelist, and the author's conception of his work in dialogue with a historical situation, all provide an entree to the theology of the Gospel.[71]

Similar approaches to Mk can be found in the works of W. Kelber and T. Weeden. Neither author finds the Mkan purpose by reconstructing in detail the tradition Mk reworks, but both concentrate on the way Mk structures his material in opposition to some inadequate theology. From an analysis of the location of the Kingdom sayings, the parallel structure of certain chapters, and the arrangement of historical allusions in Mk 13, Kelber concludes that throughout the Gospel Mk is anxious to propose a proper understanding of the Kingdom as the future revelation of God's rule in a new place (Galilee) and at a new time (the parousia) in opposition to heretical groups who claimed that the parousia had already occurred at the time of the destruction of Jerusalem in that city.[72] Weeden traces throughout the Gospel the disciples' movement from unperceptiveness through misconception to rejection of Jesus. He then suggests that Mk structures his material on the model of a Greek drama in which the characters are meant to be symbolic. The disciples in Mk are representative of members of the community who hold an enthusiastic divine man Christology in opposition to the suffering Son of Man Christology which Mk presents.[73] While such attempts to describe Mk's opponents from Mk's positive theology are always open to discussion, the approach does represent a move away from

---

70. N. Perrin, *The New Testament: An Introduction* (New York: Harcourt Brace Jovanovich, 1974), 144–45.
71. Ibid., 171–90 (Mt) and 196–216 (Lk–Acts).
72. KELBER, esp. 129–47.
73. WEEDEN, esp. 20–51; 64–69; 138–68.

bondage to the distinction between tradition and redaction as the only gateway to Mkan theology.

An objection often raised to this type of Mkan redaction criticism is that a first century author could not have intended the sophisticated nuances of meaning and themes found by such analysis. But to raise this objection is to pose a false question, for when the intention of Mk is discussed what is treated is the intention of the Mkan text. To say that an author could not have "intended" a certain meaning is to resurrect the "intentional fallacy" which modern literary critics reject as a valid tool of literary criticism.[74] Just as the text of a James Joyce or a T. S. Eliot may yield more than the author consciously intended, so too may the text of Mk admit of levels of meaning beyond the conscious intention or even the historical situation which occasioned the Gospel.

A final word must be said about the emerging method of structuralist exegesis and its application to the New Testament. Structuralist or "semiotic" exegesis is the general term for the application to biblical texts of methods of literary criticism taken from three areas: the analysis of linguistic structures—how words function in sentences; the study of the structures of narrative, or better, how narrative "works" in material as divergent as Russian folktales and French drama; and the attempt to find the deep symbolic structures of human thought which underlie myth making and story telling. Presently structuralism is not a single method but rather the convergence of many methods in the study of a given text.[75]

The method has been used by English speaking scholars principally in the study of New Testament parables, but a recent work by D. O. Via

---

74. W. K. Wimsatt, *The Verbal Icon* (New York: Noonday Press, 1954), 3–18.

75. At present structuralist exegesis has two major centers, a French school drawing on the studies of F. de Saussure (linguistics), R. Barthes and A. Greimas (narrative), and Lévi-Strauss (myth), and a German school which follows the lead of E. Güttgemanns, *Offene Fragen zur Formgeschichte des Evangeliums* (Munich: Kaiser Verlag, 1970); cf. also the editions of *Linguistica Biblica*; R. Scholes, *Structuralism in Literature: An Introduction* (New Haven: Yale University Press, 1974), with a superb introduction and bibliography; D. O. Via, *Kerygma and Comedy in the New Testament* (Philadelphia: Fortress Press, 1975), 1–38 surveys the method; on the structuralism of the parables, see *Semeia* I and II (1974); an excellent bibliography on structuralism is compiled by J. D. Crossan in *Semeia* I (1974), 256–74; *Interpr* 28 (1974), 131–220; *Structural Analysis and Biblical Exegesis*, Pittsburgh Theological Monograph Series 3, general editor D. Y. Hadidian (Pittsburgh, Pa.: Pickwick Press, 1974); G. Bucher, "Elements for an Analysis of the Gospel Text: The Death of Jesus," *Modern Language Notes* 86 (1971), 835–44.

applies it to the Mkan Gospel.[76] Since the value of the method is to call attention to a complex of details and relationships within the Mkan text, any summary of its results sounds commonplace. Via works with the internal relationships of Mk without concern for the distinction between tradition and redaction and concludes that "Mark is primarily tragicomedy because of the global and detailed presence of the death and *resurrection* or *life*-through-death motif."[77] The key words in Via's conclusion are "global" and "detailed," for the exciting aspect of the work is the manner in which he shows how the dialectic of life through death functions in parts of the Gospel which, on the surface, have nothing to do with this theme.

Via feels that structuralism is in tension with redaction criticism because he views redaction criticism as primarily a historical discipline which seeks the setting in life of the text to the detriment of study of the text as literature.[78] His objection is problematic on two grounds. First of all, the redaction criticism he attacks is only one aspect of redaction criticism and does not represent the approach to the text urged by Perrin and others. Secondly, as R. Scholes remarks, structuralism itself "seeks to explore the relationship between a system of literature and the culture of which it is a part."[79] To see the Mkan text as an entree to the cultural milieu in which it originated is equally the aim of redaction criticism and structural exegesis. When, therefore, redaction criticism is loosened from the moorings of the distinction between tradition and redaction, the insights of structuralism and redaction criticism should provide much cross-fertilization. However, when structuralism itself moves into the realm of deep structure and attempts to describe universal patterns of human thought it moves away from the richness and particularity of a given text.[80]

---

76. Via, *Kerygma and Comedy*, 71–169; cf. also L. Marin, *Sémiotique de la Passion: Topiques et Figures* (Aubier, Montaigne: Éditions du Cerf; Delachaux et Niestlé: Desclée de Brouwer, 1971).

77. Via, *Kerygma and Comedy*, 101.

78. Ibid., 71–78.

79. Scholes, *Structuralism*, 11.

80. Via, *Kerygma and Comedy*, 10: "The program of Lévi-Strauss is to discover the hidden structure that *unconsciously* informs the various aspects of a society—economics, marriage customs, law, language, art, myth, ritual, religion, etc. . . . Lévi-Strauss's ultimate goal is to discover the very structure of the human mind."

4. CONCLUSION

The Mkan Passion Narrative is no longer the neglected child of redaction criticism. It can no longer be viewed as a rather traditional and historical account which Mt and Lk adopt and adapt to their own purpose. It is itself the end product of a varied and complicated development, but a text which owes its final form and coherent structure and meaning to Mk. Nor is it a section of the Gospel which can be considered in isolation from other sections of the Gospel. The Passion Narrative as a whole and, to a certain extent, each individual part of it bears the imprint of the theology of the whole work. In this sense the exegete of the Passion Narrative is in a "hermeneutical circle." On the basis of the study of one part of the Mkan narrative certain tentative judgments will have to be made about the theology of the whole work, at a time when there is no consensus about the theology of the whole. Therefore judgments about Mk as author and theologian must be continually refined and revised in light of the ongoing study of the whole Gospel. The essays in this volume are an attempt to see the whole in the part and to contribute to this ongoing study.

II.

Last Meal:
Preparation, Betrayal, and Absence

(Mark 14:12–25)

Vernon K. Robbins

Mk presents the Last Supper (LS) in three scenes, and the unfolding drama reaches its highpoint as the cup gives meaning to Jesus' absence. My thesis is that this final meal completes the drama of the Feeding Stories (Mk 6:30–44; 8:1–10). The purpose of this dramatization is to defuse a view that Jesus' miraculous powers are the basis for belief and to link the Christian meal with Jesus' suffering and death and resurrection into heaven.[1]

The eucharistic dramatization portrayed by Mk 14:12–25 is distinctive in the New Testament. In contrast, the Pauline LS (1 Cor 11:23–26) contains only sayings about bread and the cup, and after

---

1. For a comprehensive discussion of the eucharistic traditions see: (1) Eucharistic texts, A.D. 100–1947: P. F. Palmer, *Sources of Christian Theology. Vol. I: Sacraments and Worship* (Westminster, Md.: Newman, 1955), 38–215; (2) essay collections: O. Cullmann and F. J. Leenhardt, *Essays on the Lord's Supper*, trans. J. G. Davies (Richmond, Va.: John Knox, 1958); J. Delorme, et al., *The Eucharist in the New Testament: A Symposium* (Baltimore, Md.: Helicon, 1965); H. Küng, *The Sacraments: An Ecumenical Dilemma*, Conc 24 (New York: Paulist, 1967), 43–112; R. E. Clements, et al., *Eucharistic Theology Then and Now*, Theological Collections 9 (London: SPCK, 1968); P. Benoit, R. E. Murphy, B. van Iersel, eds., *The Breaking of the Bread*, Conc 40 (New York: Paulist Press, 1969); (3) recent books: E. Schweizer, *The Lord's Supper According to the New Testament*, FBBS 18 (Philadelphia: Fortress Press, 1967); W. Marxsen, *The Lord's Supper as a Christological Problem*, FBBS 25 (Philadelphia: Fortress Press, 1970); R. Feneberg, *Christliche Passafeier und Abendmahl*, StANT 27 (Munich: Kösel, 1971); G. Wainwright, *Eucharist and Eschatology* (London: Epworth, 1971); H. Patsch, *Abendmahl und Historischer Jesus*, Calwer Theologische Monographien, Bibelwissenschaft 1 (Stuttgart: Calwer Verlag, 1972).

each saying is a command to repeat this act "in remembrance."[2] The Johannine LS (Jn 13:1–30) does not speak of "bread" and "cup"; instead, a poignant footwashing episode leads to a scene where Jesus dips a morsel and gives it to Judas, his betrayer. Unique eucharistic language is found in the setting of the Feeding of the 5,000 (Jn 6), where Jesus delivers a discourse in which he refers to "bread which came down from heaven" (Jn 6:41) and eating the flesh and drinking the blood of the Son of Man (Jn 6:53–57). The Lkan account (22:7–23) is partly dependent upon the Mkan account, yet its singularity is so evident that some interpreters propose that it stems from an independent tradition.[3] Only the Matthean account (26:17–29) is like the Mkan drama, but the verbal agreement indicates direct copying.

Each scene in the Mkan portrayal of the LS reflects Mkan theology. The preparation (14:12–16) forecasts Passover Day as the period of time in which the meal, arrest, trial, and crucifixion occur; the meal (14:17–21) delineates betrayal as the act of a disciple who fulfills scripture but evokes the judgment of God; and the bread and cup (14:22–25) interpret the death of Jesus and anticipate his return. Jesus' explanation of the meaning of the bread and the cup contrasts with Mk 6–8, where the disciples never grasp the significance of Jesus' distribution of bread and fish to large crowds. Therefore the drama of the LS, in which eating is linked with Jesus' death, resurrection, and absence, completes the drama of the Feeding Stories; without the LS, Mk would contain eucharistic overtones more compatible with Johannine language than Mkan thought.

1. PREPARATION FOR ENTRANCE INTO THE PASSION

The first scene in the Mkan LS (14:12–16) is initiated by the disciples as they ask Jesus, "Where will you have us go and prepare for you to eat the passover?" The occasion for the question is presented in

2. 1 Cor 10:16–21 discusses "the bread" and "the cup of blessing" in relation to the table of the Lord and the table of demons.

3. E.g., H. Schürmann, *Der Paschamahlbericht Lk 22, (7–14.) 15–18. I. Teil einer quellenkritischen Untersuchung des lukanischen Abendmahlsberichtes Lk 22,7–38,* NTAbh 19, 5 (Münster: Aschendorff, 1953); *II. Der Einsetzungsbericht Lk 22,19–20,* NTAbh 20, 4 (1955); *III. Jesu Abschiedsrede Lk 22,21–38,* NTAbh 20, 5 (1957); "Jesus' Words in the Light of His Actions at the Last Supper," Conc 40 (New York: Paulist Press, 1969), 119–25.

14:12: it was the day when the passover lambs were being slaughtered to be eaten after sundown. But as the scene unfolds, the actual preparation of the passover is an addendum—"and they prepared the passover." Entering into Jerusalem, finding the man carrying a water jar, and following him to a guest room comprise the scene. Since these actions constitute an extraordinary prelude to a meal which interprets Jesus' arrest, death, and resurrection, the scene highlights Jesus' foreknowledge and authority rather than the food which must be prepared for the meal.

The structure of this scene is parallel to the preparation for Jesus' entry into Jerusalem (11:1–6). The parallel construction of the stories makes it obvious "that the two stories are composed by the same writer...."[4] The common features emerge when the scenes are placed in parallel columns:

11:1–6	14:13–16
1: *he sent two of his disciples*	13: *he sent two of his disciples*
2: *and said to them,*	*and said to them,*
"Go into the village . . .	*"Go into the* city . . .
and . . . you *will* find	*and . . . will* meet you . . .
3: *Say, 'The* Lord . . . '"*	14: *Say . . . , 'The* Teacher . . . '"*
4: *And they went* away,	16: *And they went* out . . .
and they found . . .	*and found*
6: *as* Jesus *had said,*	*as* he *had* told them;
and . . .	*and* . . .

The parallels draw attention to three common elements: (a) in 14:13, 14a and 11:2 the two disciples are given a promise that they will encounter a phenomenon through which they can fulfill their instructions; (b) in 14:14b and 11:3b Jesus gives them a special formula to use so that the people whom they meet will cooperate with them; and (c) in 14:16 and 11:4–6 the disciples come upon the circumstances, act according to the instructions, and everything works out well because they do "just as he said."[5]

The imprint of the hand of Mk, visible in the parallel features, is

4. TAYLOR, 536.
5. DORMEYER, 91–93.

pervasive in the first LS scene. The author linked eleven clauses simply with "and."[6] The final verse (14:16) discloses its thoroughly Mkan character not only by this but also by the exit and entry statements which reflect Mkan patterning throughout the Gospel.[7] The opening verse of the story proper (14:13) reflects Mkan composition as it introduces the action of Jesus through clauses containing historical present verbs.[8] But the particular features of the story—the man carrying the jar of water, the formula "The Teacher says..." and the large upper room—point to tradition. A story, perhaps available to Mk from oral tradition, has been written down in Mkan format.

For Mk the instruction to the disciples for the preparation of the passover (14:13–16) has the same introductory function for the passion as 11:1–10 has for the Jerusalem entry of Jesus. In both scenes the foreknowledge implied by the instructions, the titles "Lord"/"Teacher" in the formulaic response they are to use, and the fulfillment of the incidents "just as he said" depict Jesus as authoritative.[9] Not only the conflicts which arise after Jesus' initial entry into Jerusalem, but also the arrest, trial, and death of Jesus are interpreted through prefatory scenes that evoke an authoritative aura around Jesus. Although there is conflict and death, investment of Jesus with authority assures the reader of some resolution of the tragedy.

One feature, however, is remarkably different between the entry into Jerusalem and the first LS scene. In the first story a promised encounter (11:2–3) is recapitulated with detail (11:4–6), and this narration leads directly to the Jerusalem entry on the colt (11:7–10). In the opening LS scene, no detailed recapitulation follows the promise (14:13–15), and no continuous narration leads directly to the meal: narration is suppressed so that an abrupt change takes us to the evening

---

6. This paratactic style, the alignment of clauses in a sequence through the use of *kai*, "and," is one of the most striking characteristics of Mk's composition; see HAWKINS, 150–52; ZERWICK, 1–21; TAYLOR, 57–58; DONAHUE, 55–56.

7. See U. Luz, "Das Geheimnismotiv und die markinische Christologie," *ZNW* 56 (1965), 14–15; DONAHUE, 114.

8. The use of the historical present, i.e., the use of the present tense in place of the aorist, is another characteristic of Mkan style; see HAWKINS, 144–49; BLASS-DEBRUNNER, 167; TAYLOR, 46–47; DONAHUE, 54–55.

9. As for the aura these motifs evoke for Samuel's personage in 1 Sam 10:1–10, see the recent analysis by B. C. Birch, "The Development of the Tradition on the Anointing of Saul in 1 Sam 9:1–10:16," *JBL* 90 (1971), 55–68.

meal. Detailed narration would describe the food that they found and prepared, and the room in which the food was to be eaten. The comment, "and they prepared the passover" (14:16d), must be compared with the actions in 11:7–8 which elongate the scene into the Jerusalem entry: "and *they* brought the colt to Jesus and *they* threw *their garments* on it; and he sat upon it. And *many* spread *their garments* on the road...." With striking contrast, once the comment in 14:16d is made, the scene shifts to Jesus "with the twelve" in the evening.

As a result of the abrupt change in scene, "the passover" is not mentioned in the entire Passion Narrative.[10] If an account of a *passover* celebration ever existed (fragments have been suggested in Mk 14:25, 26), the scenes which now succeed it do not develop naturally out of it. The eating scenes which stand at 14:17–21 and 14:22–25 do not recount passover activities for two major reasons: (a) no bitter herbs are mentioned, and (b) there is no recitation of liturgy related to eating the passover lamb.[11] A third possible reason is that the LS presupposes a common bowl rather than an individual dish for each participant, although it is impossible to verify the existence of this tradition as early as first century A.D.[12]

For Mk, therefore, passover presents a general framework for the last meal, but direct interest in passover traditions is lacking. Perhaps it is well to recall that in the entire New Testament only Lk 22:15 recounts a saying that suggests a passover narrative may have existed with Jesus as the leader of the meal. Even though the Fourth Gospel refers to three occasions when Jesus went to Jerusalem for passover—(1) 2:13, 23; (2) 6:4; (3) 13:1—it does not contain a narrative recounting eating of the lamb and recitation of the passover liturgy.[13] In all likelihood Jesus did participate in a passover celebration at some point

---

10. *To pascha* occurs only five times in Mk, and these instances are localized within 14:1, 12 (twice), 14, 16.

11. Num 9:11 requires the presence of bitter herbs and unleavened bread at the meal; Pes 10:5 attributes to R. Gamaliel (first century A.D.) a tradition that whoever does not mention the lamb, unleavened bread, and bitter herbs at the meal has not fulfilled his passover obligations; cf. Y. Pes 9:3 (36d).

12. B. Pes 115b (fifth century) interprets Pes 10:3 as requiring that unleavened bread, herbs, and haroseth be set in individual dishes before each person. Cf. BULTMANN, 264.

13. For the importance of distinguishing between a general reference to an event and a narrative account of that event, see J. D. Crossan's essay in the present volume, "Empty Tomb and Absent Lord."

in his life (or many times), but the Evangelists have little interest in such a thoroughly Jewish activity. This opens the possibility that the eucharistic stories which they recount are fashioned by Christian practice and theological concerns.

From this perspective the beginning of the scene has special significance. When the disciples ask Jesus if they should go away to prepare the passover, they are mimicking their action in the Feeding of the 4,000 when they asked Jesus if they should go away to buy food for the crowd (6:37). The disciples take an active role in both Feeding Stories (6:30–44; 8:1–10), and this activity entwines discipleship with eating.

Still another feature links this first scene with the Feeding Stories: the Feast of Unleavened Bread referred to in 14:12. This verse places the first day of the Unleavened Bread Festival on Nisan 14, the day of preparation, although the majority of Jewish traditions assign it to Nisan 15, the day of passover.[14] Its importance is signaled by the discrepancy it creates with Mk 14:1, which presupposes, correctly, that the festival begins with the passover. This discrepancy shows Mk's specific interest in unleavened bread as he presents the LS, and he creates a chronological conflict by emphasizing the Unleavened Bread Festival in the opening sentence of the first scene.[15] Why did such a contradiction arise in Mk's narration?

Although Mk uses passover day as the setting for the death of Jesus, he uses the Festival of Unleavened Bread for polemical imagery. In the context of the Feeding Stories, where the meaning of bread is being discussed with the disciples, the imperceptiveness of the disciples is linked with "the leaven of the Pharisees and the leaven of Herod" (8:15). The difficulty in ascertaining the meaning of these phrases is well documented by Q. Quesnell. In order to discover the meaning, he found it necessary to move outside the Gospel context into the eucharistic overtones surrounding 1 Cor 5:7.[16] I suggest that the leaven-bread

---

14. J. Jeremias, *The Eucharistic Words of Jesus*, trans. N. Perrin, 3d ed. rev. (New York: Scribner's, 1966), 17–18.

15. See J. D. Crossan, "Redaction and Citation in Mark 11:9–10, 17 and 14:27," *SBL Proceedings* (n.p., 1972) I, 18: a feature within the Markan text "can be probably judged as redactional which (i) creates some awkwardness, discrepancy, contradiction, anomaly, etc., by its presence . . . ; and (ii) this awkwardness is signalled as such by its absence (removal?) in the parallel passages of Matthew and/or Luke, and sometimes even by scribal corrections in the Markan textual tradition. . . ."

16. Q. Quesnell, *The Mind of Mark*, AnBib 38 (Rome: Pontifical Biblical Institute, 1969), 232–42.

imagery be construed in the setting of the overall Mkan narrative. References to leaven occur in the section of Mk which not only recounts the two Feeding Stories but also contains statements about bread in six of the ten episodes (6:7–8:13).[17] The concern over bread in Mk 6–8 represents a development of the leitmotif of eating which is introduced in controversy stories in Mk 2–3.[18] These controversies culminate in a meeting of "the Pharisees with the Herodians" to plot the death of Jesus (3:6). In like manner, the episodes in Mk 6–8 reach their zenith in a scene in which the disciples are warned: "Beware of the leaven of the Pharisees and the leaven of Herod" (8:15). In other words, Mk's sequential arrangement of the narrative produces two clusters of episodes which correlate eating with conflict. In Mk 2–3 the conflict includes the scribes, the Pharisees, and the Herodians; in Mk 6–8 the conflict expands to the disciples.

Controversy with the Pharisees has been focused through 7:1–23 where Jesus pronounces "all foods clean" and through 8:1–13 where a request for "a sign from heaven," juxtaposed with the Feeding of the 4,000, is refused by Jesus. The controversy about "clean food" reveals Mk's concern for preaching the Gospel to the whole world, including Gentiles; Jesus' refusal to give a sign in this setting points to a rejection of manifestation of the risen Lord in miraculous feedings.[19] The community must accept the absence of Jesus until the true "sign from heaven" occurs, i.e., Jesus' return as Son of Man (13:24–27).[20]

Correspondingly, the problem with Herod is indicated in 6:14–29. Herod not only created the setting for the death of the Baptist, but also proposed an erroneous view of the person of Jesus: Jesus was John the Baptizer raised from the dead, and for this reason the powers were at work through him (6:14). The "leaven of Herod" appears to peak

17. The term *artos*, "bread," occurs in Mk 6:8; 6:37, 38, 41, 44; 6:52; 7:2, 5; 7:27; 8:4, 5, 6—in these six episodes.
18. The term *artos* occurs in 2:26, 3:30; problems in regard to eating occur in 2:13–17, 18–22, 23–28; 3:20–29. J. Dewey ("The Literary Structure of the Controversy Stories in Mark 2:1–3:6," *JBL* 92 [1973], 397–400) suggests that contention over eating habits has been intensified through Mkan redaction. Cf. J. A. Grassi, "The Eucharist in the Gospel of Mark," *AER* 168 (1974), 595–608; D. O. Via, *Kerygma and Comedy in the New Testament* (Philadelphia: Fortress Press, 1975), 133–34, 144.
19. Cf. P. J. Achtemeier, "The Origin and Function of the Pre-Marcan Miracle Catenae," *JBL* 91 (1972), 198–221. The presence of this emphasis in some early Christian circles is evident from Lk 24:13–35; Acts 10:40–41; Jn 21:1–14.
20. See the author's "*Dynameis* and *sēmeia* in Mark," *BR* 18 (1973), 1–16.

in this view about Jesus, since Mk emphasizes it through repetition in 6:14, 16 and puts it on the lips of the disciples as the most prominent conception "among men" concerning the identity of Jesus (8:28). Mk discredits such a view of Jesus by placing it on the lips of a confused and manipulated Herod—confused over the identity of Jesus and manipulated into killing the Baptist.

Mk associates the disciples with the misunderstanding promoted by Herod and the Pharisees through the scene in 8:14–21. The leitmotif of eating bread is the literary medium through which the association is made. The disciples' anxiety about forgetting to bring bread is countered by the warning, "Beware of the leaven of the Pharisees and the leaven of Herod." The misunderstanding by the disciples implicates them along with the Pharisees and Herod.

In Mk 6–8, therefore, leaven pervades mistaken perceptions held by the Pharisees, Herod, and the disciples. In contrast, the LS takes place on the first day of "unleavened bread." Evidently for Mk leaven signifies power which inflicts death upon others but refuses to internalize the meaning of suffering and death. The urge for immediate transformation of death into life pervades their theology. The leaven of the Pharisees and the leaven of Herod are thoroughly removed when Jesus eats with disciples in the setting of betrayal and death.

In summary, the prefatory scene to the LS (14:12–16) harks back to the first Feeding Story (6:30–44). When the disciples ask Jesus if they should go away to prepare the food for the passover (14:12), the reader begins the drama of the Feeding Stories again (6:37). But this time the setting is demarcated by "unleavened bread." In other words, in the LS the power of Jesus is qualified. Mk 14:12–16 portrays Jesus' sovereignty over the passion events, as the preparation for entry into Jerusalem (11:1–6) depicts his authority over the Jewish Temple and its cult. However, this is not the miraculous power which Herod and the Pharisees envision; such a perspective contains leaven. The setting for the proper ("unleavened") view about Christian eating and about Jesus takes us into a meal which evokes the arrest, death, and resurrection of Jesus.

2. "TABLE-INTIMATE" AS BETRAYER

The second scene takes us abruptly to an evening meal. At this meal the betrayer, with the other disciples, eats with Jesus. The name Judas never appears in the scene, because scripture passages furnish the language to identify the betrayer. Ps 41:9 says, "Even my bosom friend in whom I trusted, who ate of my bread, has lifted his heel against me." The dramatic portrayal of this scriptural verse during the last night of Jesus' earthly life concludes with a pronouncement of "woe" which interprets the act of betrayal as evil but the result of the action as a fulfillment of the will of God. This scene depicts conflict which arises out of the circle of discipleship itself. It is only rivaled by Peter's denial of Jesus (14:66–72) and encounters between Jesus and Pharisees. If discipleship as portrayed by Mk relates to discipleship in Mk's own community, then the community in which he lives experiences bitter conflict. Misunderstanding, dissension, and even betrayal reside within the Christian community itself, and these acts are evil. In this arena of conflict, however, the sovereign purpose of God is fulfilled.

After the preparation, only one more scene is expected—a meal. There is only one meal, as the clauses in 14:18, 22 indicate: "while they were reclining and eating" Jesus spoke about the betrayer, and "while they were eating" Jesus took the bread and the cup. But the author created two scenes by repeating the statement that they were eating a meal. Such repetition of a phrase or clause to add a scene is a common feature of Mkan composition called "the Markan insertion technique."[21] Mk inserted a scene about Jesus' betrayer (14:18–21) into a story about a special meal Jesus ate with his disciples (14:22–25).[22]

Before we ask why Mk inserted this scene, we need to make some

---

21. DONAHUE, 242: the clause *kai anakeimenōn autōn kai esthiontōn* in 14:18 is intentionally reiterated with *kai esthiontōn* in 14:22. He suggests that this technique is "used by Mark for a variety of functions, and not simply to call attention to 'inserted' material" (241). Cf. DORMEYER, 101, who calls *esthiontōn autōn* in 14:22a a doublet of 14:18, and therefore designates it as redactional.

22. This is a rare instance in which the "insertion" technique coincides with Mkan "intercalation" (DONAHUE, 59). Following BEST (91), Donahue speaks of a "double sandwich" here because comments about the betrayer (14:10–11, 18–21) frame the preparation just as preparation and distribution (14:12–16, 22–25) frame the scene about the betrayer. However, 14:10–11 relates directly to 14:1–2, and these passages frame the anointing of Jesus at Bethany (14:3–9). Therefore, it is preferable to describe 14:1–25 in terms of two intercalated episodes in sequence: (1) 14:1–2, 3–9, 10–11, and (2) 14:12–16, 17–21, 22–25. In the second episode the Mkan "insertion technique" is employed to create the intercalation.

estimation concerning the form of the scene as he knew it. This short scene, perhaps from oral tradition, features the saying, "Verily I say to you, one of you will betray me." This saying, which is common to Jn 13:21, Mk 14:18, and Mt 26:21, was part of a tradition in which Jesus confronted his disciples with betrayal from within the group. The story portrays the disciples' inquiry about the identification of the betrayer (Jn 13:25; Mk 14:19; Mt 26:22), and Jesus identifies the betrayer as one who participates in the table fellowship (Jn 13:26; Mk 14:20; Lk 22:21; Mt 26:23).

It is impossible to know if the meal was construed to be the last one Jesus ate with his disciples. But this story attracted, probably already before Mk, part of an exegetical tradition which furnished a scriptural basis for betrayal from within the group. This apologetic, based on scriptural fulfillment, has influenced the last part of 14:18, which contains wording from Ps 41:9. The Qumran community's use of the same psalm verse, which states that "a friend who ate my bread turned against me," reveals an interest in this passage by groups who were reading the Old Testament.[23] Since the Christian community was especially interested in its potential for explaining the betrayal of Jesus by a close associate, this passage occurs, with different wording, in Jn 13:18. The different wording indicates that Ps 41:9 had given rise to a Christian exegetical tradition, so that Christians in different locations reflected on the interpretational Christian form of the passage rather than the actual Old Testament passage in its context.[24]

Mkan redaction within 14:17–21 suggests that Mk wove the scriptural wording into the scene. Mk composed 14:17 as a transition from the preparation to the meal. Since two disciples had already been sent into the city for preparation, technically only ten would accompany Jesus in the evening. But Mk brings "the twelve," an important concept within his theology, into the meal scene through verse 17, and he adds "one of the twelve" to the saying in 14:20.[25] The first part of

23. 1QH V. 22–26, 33, 35; see M. Mansoor, *The Thanksgiving Hymns*, Studies on the Texts of the Desert of Judah 3 (Grand Rapids, Mich.: Eerdmans, 1961), 135–37.

24. B. Lindars, *New Testament Apologetic* (Philadelphia: Westminster Press, 1961), 98–99; cf. E. D. Freed, *Old Testament Quotations in the Gospel of John*, NTSup 11 (Leiden: E. J. Brill, 1965), 89–93.

25. DORMEYER, 83, considers *dōdeka*, "twelve," to be redactional in every instance in Mk except 3:16.

14:18 is traditional except for the clause "and eating," but the last clause, "he who eats with me," appears to be a redundant insertion by Mk. The opening words in 14:19 are redactional, but the last part comes from the traditional scene.[26] Therefore, Mk himself appears to introduce the allusion to Ps 41:9, "he who eats with me," as he depicts the conflict arising within the inner circle.

Through this redactional activity, Mk composed a balanced pair of sayings in a chiastic pattern. The result is that 14:18b–20 form an ABA' pattern:

A   Jesus said, "Verily I say to you, one of you will betray me, who eats with me."

B   They began to grieve and to say to him one by one, "Is it I?"

A'   And he said to them, "one of the twelve, who dips with me in the bowl."

The function of chiastic composition is twofold: it emphasizes the center part and distributes parallel ideas in the outer parts.[27] Emphasis on the center makes the betrayal by Judas the medium for placing the possibility of betrayal before anyone who enters discipleship. Parallelism between the outer parts identifies "one of you" as "one of the twelve." In addition to being balanced pairs, these statements present a linear heightening of the identification.[28] The progression to "one of the twelve," a specific identification of the betrayer within the inner circle of disciples, contributes to the dramatic portrayal of the scene.

The formula, "as it is written," continues the idea of scriptural fulfillment in 14:21. Moreover, it provides the rationale for the specific identification of one of the twelve as the betrayer. This feature gives the story a dynamic similar to the story in which Jesus asks the disciples about his own identity (Mk 8:27–30; Mt 16:13–20; Lk 9:18–21; Jn 6:67–71). As Mk interprets the scene concerning Jesus' identity with the saying, "that the Son of man must suffer many things and be rejected . . ." (8:31), so Mk interprets the scene concerning the betrayer's identity with the oracle, "For the Son of man goes as it is written of him,

26. Ibid., 95–96.

27. See an example in J. Dewey, "Literary Structure," 398–401.

28. F. W. Danker calls this feature "explanatory heightening" in "The Literary Unity of Mark 14:1–25," *JBL* 85 (1966), 470–71. Including this instance, Danker finds fifteen examples in Mk. Mt alters ten of the instances.

but woe . . ." (14:21). In both instances Mk interprets the story through a passion statement which indicates that these things must happen.

But the "woe-oracle" in Mk 14:21 is unique; there is no other like it in the biblical tradition. The peculiar force is evident when it is compared with the basic structure of biblical woe-oracles. The opening sentence of such an oracle customarily contains "woe" or "alas" and identifies the recipient of the oracle, the second part contains an explanatory sentence specifying the offense (usually introduced by "for" or "because"), and the third part is the announcement of divine judgment.[29] In Mk 14:21 the woe statement and the explanatory sentence specifying the offense are reversed from the traditional order.[30] Mk has adapted the oracle to make it a fitting conclusion for the scene identifying the betrayer.

Why has Mk given this woe-oracle a peculiar twist? If the betrayer is a disciple, then an unusual situation arises. The recipient of the woe-oracle in the Old Testament is characteristically haughty: he acts in self-reliant independence of Yahweh. This action leads to false security, defiance of covenant obligations, and disloyalty to Yahweh, and therefore he must fear the "greater sovereignty of Yahweh in a terrifying visitation."[31] Although Judas appears to be self-reliant in Mk, his action fulfills the sovereign purpose of God. In other words, it is necessary to separate the action (which is judged as wrong) from the result of the action (which fulfills the plan of God). This is expressed by introducing two subjects in the oracle rather than one—"that man" (who does the evil deed) and "the Son of man" (who fulfills the sovereign will of God). The proper subject of the woe-oracle is "that man," and the evidence of such an oracle is implied in Mk 14:21b, c:

29. W. E. March, "Prophecy," *Old Testament Form Criticism*, ed. J. H. Hayes, Trinity University Monograph Series in Religion 2 (San Antonio, Tex.: Trinity University Press, 1974), 164–65. For examples in the New Testament with all three parts, see Lk 10:13–14; 11:46–51. For the persistance of the first two parts, with *ouai* in the first part and *hoti* in the second, see Mt 11:21; 23:13, 15, 23, 25, 27, 29; Lk 6:24, 25; 11:42, 43, 44, 52; Jude 11; Rev 12:12; 18:16–17, 19–20; with *gar* in the second part, see Lk 6:26; 21:23.

30. Because of the reversal, this is the only "woe-oracle" in the biblical tradition which contains *men . . . de* (on the one hand . . . on the other hand) at the beginning of the first two members. The only exception is its parallel in Mt 26:24.

31. W. Janzen, *Mourning Cry and Woe Oracle*, BZAW 125 (Berlin: W. de Gruyter, 1972), 81–82.

> *woe* to that man,
> *for* he betrayed the Son of Man;
> better if that man had not been born.

But the second line of the oracle could never have taken this form, because the tradition which linked the Son of Man with betrayal uses the verb "in the passive which expresses the divine activity."[32] Introduction of the betrayal of the Son of Man into the oracle brings with it the passive form of the verb and implies God as the one who causes the betrayal. This brings two subjects into the oracle and allows the cause for the woe to be stated only implicitly. The oracle has to be couched in the form which it has in Mk 14:21b, c.

My view is that Mk found an independent woe-oracle in the tradition with this form, and he added a preceding clause to make it a conclusion to this scene. There are three reasons why I conclude this. First, in this form the saying has individual autonomy requiring no special context for it to be understood; especially the catchword construction ("that man") would help it to live on in oral tradition. Second, the phrase "the Son of man" in the second member presents the natural occasion for prefixing the oracle with "for the Son of man goes as it is written of him." Third, this oracle may well have arisen in connection with a *pesher* on Ps 22:6, 9–10 (RSV). In these verses the psalmist cries out:

> But I am a worm, and no *man* (*ish*)
> the scorn of *man* ('ādām) and contempt of a people.
> . . .
> Yet thou art he who took me from the womb;
> thou didst keep me safe upon my mother's breasts.
> Upon thee was I cast from *my birth*,
> and since my mother bore me thou hast been my God.

The play upon *ish* and 'ādām in MT Ps 22:7 (RSV 22:6) in the setting of Ps 22:7–8 (RSV), which plays such an important role in crucifixion apologetic,[33] and the direct reflection upon 22:9–10 (RSV) could well have been the occasion for the origin of the woe-oracle:

32. N. Perrin, "The Use of *(para)didonai* in Connection with the Passion of Jesus in the New Testament," *Der Ruf Jesu und die Antwort der Gemeinde*, ed. E. Lohse et al. (Göttingen: Vandenhoeck & Ruprecht, 1970), 210; reprinted in *A Modern Pilgrimage in New Testament Christology* (Philadelphia: Fortress Press, 1974), 101.
33. Lindars, *Apologetic*, 89–93.

But woe to *that man* (*ish*)
by whom *the Son of Man* ('ā<u>d</u>ām) is betrayed:
... better if *that man* (*ish*) had not been *born.*

Mk composed 14:21a to link the woe-oracle (14:21b, c) with the eating scene which defines the betrayer on the basis of Ps 41:9. In this clause (14:21a) Mk uses the exact formula for citing scripture that he did with the Baptist in Mk 1:2 ("as it is written"). The saying is an embellishment of the last half of 14:21b, "by whom the Son of man is betrayed." When it precedes the woe-oracle it produces a strange sequence of thought, because it belongs to the sphere of "because" or "for" clauses which customarily stand after the "woe" clause.

The purpose of the Mkan adaptation of the woe-oracle is to intensify the scriptural necessity for the betrayer to be one who "shared table" with Jesus. But more than this is at stake. We must ask why Mk inserted this scene into the LS. The answer, I suggest, brings up an earlier observation. If the LS scene is completing the drama of the Feeding Stories, then the conflict that builds around the eating scenes from Mk 2–8 is interpreted in this scene. Mk is saying that a person cannot eat with Jesus without also facing the possibility that he might betray him, and, as soon as this possibility is faced, eating with Jesus includes an emphasis upon his death, resurrection, and absence. If there is conflict in Mk's community over the meaning of eating with Jesus, and I suggest there is, then the conflict itself indicates that eating with Jesus must include the theology connected with his death, resurrection, and absence. The "betrayer-tradition" in the center of the LS interprets the conflict which Mk faces in his own community. The acts of conflict are evil and the perpetrators of this action are judged by God, but the will of God will be fulfilled in the arena of this conflict.

3. THE CUP OF THE SON OF MAN

The last scene in the LS portrays Jesus' taking bread and blessing it, then passing a cup from which all drink. The descriptive words in the first verse (14:22) are amazingly close to the narration of Jesus' acts with the bread and fish in the Feeding Stories (6:41; 8:6–7). Most noticeable is the sequence of "take," "bless," "break" and "give." Through these words, the LS recaptures the drama of the Feeding Stories and brings it to a conclusion. At the end of the Feeding Stories, Jesus discovers that the disciples do not understand the meaning of the bread (8:17–21). Instead of explaining the bread to them, he begins to teach them about the suffering, death, and resurrection of the Son of Man (8:31). In the LS, Jesus abruptly interprets the meaning of the bread and adds a new feature by introducing a cup and interpreting its meaning. He interprets the bread as the body which has been prepared for burial (14:8, 22), and with the cup he invokes the Son of Man Christology which points to his absence until his return in a future, cosmic scenario. The conflict and misunderstanding which surrounds eating scenes in the Gospel finds its conclusion here. If some members of Mk's community invoke the presence of Jesus through their eating, Mk stands this on its head through this scene which announces his absence.

The form of the sayings in Mk 14:22 and 14:24 has been one of the most difficult features to explain in the Mkan LS account. The problem is that the bread-word (BW) in 14:22 contains the basic part of the first half of the Pauline BW in 1 Cor 11:24, but nothing else. In Mk the statement is simply, "Take, this is my body." In the Pauline account there are additional items consisting of "for you" and instruction that this be performed by the Christian community "in remembrance of me." If Mk knows a longer form of the BW, then he has shortened it. Only fifteen Greek words are used by Mk to describe the blessing, distribution, and interpretation of the bread; in contrast, fifty-one words are devoted to the thanksgiving, distribution, and interpretation of the cup. Unfortunately we are not able to know whether Mk knew the Pauline form of these sayings and intentionally omitted some of the words to interpret the bread. But the limited attention given to the bread distribution results in a de-emphasis of the bread.

Why did Mk give such limited space to the interpretation of the bread? The answer lies in relation to the Feeding Stories. For Mk, the bread invokes the death and absence of Jesus rather than his presence manifested in miraculous powers. Mk asserts this by placing the anointing at Bethany just before the LS, then referring only briefly to the bread in the LS. Because of this, we must look briefly at the anointing story (14:3–9), which has two features that link it with the third LS scene. (a) Through 14:8, in which Jesus speaks of "my body," Jesus' body is interpreted through death and burial. This understanding is reinforced through the saying in 14:7 which ends with the comment that "you do not always have me [with you]." In this way Mk asserts the absence of Jesus from the community, which is the basis for his expectation of the Son of Man "coming in clouds with great power and glory" (13:26). (b) In 14:9 Jesus speaks of "remembrance." A remarkable difference between Mk's LS and the Pauline account (1 Cor 11:23–26) is the lack of instructions in the Mkan account to eat and drink "in remembrance of me." In the anointing story the reader discerns the overriding interest of Mk. Remembrance is to take place in the context of "preaching the Gospel to the whole world." Further, the act of anointing "my body for burial" represents the specific item to "be remembered." Did Mk know the Pauline "in remembrance of me" statements? We can surely never have this information. But the effect of Mkan composition is to construe "remembrance" in "Gospel framework" which ends in crucifixion rather than the "meal setting" which may cause misunderstanding with its focus upon "the bread" (*qua* 8:14–21).

The short description of bread distribution in 14:22 effects a direct movement to the cup distribution which is elaborated to present Mkan theology. First, Mk constructs a description of thanksgiving for the cup which parallels the blessing and breaking of bread. Such a description does not occur in the Pauline LS since the cup is introduced "in like manner after supper." The Pauline account gives the impression that "thanksgiving" is said over both the bread and the cup. Pre-Mkan tradition of the Feeding Stories seems to have linked "thanksgiving" with the breaking of the bread (8:6), but, in contrast, Mkan redaction links bread (and fish) with "blessing" (6:41; 8:7; 14:22) and cup with "thanksgiving." Second, the CW is structured in imagery parallel to the BW:

This is my body . . .
this is my blood . . .

This is a variation from the basic Pauline sayings which lack this parallelism:

This is my body . . .
this cup is the new covenant . . .

The Pauline sayings indicate a direct interest in the church as a "covenant of fellowship." In this setting the bread as the "body of Christ" and the cup as the "new covenant" connote special communal significance. But the Mkan sayings have emerged through direct reflection on the relation of the bread and cup to the passion events: " 'Body and blood' are now the two 'components' of the Christ who gave himself in death."[34] Third, interest in the passion events is also present in the descriptive clause "which is poured out for many." With this addition the CW evokes a full image of the crucifixion as the event which furnishes the covenant. The fourth feature is perhaps the most important: the bread and cup scene has the form of an apophthegm.[35] Jesus tradition in this form contains a saying near the end, and the main emphasis culminates in the saying. In this scene, Mk 14:25 expresses the most important aspect for the Evangelist. As Jesus solemnly swears not to drink of the fruit of the vine until the final Messianic banquet, the weight of the entire scene falls on the cup. With this saying, Jesus refers to his approaching absence from the community and the reunion which will occur with his return as Son of Man.[36]

The saying in 14:25 has no introductory phrase which suggests that Mk was the first to combine this saying with the BW and the CW. However, this saying was not an integral feature of the tradition which transmitted the words about the bread and the cup.[37] This suggests that Mk is recounting the liturgical practice of the portion of the church which he represents. He recalls this tradition in its oral form and composes it in Mkan style. Accordingly, Mkan style is apparent in 14:22 not only in the opening clause, "and as they were eating," but also in the participial sequence, "having taken bread having blessed" and the phrase, "and he gave to them."[38] Mk has composed the first half of 14:23 by analogy to his description of the bread in 14:22 ("having taken a cup having given thanks he gave to them"), then he

---

34. Marxsen, *Lord's Supper*, 15, cf. 4–16.
35. Cf. A. M. Ambrozic, *The Hidden Kingdom*, CBQMS 2 (Washington: Catholic Biblical Association of America, 1972), 199.
36. Ibid., 183–202.
37. Ibid., 197.
38. Both the asyndetic participial construction and the phrase "and he gave to them" are absent in 1 Cor 11:23–24 and avoided in Mt 26:26.

adds "and they all drank of it."[39]   The saying in 14:25, however, has
no Mkan introductory formula like "and he said to them"; it represents
the climactic logion in the form of the tradition as it is recounted orally
in Mk's community.

Overall Mkan composition places the scene in tensive relationship
with the Feeding Stories and in direct relationship with the passion
events.   Moreover, when Mk adds, "and they all drank of it" (14:23b),
his community fully shares in the destiny of Jesus.   In 10:39 Jesus tells
James and John that they will drink the cup which he drinks, and in
14:36 Jesus refers to the passion events as "the cup."   Drinking the cup
therefore evokes the entire "Gospel story" which ends in death, resurrection into heaven, and anticipated return of Jesus as Son of Man.

In summary, the last scene links the bread with "the body of Jesus"
which undergoes death.   "Remembrance" of this is to take place in the
activity of "preaching the Gospel to the whole world" (14:9).   Drinking the cup represents the emphatically Mkan emphasis, for this activity
unites the believer with the fate of Jesus, and it evokes anticipation of
the coming of the Son of Man.   The cup gives meaning to the absence
of Jesus; he will not drink again until he drinks anew in the Kingdom of
God.

4. MARKAN "MEAL" CHRISTOLOGY

In this study I have taken the position that Mk arranges and redacts
stories and sayings about Jesus to produce emphases different from
those which some Christians within his purview were making.   One of
the differences centers on Christian ceremonial eating.   Analysis of the
miracle stories in Mk 6–8 indicates that Mk knows Christians who
recount miracles of Jesus in the setting of ceremonial eating and focus
upon breaking bread as the act through which the powers of the risen
Lord are manifested in their midst.   Mk places these stories in the first
half of his Gospel and portrays the result of participation in them in
terms of misunderstanding.   Disciples who participate in these events do
not properly comprehend the meaning of breaking the bread.   Under-

---

39. This description of the action with the cup is missing in 1 Cor 11:25 and Lk
22:20; the redactional character of the last half is apparent to many interpreters: cf.
Schürmann, *Paschamahlbericht*, 133 n. 145; Ambrozic, *Kingdom*, 197.

standing can only be attained through awareness of the entire "Gospel story" as narrated by Mk. The bread must be perceived in the context of the passion events where Jesus' body is prepared for death and burial; and the bread is subservient to the cup which poignantly evokes the crucifixion and absence of Jesus, and anticipation of his return as Son of Man when he will drink "anew" with them.

Mk introduces the entire LS account with a reference to "the first day of the Feast of Unleavened Bread." The irony is that Mk seems to have no interest in this feast *per se*. We have discovered that Mk has no direct interest in the passover feast either, but he has great interest in it as a general framework for emphasizing the importance of the death of Jesus. I suggest that the reference to unleavened bread is a polemical feature. The LS scenes present the unleavened view of "eating with Jesus" as opposed to the leaven of the Pharisees and of Herod by which Mk is countering christological views within Christian circles of his own time. If some Christians believe that Jesus is the Baptist raised from the dead, then they are still looking for the Messiah at the end of time. In Mk's time some are making a claim to come "in the name of Jesus" saying "I am he" (13:6), and they are successfully leading members of the Christian community astray. These Messianic claimants have an especially strong appeal within Christian circles, because they base their activity not on "new Moses" typology (as those reported in Josephus) but on "new Jesus" typology. A highpoint of their leadership has its locus in miraculous "breaking and distribution of bread" through which the powers of the resurrected Baptist-Jesus are again evident.

The LS scenes will not allow anyone to be misled by "false Christs and false prophets" who come "in my name" saying "I am he." On its own terms, the meal signifies that the Son of Man goes as it is written, and Jesus will no longer be present with the community "as they all drink the cup." His presence will be unmistakably "seen" when "the Son of man comes in clouds with great power and glory" (13:26); then he will drink it anew in the Kingdom of God.

Perhaps the greatest achievement of Mk lies in his interpretation of the conflict within his Christian community by the second scene. In this scene the conflict between Jesus' purpose and the disciples' view of him becomes calamitous; the intimate act of eating with Jesus is forever slandered by Jesus' betrayal to death. Or is it slandered? After Mk, no Christian can eat the holy meal without asking himself, "Am I myself a betrayer of Jesus?" As soon as this question is asked, there is no way to avoid the story of Jesus' arrest, death, and absence as the meal is celebrated.[40]

40. I am deeply grateful to the Institute for Ecumenical and Cultural Research, Collegeville, Minnesota, for the setting to write this essay during spring semester, 1975.

III.

The Hour of the Son of Man and the Temptation of the Disciples

(Mark 14:32–42)

Werner H. Kelber

Interpreters are widely agreed that the text of Mk 14:32–42 features an unusual amount of doublets and contradictions. The most striking double features are: the introduction of two groups of disciples (14:32, 33), Jesus' prayer in both indirect and direct discourse (14:35, 36), and two climactic sayings of Jesus (14:38, 41). Among logical, theological discrepancies, the following three are frequently pointed out: an eschatological use of the "hour" motif (14:35, 41) versus a profane use (14:37), Jesus' reproach of Peter being abruptly deflected toward the disciples (14:37–38), and the disciples' reported failure to "answer" (14:40) without antecedent reprimand or questioning.

These observed duplicate features and thematic inconsistencies became the basis for complex source and tradition theories which in turn contributed to an understanding of the text as a product of sources or a blending of tradition and redaction.[1] Methodologically, all these studies share the conviction that the Mkan text is ideally interpreted in dialogue with pre-Mkan stages or sources.

---

1. E. Hirsch, *Frühgeschichte des Evangeliums*, 2d ed. (Tübingen: J. C. B. Mohr [P. Siebeck], 1951), I, 156–58; K. G. Kuhn, "Jesus in Gethsemane," *EvT* 12 (1952), 260–85; T. Boman, "Der Gebetskampf Jesu," *NTS* 10 (1964), 261–73; T. Lescow, "Jesus in Gethsemane," *EvT* 26 (1966), 141–59; R. S. Barbour, "Gethsemane in the Tradition of the Passion," *NTS* 16 (1970), 231–51; LINNEMANN, 11–40; SCHENKE, 461–560; SCHENK, 193–206; DORMEYER, 124–37; W. Mohn, "Gethsemane (Mk 14, 32–42)," *ZNW* 64 (1973), 194–208.

41

With redaction and composition criticism, however, the hermeneutical focus is shifting from pre-Mkan traditions to the given entity of the Mkan text. The text is now understood as the purposeful composition of a theologian who works selectively with traditions and creatively with a definite theological project in mind.

From this perspective many alleged contradictions turn out to be illusory when examined in the context of the Mkan story line, the Mkan character development, the Mkan plot structure, and Mkan theological themes. What looks like a flawed text, controlled by disparate pre-Mkan traditions, may well prove to be under Mkan control, if we persist in reading the text within the Mkan theological framework.

This new appreciation of Mkan authorship extends to matters of style and language. With regard to the observed redundant features, for example, F. Neirynck[2] has demonstrated that duality in the broad sense of the word, including double phrases, repetition of single words, double questions, doublets of indirect and direct discourse, and pleonastic constructs of various kinds form an integral part of Mkan style and syntax.[3]

In an earlier study on Mk 14:32–42 we arrived at the conclusion that "Mark is not merely the redactor, but to a high degree the creator and composer of the Gethsemane story."[4] Neirynck's observations, which we failed to consider at the time, further confirm the intensely redactional nature of the Mkan Gethsemane story.[5]

The task before us now is to make 14:32–42 more readily understandable as an integral part of Mk's total narrative scheme. We shall begin our study with an analysis of the story's two principal scenes, the lamenting Jesus (1) and the sleeping disciples (2). We shall next ex-

---

2. See NEIRYNCK.

3. The practical impact of Neirynck's work is easily obscured by the technical, statistical nature of his presentation. By demonstrating a fairly homogeneous Mkan character of the Gospel's language, Neirynck sets definite limits to source critical theories and challenges the feasibility of separating tradition from redaction on linguistic grounds. After Neirynck, all source and decomposition theories have to pass the test of his studies.

4. W. H. Kelber, "Mark 14:32–42: Gethsemane," *ZNW* 63 (1972), 176. This article, while largely based on linguistic analysis, already followed a less decompositional, more constructive line of approach represented by the following three scholars: M. Dibelius, "Gethsemane," trans. M. S. Enslin, *The Crozer Quarterly* 12 (1935), 254–65; E. Lohmeyer, *Das Evangelium des Markus*, 17th ed. (Göttingen: Vandenhoeck & Ruprecht, 1967), 313–21; E. Lohse, *History of the Suffering and Death of Jesus Christ*, trans. M. O. Dietrich (Philadelphia: Fortress Press, 1967), 55–68.

5. NEIRYNCK, 30–31, 63–64, 70–71.

plore the relationship between the Gethsemane unit and the Mkan sequence at large (3), and then view the story in relation to its cultural milieu to which it was intended to speak (4).

1. THE SPARING OF THE HOUR

In 14:32–36 Mk develops a three-stage drama which serves to focus upon the solitary prayer of Jesus. In anticipation of his prayer Jesus asks a group of disciples, presumably the twelve (cf. 14:17, 20), to stay behind and pray (14:32). Next Jesus singles out Peter, James, and John, laments his state of trepidation, and advises the three to stay awake (14:33–34). Leaving the three behind, Jesus then turns to his Father in solitary prayer (14:35–36).

In his lament Jesus evokes the crucial death motif (14:34: *heōs thanatou*). His suffering is until death or on account of death.[6] It is not terminated by death, but it culminates in it, for death, the story will tell, is what ultimately causes the anguished lament. Partly drawn from Ps 41:6 (LXX), this lament suggests the image of the Righteous One who submits to a life in suffering climaxing in death. On one level this belongs to the logic of Mk's passion Christology. Suffering and a climactic death are the fate of the Son of Man (8:31; 9:31; 10:33–34). In a deeper sense, however, the lamenting Jesus is not the Righteous One who affirms his vindication through suffering and death. The lament together with the prayer reveal a new depth of anxiety over the prospect of suffering. The verbs *ekthambeisthai* and *adēmonein* (14:33) portray a Jesus who is overcome by anguish and horror in the face of death. This fear of death drives him into solitary prayer which both in its indirect and direct form aims at the elimination of suffering from his Messianic ministry. To be sure, the prayer allows for the possibility of ultimate consent to the divine plan of passion (14:35: *ei dynaton*; 14:36 closes with a formula of submission). But the request for the passing of the hour and the removal of the cup has every indication of a desire to bypass the cross.

The passion predictions had spoken of Jesus' voluntary acceptance of

---

6. Both meanings may be implied in the Mkan context. For suggested translations of the preposition *heōs* with the genitive, see BLASS-DEBRUNNER, 116.

the divinely ordained suffering from the hands of sinful men. This suffering embraced by the passion predictions no longer is affirmed by Jesus' lament and prayer at Gethsemane. The lament articulates his personal fear in view of death, and the prayer even seeks a way out of the cross. In his lament and prayer Jesus is therefore on the verge of retracting his passion predictions and close upon disavowing his vocation as the suffering Son of Man. The lamenting, praying Jesus is not the suffering Righteous One, but one who seeks to escape his appointed fate of righteous suffering.

This desire to bypass the cross is articulated in Jesus' prayerful request that he be spared "the hour" (14:35). We shall in the following reflect on this motif of "the hour" because it discloses the full implications of Jesus' Gethsemane prayer.

"The hour" from which Jesus prays to be spared is identified as "the hour" of the Son of Man's being "delivered up" (*paradidonai*) into the hands of sinners (14:41). In the crucifixion scene Mk resumes the hour motif and extends it, in typical redactional fashion, into a threefold pattern[7] to indicate the heightening of Jesus' being "delivered up" on the cross (15:25, 33, 34). "The hour" is therefore a symbol for Jesus' passion (being "delivered up") which commences with the arrest immediately following the Gethsemane story and culminates in the cross.

Still more is at stake in "the hour" of the Son of Man. "The hour," used in this absolute sense, not merely attaches weight to the period of passion proper, but it qualifies this suffering in an eschatological sense. In the Gospel's apocalyptic discourse (Mk 13) "the hour" of the Christians' being "delivered up" (*paradidonai*) coincides with the intercession of the Spirit (13:11). In this case, the eschatological dimension of the Spirit is revealed through the medium of "the hour" of suffering. In this same discourse "the hour" points to the future, but incalculable *kairos* of the Son of Man (13:32). "The hour" is therefore a cipher for suffering (14:35, 41), for the eschatological quality of suffering (13:11), and for eschatological revelation in a purely futuristic sense (13:32).

---

7. On the use of threefold patterns in Mk, see D. E. Nineham, *The Gospel of St. Mark* (Baltimore, Md.: Penguin Books, 1963), 392; T. A. Burkill, *Mysterious Revelation* (Ithaca, N.Y.: Cornell University Press, 1963), 232 n. 24, 243–44; NEIRYNCK, 110–12; DORMEYER, 130–31, 153, 199, 213–14.

The eschatological dimension of Jesus' passion is confirmed by the following two observations. There is first the use of *ēngiken* at the very end of the Gethsemane story (14:42). The verb announces the "coming" of Judas. Significantly, the betrayer is at this point not introduced by his name, but by titular derivation from *paradidonai*. As the one who "delivers up" Jesus (*ho paradidous me*) Judas "comes" to set into motion the passion proper.[8] It is this "coming" of Judas for the purpose of initiating the passion of Jesus which is expressed by *ēngiken*, an eschatologically loaded term which recapitulates the *ēngiken* of 1:15. In 1:14–15, a carefully worded Mkan summary, *ēngiken* had served to announce the Mkan Jesus' programmatic message and the Gospel's principal theme: the arrival of the Kingdom of God.[9] Not until 14:42 is the crucial term repeated, and now in reference to the imminent passion. The "coming" of the passion is thus correlated with the "coming" of the Kingdom, and Jesus' being "delivered up" is given an eschatological perspective.

The eschatological dimension of the passion, i.e., this inner connection between the arrival of the Kingdom and that of the passion, is further suggested by the emergence of the designation King (*ho basileus*) in the Passion Narrative (15:2, 9, 12, 18, 26, 32). In reference to Jesus, King is not used prior to Mk 15.[10] This seems surprising in view of Mk's guiding theme of the Kingdom of God. Yet this showing of the title King in Mk 15 is comprehensible as the result of Mk's eschatologically conditioned theology of the cross. "The hour" is the period of passion, i.e., Jesus' last hour, just as it is the eschatological hour, i.e., the time which reveals the full identity of the Kingship of Jesus.

A survey of the title in its dramatic settings discloses a curiously ambiguous and ironic quality. Jesus' own response to Pilate's question (15:2: *sy legeis*) remains obscure and is open to interpretations in an affirmative, negative, or ironic sense. Pilate's adoption of the title (15:9, 12) may be contemptuous, ironic, or out of secret conviction.

---

8. Judas' act of betrayal is consistently described by the term *paradidonai:* 14:10, 11, 18, 21, 42, 44.

9. See KELBER, 7–15.

10. In 6:14, 25, 26, 27 king is used in reference to Herod Antipas, and in 13:9 with regard to secular rulers.

The salutation of the soldiers (15:18) creates a cruel mock scene. The *titulus* (15:26) is expressly designed to state the nature of the crime. The reaction of the guardians of the Jewish religion, finally, reflects open ridicule and establishment ideology (15:32). Is the title then affirmed or negated by Jesus' cross? For Mk, is Jesus the King or is he not the King?

Both the sudden flare of the royal title and its ambiguous status in Mk 15 may be the desired effect of Mk's theological reflection. The title itself resumes and brings to new heights Mk's theology of the Kingdom, while its double meaning results from the paradox of a suffering King. The Jesus whose enemies speak the truth in ignorance and infamy, whose crime reveals his honor, and whose crown is made of thorns is precisely the kind of King Mk wishes to portray. It is the paradox of the crucified King which finds dramatic expression in the ironic ambivalence surrounding the royal title in the Passion Narrative.

The full meaning of Jesus' Messiahship is thus rooted in suffering and realized on the cross. The cross confirms the coming of the Kingdom and legitimizes Jesus as King. Far from contradicting the Gospel of the Kingdom (1:14–15), "the hour" of crucifixion is paradoxically "the hour" of coronation.

In returning to Jesus' request for the passing of "the hour," we can see what is truly at stake in Gethsemane. This plea for release from the passion raises the question whether Jesus will live out the truth of the Gospel of the Kingdom which is contingent upon his suffering and death. The Kingdom itself is at stake in Gethsemane.

In view of Mk's systematically presented passion Christology (8:31; 9:31; 10:33–34) and closely related Kingdom theology one must probe the question why the Evangelist challenges the theme of suffering as severely as he does in the Gethsemane scene. Obviously, Jesus' conflict at Gethsemane is resolved with his acceptance of the previously chosen fate of suffering and death. What needs to be explored, however, is the Mkan reason for forcing Jesus to the brink of refuting his mission of Kingdom through passion which he (the Mkan Jesus) had earlier affirmed with authority and conviction. To this issue we will turn in the concluding section.

2. THE SLEEPING DISCIPLES

As Jesus' lament and prayer form part of a threefold progression, so is also the scene of the sleeping disciples (14:37–42) distinguished by three acts.[11] Three times Jesus leaves his place of prayer to call upon the disciples, and three times he finds them asleep. It is our contention that this threefold structure of 14:37–42 serves both an internal (within the Gethsemane unit's frame of reference) and external (in relation to the total Gospel context) purpose. We will at this point develop the internal significance.

What should be noted first is a shifting of the spotlight away from Jesus. His continued prayers are mere encores of the initial prayer,[12] and his terror-stricken soul is no longer the issue. Nor is the tripartite drama staged to act out Jesus' inner development. There is no indication that 14:37–42 is designed to dramatize the protagonist's metamorphosis, as if each prayer stage carried with it a new measure of insight, until at stage three Jesus has arrived at the supreme decision to take the cross upon himself. Although Jesus does emerge in the end with a resolve that seemed in jeopardy at the outset, and although it is through prayers that he gains the freedom of decision, Mk does not focus upon the inner thoughts and progress of the praying Jesus.

On the contrary, the spotlight in 14:37–42 is on the disciples. Peter, James, and John are chosen to be present at Gethsemane, as they were earlier selected to witness Jesus' power over death (5:35–43; see 5:37) and the epiphany of his eschatological glory (9:2–8; see 9:2).[13] The singling out of the three at Gethsemane, therefore, signifies the importance of what transpires there, as conversely their lack of performance raises the issue of failure in leadership.[14]

11. The structure of the Gethsemane unit consists of two threefold units (14:32–36, 37–42). In view of Mk's predilection for units of three, this is further confirmation of Mk's composition of the whole pericope. See note 7.

12. 14:39: . . . *ton auton logon eipōn*; a third prayer is only implied.

13. Apart from the singling out of the three for special occasions, see the bestowal of a name at their appointment (3:16–17).

14. The separation of the three confidants from the remainder of the disciples is thus not the result of the mingling of two sources, or a clash between tradition and redaction. Source and tradition theories of this kind were advanced by Kuhn, "Gethsemane," 263, 266; BULTMANN, 268; LINNEMANN, 11, 31–32; SCHENKE, 472, 480–83; E. Schweizer, *The Good News According to Mark*, trans. D. H. Madvig (Atlanta, Ga.: John Knox Press, 1970), 309–10.

On his first return to the three sleeping disciples Jesus singles out Peter and censures him on account of his inability to stay awake (14:37). Jesus' reprimand of Peter changes in mid-sentence into the second person plural (14:38), as a result of which it is directed to the three, and through them to the disciples at large. This broadening of the audience perspective in 14:38 is accompanied by efforts to transcend the immediacy of the plot. The issue of waking is expounded in terms of prayer, and the disciples' failure to wake and pray is said to constitute temptation. Be it noted already that temptation does not refer to Jesus' own agonizing lament and prayer in the sense that 14:32–36 might be understood on the analogy of 1:12–13. At Gethsemane it is the disciples who undergo temptation! The exact nature of their temptation, what precisely their sleeping signifies, and what the call to wake and pray enjoins them to do is as yet not fully clear. But it seems that in the temptation to succumb to the weakness of the flesh (14:38) more is involved than man's natural inclination to yield to physical weariness.

It is noteworthy that within the larger Gospel framework the motif of watching/waking and the corresponding topics of coming, finding, and sleeping had occurred earlier in the parable of the doorkeeper (13:33–37).[15] *Grēgorein* is restricted in Mk to the parable of the doorkeeper (13:34, 35, 37) and to the Gethsemane scene (14:34, 37, 38). The exhortation to watchfulness is issued only in the conclusion of the apocalyptic discourse and at Gethsemane. As for the motif of sleep, *mē elthōn exaiphnēs heurē hymas katheudontas* (13:36) strikingly parallels two clauses in the Gethsemane unit: *kai erchetai kai heuriskei autous katheudontas* (14:37a), and *kai palin elthōn heuren autous katheudontas* (14:40a). Watching-coming-finding-sleeping forms a cluster of associations both in 13:33–37 and in 14:32–42. In both instances waking is virtue and sleeping is fault. In the parable waking is demanded by the expected *kairos* of the master of the house, while sleeping causes one to miss the eschatological coming of the Son of Man. The resumption of this watching-sleeping theme in 14:32–42 casts an eschatological light on the conduct of the disciples at Geth-

---

15. After the "hour" motif this is the second time we observe a correlation between Mk 13 and 14:32–42. Thematic connections between the Mkan apocalypse and the Gethsemane story were observed among others by R. H. Lightfoot, *The Gospel Message of St. Mark* (Oxford: Oxford University Press, 1950), 48–59; F. Dewar, "Chapter 13 and the Passion Narrative in St. Mark," *Theology* 64 (1961), 99–107.

semane. As "the hour" of Jesus carries eschatological quality, so does also the disciples' "sleeping" and failure to "wake" have eschatological repercussions. Whatever it is that the disciples fail to do by "sleeping," it carries consequences which far transcend the particular moment of Gethsemane.

What is highlighted at the second stage (14:39–40) is not the prayer of Jesus, but again the scandal of the sleeping disciples (14:40). Indeed the depth of their sleep is emphatically expressed: *ēsan gar autōn hoi ophtalmoi katabarynomenoi*. This brief descriptive phrase belongs to the established form of *gar*-clauses[16] which serve to draw the attention of the reader to a level of perception lying beneath, or outside, the immediate plot structure. In the case of 14:40, the description of the disciples' "heaviness of eyes" does therefore appear to point to a blindness on a deeper level. It is only on the story level (linear plot structure) that the three close their eyes as a result of physical exhaustion. On the discourse level (the narrator's communication to the readers) they close their eyes to what essentially transpires at Gethsemane. Their natural sleepiness is but the outward manifestation of a nonphysical, religious blindness.

The final description of the disciples' response (14:40: *ouk ēdeisan ti apokrithōsin autō*) is immediately reminiscent of Peter's mistaken reaction to the transfiguration epiphany (9:6: *ou gar ēdei ti apokrithē.*)[17] In the transfiguration story Mk had used this phrase to disqualify Peter's suggestion to build three booths; Peter had not understood the significance of Jesus' metamorphosis. In like manner, the parallel statement in 14:40 records the disciples' incomprehension. They do not know how to respond properly to Jesus at Gethsemane, not merely out of natural drowsiness, but due to their failure to grasp the significance of the hour. In sum, the principal theme of the second visit is the disciples' continuing lack of understanding.

At the outset of the third and last stage (14:41–42) attention is one more time drawn to the weakness of the disciples. Jesus' response, his last words to the disciples, opens with a rebuke: "Do you still sleep and

16. Their Mkan authorship and function were first argued by C. H. Bird, "Some *gar*-clauses in St. Mark's Gospel," *JTS* n.s. 4 (1953), 171–87.

17. See A. Kenney, "The Transfiguration and the Agony in the Garden," *CBQ* 19 (1957), 444–52; see also DORMEYER, 137.

rest?" (14:41b)[18] It seems, therefore, that Jesus' three visits to the disciples prove futile because sleeping had been their inclination from the outset, and sleeping remains their inclination to the end.

The foregoing analysis suggests that the chief purpose for dramatizing Jesus' three visits to the disciples lies neither in the inner life of the praying Jesus nor in the content of his prayer, but in the negative role played by the disciples. Jesus' thrice-told visits form the background against which the disciples' failure is displayed. This, then, is the internal function of the three-stage dramatization of Jesus' visits: it demonstrates the recurrent and incorrigible blindness of the disciples.[19]

3. THE NARRATIVE POSITION

Gethsemane marks a climactic point not only in the Mkan Passion Narrative but in the Gospel's total thematic development.

The dramatic movement which peaks at Gethsemane gets notably under way at Caesarea Philippi. There Peter's "confession" (8:29) comes into conflict with Jesus' first prediction of passion and resurrection (8:31). Peter's Christ (*ho Christos*) receives correction through Jesus' suffering Son of Man, and the chief disciple's rejection of a suffering Messiah earns him the accusation of playing the role of Satan. At Caesarea Philippi the final outcome of the Gospel story is already within sight. Jesus is the Messiah of passion and committed to life through death—the cross is anticipated. Peter rejects the necessity of suffering and thereby qualifies himself as his master's leading opponent—the denial is anticipated.

Jesus' second pronouncement of his fateful suffering meets incomprehension and fear on the part of the disciples (9:31–32). Not grasping the issue of suffering and failing to ask for clarification, they in effect join the ranks of Peter. The disciples choose the leadership of Peter over that of Jesus—their apostasy is anticipated.

The third passion prediction of the Son of Man's death and rising (10:33–34) contrasts sharply with James's and John's request for posi-

---

18. Contextually 14:41b must be read as a question and not as a command.

19. Very much to the point is SCHENKE, 532: *"Nicht das dreimalige Gebet Jesu soll also geschildert werden, sondern das dreimalige Versagen der Jünger. Nicht der Gebetskampf Jesu wird durch die Schilderung gesteigert, sondern das Versagen der Jünger."*

tions of power and honor (10:35–37). By rejoinder Jesus summons them to drink the cup which he will drink (10:38–39). The cup is a symbol of suffering and death[20] and therefore a controversial cipher in the growing conflict over the wisdom of the passion.[21] James's and John's inclination to prefer glory over the cup anticipates their break with Jesus over the issue of the cup.

Jesus' recurrent teaching about the suffering Son of Man and the disciples' consistently negative response dramatizes an ideological division between Jesus and the disciples. Jesus the suffering Son of Man is opposed by the disciples' nonsuffering Christ (cf. 8:29), and passion Christology is set over against discipleship failure. At Gethsemane the christological structure represented by Jesus and the disciples' counter-structure come to a climax.

Recent work on the Mkan Son of Man Christology has developed the view that the Evangelist in part adopted, in part shaped and created, and above all strategically placed Son of Man sayings throughout the Gospel.[22] The *suffering* Son of Man sayings occur in two Gospel units: 8:27–10:52 (cf. 8:31; 9:12; 9:31; 10:33–34), the section which develops the pattern of the *via crucis*, and 14:1–42 (cf. 14:21, 41), the prelude to the passion proper, as we shall argue. While the passion predictions speak of suffering and rising (8:31; 9:31; 10:33–34), the scope of the sayings immediately preceding the passion is limited to suffering (14:21, 41). Beginning with 9:31 and down to 14:41—the two sayings are parallel constructions—the suffering is explicated by the passive voice of *paradidonai* ("to be delivered up"), Mk's technical term for Jesus' passion. This progression of suffering Son of Man sayings introduces a regulative theme into the Gospel which directs the plot toward its culmination, the Passion Narrative. It is at the end of the Gethsemane story that the Mkan Jesus speaks for the last time to the disciples (14:41–42), and it is at this point of parting that he leaves the

---

20. L. Goppelt, "*potērion*," TDNT VI, 152–53.

21. At the Last Supper Jesus makes the disciples drink the cup (14:23: "they *all* drank from it"), but their conduct during Jesus' passion belies their sharing of the cup (14:50: "they *all* forsook him").

22. N. Perrin deserves major credit for illuminating the Mkan Son of Man Christology, see *A Modern Pilgrimage in New Testament Christology* (Philadelphia: Fortress Press, 1974). The present state of the discussion is aptly summarized by J. Donahue: "The Son of Man Christology as it is found in Mark is then in a real sense a Marcan creation" (DONAHUE, 182).

disciples with the last suffering Son of Man saying: *idou paradidotai ho hyios tou anthrōpou eis tas cheiras tōn hamartōlōn* (14:41d). At Gethsemane, therefore, Mk's christological explication of the suffering Son of Man has reached a high point.[23] What up to this point was expounded conceptually will from now on be enacted dramatically. With this last suffering Son of Man saying Jesus ceases publicly to pronounce or reflect upon his *suffering* role. Henceforth, he undergoes suffering itself, and he does so in almost complete silence.[24] Gethsemane thus stands on the threshold of the actualization of Jesus' suffering. It summarizes the suffering Son of Man Christology, and effects the transition toward the passion proper.[25]

Parallel to passion Christology runs the drama of the disciples' apostasy. Their principal weakness lies in the inability to apprehend the full implications of a suffering Messiahship. As D. O. Via correctly observed,[26] theirs is an existential, not an intellectual problem. At rare moments they express a willingness "to drink the cup" and die with Jesus (10:39; 14:29, 31), but in the light of the total perspective generated by Mk, suffering goes against the grain of their humanity.

The double structure of passion Christology and discipleship failure on one level carries the plot toward certain disaster. Ever since the conflict erupted at Caesarea Philippi, the disciples and their master embarked upon a collision course. The disciples walk the way of Jesus, but they are oriented toward a goal which is different from what he had in mind. Unless there is a dramatic change of heart, Jesus and the disciples will inevitably come to grief in the passion days of his ministry. Opposition to passion is, however, against the express will of Jesus, and the disciples are therefore to be held accountable for their failure. The cumulative effect of the passion predictions makes their

---

23. As for the redactional nature of 14:41, see Perrin's change of opinion: from traditional ("The Creative Use of the Son of Man Traditions by Mark," *USQR* 23 [1968], 359) to redactional (*Pilgrimage*, 132).

24. The silence is broken by the two Messianic confessions (14:62; 15:2) and the two cries of dereliction and expiration (15:34, 37).

25. The retrospective-prospective function of Mkan units was explored by V. Robbins, "The Christology of Mark" (Ph.D. dissertation, University of Chicago, 1969). See also N. Perrin's essay in the present volume, "The High Priest's Question and Jesus' Answer."

26. D. O. Via, *Kerygma and Comedy in the New Testament* (Philadelphia: Fortress Press, 1975), 141.

conduct appear inexcusable. Three times Jesus pronounces in plain terms what to expect from associating with and following after him. And three times they only hear what they want to hear. In the end, their desertion of Jesus introduces an additional element of crisis into the Passion Narrative.[27]

While Jesus' three visits to the disciples (14:37–42) function internally to emphasize their inexcusable blindness, they link up externally (in relation to the total Gospel context) with the three passion predictions, Peter's three denials, and the three "hours" on the cross. Three times Jesus attempts to open the eyes of the disciples to the passion reality (8:31; 9:31; 10:33–34), but three times they remain unperceptive. Three times at Gethsemane Jesus gives his chosen disciples a chance to endorse the model of a suffering Messiah, but each time they let the occasion slip by. Three times Peter denies Jesus at the very moment the latter makes his fateful Son of Man confession.[28] The tragic peak is reached with Jesus' three hours on the cross, the agony of which intensifies from the hour of crucifixion (15:25), to the hour of demonic darkness (15:33), to the hour of abandonment, mocking, and death (15:34–37). The correlation of these four threefold scenes, which variously emphasize the divine necessity and human rejection of passion, underscores the tragically irreconcilable conflict between passion Christology and discipleship failure.

Gethsemane, then, is not the first time the disciples fail to live up to Jesus' expectations. Rather, it marks a pivotal point on their collision course with Jesus. Their temptation consists in succumbing to the weakness of the flesh (14:38) by falling asleep. But on a deeper level, we noticed, their state of fatigue signaled a religious blindness which prevented them from grasping the significance of Gethsemane altogether. What had happened at Gethsemane was that Jesus, through aching lament and agonizing prayer, had come to terms with the necessity of his suffering. In effect Jesus had opted for the identity of a crucified King. His royal road would not end in triumph at the Temple,

---

27. Schweizer (*Mark*, 315) states that it is the disciples who are "the greatest cause of his [Jesus'] suffering." But the agony caused by the disciples' desertion is exceeded still by God's abandonment.

28. See K. Dewey's essay in the present volume, "Peter's Curse and Cursed Peter"; DONAHUE, 42, 62–63, *passim*.

but lead through the Temple to the cross. It is this final breakthrough toward a suffering Messiahship which the disciples overslept at Gethsemane. Their blindness amounts to, and their temptation consists in, the failure to come to terms with the passion Christology.

In the total dramatic sequence, Gethsemane constitutes the last attempt at resolving the Gospel's pervasive conflict by reconciling the disciples' counterstructure to the structure of passion Christology. For one last time the fate of Jesus and that of the disciples are closely tied together. What is at stake at Gethsemane is the very issue which had proven the major stumbling block in the disciples' following of Jesus: the necessity of suffering. In the end Jesus does not change, nor does his exemplary conduct effect a change in the disciples. Jesus overcomes his desire not to drink the cup (cf. 14:36), and the disciples evade drinking from the cup. In a sense all remains the same as before. With Gethsemane the conflict between Jesus and the disciples has been brought to a head and proven insoluble.

Henceforth, Jesus and the disciples will part company. Jesus moves into death, and through death and resurrection toward the parousia. The disciples, represented by Peter, James, and John, forfeit their last chance for entering the Kingdom. As Peter was in the case of the first passion prediction, so is he also singled out for reproach at the height of his resistance to passion. But the reproach of Gethsemane is addressed to "Simon," not to Peter (14:37). This last time Jesus speaks to Peter he refrains from calling him by his apostolic name (cf. 3:16).[29] As the bestowal of the new name had revealed Peter's ascendancy to apostolic leadership, so will the one and only recurrence of the old name on the threshold of Jesus' passion signify the apostle's fall from power.[30] The kind of discipleship and leadership exhibited by Peter founders at Gethsemane. If he and the disciples fail to wake for the "one hour" (14:37), they will not tolerate "the hour" (14:35, 41) of Jesus' passion.[31] Unable to reconcile themselves with the logic of

29. Mt makes two moves in the direction of exonerating the Mkan Peter. First, he suppresses the—for him—embarrassing item that Jesus called Peter "Simon" at Gethsemane. Second, he presents both Jesus' rebuke and his exhortation in the second person plural (Mt 26:40).

30. H. B. Swete, *The Gospel According to St. Mark* (London: Macmillan, 1898), 325.

31. The hour, like the cup, is thus also a controversial symbol, a cipher which evokes the division between Jesus and the disciples. Their hour differs from his "hour."

passion, they will lose their lives while trying to save themselves (8:35).

At the end of the Gethsemane account Jesus' last rebuke of the disciples (14:41b) is followed by the controversial term *apechei* (14:41c).[32] In both classic and Hellenistic Greek the term is used in commercial contexts, denoting the issuing of receipts and/or the completion of business transactions. Based on this technical meaning the term may be variously applied to Judas who has settled his account with the high priests (14:10–11), or to the disciples whose temptation of "sleeping" has come to an end, or to Jesus who has come to terms with his passion. Perhaps one should let the term speak in its suggested ambiguity. A moment pregnant with meaning has arrived. The fate of both Jesus and the disciples is sealed. "The account is settled."

Recognition of a break in the Mkan Passion Narrative between the Gethsemane and the arrest stories, of a caesura between 14:42 and 14:43, has played a significant role in advancing the thesis of a pre-Mkan Passion Narrative. R. Bultmann[33] and J. Jeremias,[34] among others, argued for a "primitive narrative" (Bultmann) or a "shorter account" (Jeremias) of the passion which began with the arrest and continued with condemnation, departure to the cross, crucifixion, and death. In our judgment the observed caesura after the Gethsemane story is of Mkan making. Mk portrays the story as the culmination of the suffering Son of Man Christology and the high point of the conflict between Jesus and the disciples over the issue of a suffering Son of Man. After the resolution of Gethsemane, according to the Mkan scheme, suffering itself will come to pass.

Jeremias corroborated his thesis of a pre-Mkan passion source beginning after the Gethsemane story by observing a comparatively close agreement between Jn and Mk from the arrest onward. Agreements (and disagreements) between Mk and Jn, however, need not inevitably point to these Evangelists' joint use of a pre-Mkan passion source. Redaction critical awareness of the theological competence of the four Evangelists casts increasing doubt on source dependence as the

32. Authorities of the Western textual tradition attest *apechei to telos*, a reading accepted by TAYLOR, 557. This may already constitute a plausible explication of the *lectio difficilior, apechei*.

33. BULTMANN, 279, 275–84.

34. J. Jeremias, *The Eucharistic Words of Jesus*, trans. N. Perrin, 3d ed. rev. (New York: Scribner's, 1966), 96, 89–96.

prime explanation for intra-Mkan tensions, inner-Synoptic connections, and the Synoptic-Johannine relationship. Greater allowance should be made for literary fluidity and interaction among Gospel traditions, and it would seem desirable to explore in some depth the possibility of Jn's judicious handling of passion material in Mkan/Synoptic form.[35]

The caesura following the Gethsemane story is therefore not likely to be source-conditioned. It does not mark a clash between loosely connected units prior to 14:42 and a purposefully constructed Passion Narrative after 14:42,[36] for Gethsemane coheres with the theological and dramatic development of the Gospel's total narrative. Nor does the absence of suffering Son of Man sayings after 14:42 reflect Mkan reluctance to interfere with an authoritative, ready-formed passion source.[37] Our discussion has suggested that the break between 14:42 and 14:43 is a literary, theological creation of Mk. It serves to elevate the conflict between Jesus and the disciples to a new dramatic level which signals the end of the pre-passion period and the beginning of the Son of Man's being "delivered up."

---

35. See also in the present volume K. Dewey's essay, "Peter's Curse," and the concluding essay, "From Passion Narrative to Gospel." The primacy of the Mkan Passion Narrative and a Johannine adaptation of Mkan/Synoptic material has recently been suggested by J. Schreiber, *Die Markuspassion. Wege zur Erforschung der Leidensgeschichte Jesu* (Hamburg: Furche, 1969), 18–19, 27, 53. The Gethsemane tradition itself is a case in point. We observe seven parallels between Mk and Jn: (1) Distress of the soul—Mk 14:34b (Mt 26:38b): *perilypos estin hē psychē mou* (Jn 12:27a, lacks however *perilypos*); (2) two versions of the hour motif—(a) rescue from the hour: Mk 14:35: *parelthē ap' autou hē hōra* (Jn 12:27c, d); (b) the *coming* of the hour of the *Son of Man:* Mk 14:41d (Mt 26:45c): *ēlthen hē hōra, idou paradidotai ho hyios tou anthrōpou* (Jn 12:23; cf. 12:27d); (3) the address of God with Father in conjunction with the hour motif—Mk 14:35b–36b: *parelthē ap' autou hē hōra . . . abba ho patēr* (Jn 12:27c); (4) the cup motif—Mk 14:36c (Mt 26:39a; Lk 22:42b): *parenegke to potērion touto ap' emou* (Jn 18:11b); (5) call for departure—Mk 14:42a (Mt 26:46a): *egeiresthe, agōmen* (Jn 14:31b); (6) the singling out of Peter—Mk 14:37a (Mt 26:40a): *kai legei tō Petrō* (Jn 18:11a); (7) the titular use of *paradidonai* in reference to Judas—Mk 14:42b (Mt 26:25, 46, 48; Lk 22:21): *ho paradidous me* (Jn 18:2, 5c; cf. 13:11a; 19:11b). All available Johannine fragments of the Gethsemane tradition (Jn 12:23, 27; 14:31b; 18:2, 5c, 11) appear to stem from a Mkan-type version, while the fragmentation itself is attributable to Jn's *theologia gloriae.*

36. This assumption underlies Jeremias' consideration of a pre-Mkan Passion Narrative beginning with 14:43.

37. Thus H. E. Tödt, *The Son of Man in the Synoptic Tradition,* trans. D. M. Barton (Philadelphia: Westminster Press, 1965), 148.

4. THE MARKAN DIALECTIC

"Perhaps the best name for the Markan sequence in its totality is conflict," observes D. O. Via.[38] The story of the Mkan Gospel reveals a conflict in which the protagonist encounters and provokes a deepening opposition which in turn precipitates the movement toward passion.[39] Specifically, the Gospel informs us of a clash between Jesus and the disciples which reaches a high point in the Gethsemane scene.

Manifestly, the discord arises over the issue of passion Christology. One of the chief characteristics of the disciples in Mk is their rejection of a suffering Messiah. For this reason the conflict is most sharply dramatized in the Passion Narrative. There is, one might say, a dramatic necessity imposed upon Mk to make the disciples deteriorate as Jesus moves toward death. Such features as flight and denial are thus in full keeping with the dramatic role assigned to them by Mk the theologian. The disciples' disappearance—at the outset of Jesus' being "delivered up"—and the chief disciple's denial of his master—at the very moment Jesus makes his crucial Messianic confession—bring to an effective and logical conclusion their role as opponents of a suffering Messiah.

Within this conflict Mk develops the Gethsemane scene as a threshold event. Immediately preceding the passion proper Mk presents a closing argument for a Christology of the suffering, dying Jesus, and he makes his case against the leading disciples. Both the inescapable necessity of the Son of Man's passion and the inexcusable conduct of the disciples are brought into focus.[40] With Gethsemane Mk has made it unmistakably clear that it was over the issue of suffering Messiahship that Jesus and his disciples parted in conflict.

In a biographical narrative, Via points out, conflict serves a "maintaining function," because "the process of amelioration needs the

---

38. Via, *Kerygma and Comedy*, 115.

39. On the one hand, Jesus' authority, his violation of the taboos of cleanliness and his mission against the Temple, causes hostility. On the other hand, Peter's "confession" prompts Jesus' confession, Judas's betrayal "delivers up" Jesus, and the High Priest's question provokes Jesus' Messianic confession.

40. The motif of inexcusability does not exhaust the significance of the disciples in Jesus' passion. In a deeper sense for Mk the cross is both the will of God and the fault of man. Human weakness and divine necessity belong together in inscrutable logic. See note 39. Cf. also Via, *Kerygma and Comedy*, 129.

process of degradation in order to attain its goal."[41]   This may well be
true from a global, structuralist viewpoint. Undoubtedly the Mkan conflict accentuates "the existential problem of the difficulty of man's grasping the revelation of God in a suffering messiah."[42]   In this general
sense Gethsemane will continue to speak to Christians and indeed to
human beings universally.[43]   But redaction criticism is curious about
the *Mkan condition* which helped shape the *specific nature* of this
fundamental conflict.   What is there in the Mkan setting that makes
Jesus' humiliation at Gethsemane a necessary feature of the Gospel?
What causes the Evangelist systematically to undermine the leadership
of the disciples?   What is the point of contact between the Gospel's
readers and a story which denies them Petrine patronage?

In Mk's view the three disciples form a triumvirate which is set apart
from the larger group of the twelve. The three are the representatives
of the twelve. The conduct of these three, under the leadership of
Peter, typifies that of the twelve, and of Christian discipleship in general.
Ideally, Christians ought to trace their own existence to these leaders,
and model their infant movement after the chosen three and the appointed twelve.[44]   And yet, Mk focuses critically upon the three.
Their bearing is uninspiring and indeed detrimental to Christian discipleship.   The manner in which they succumb to temptation is precisely the way in which Christians ought *not* to conduct themselves.

The disciples' objection to passion Christology, while understandable
as a universally human feature, might find a historical explanation in the
specific Mkan setting and in the general environment of early Christianity.

As is well known, dispute and dissension arose in early Christian

41. Via, *Kerygma and Comedy*, 116, 128.
42. Ibid., 75–76.
43. After a lengthy period of doctrinal generalizations and harmonizations in the history of New Testament interpretation redaction criticism now pays respect to the historical circumstance of individual texts and to authorial intention.   Will structuralism
take us back to a priori generalizations and into the "magic land of meanings outside
human consciousness"?   (E. D. Hirsch, *Validity in Interpretation* [New Haven, Conn.:
Yale University Press, 1967], 4).   Philosophically, structuralism and redaction criticism
part over the issue of semantic autonomy versus historical authenticity, and authorial
irrelevance versus authorial significance.   Is language ontologically prior to history and
independent of authors, or is it shaped by authors in creative response to social conditions?   Is the author controlled by the semantic status quo, or can he break it, subject it to his authorial intent, produce semantic mutations and conceptual innovations?
44. K.-G. Reploh, *Markus-Lehrer der Gemeinde*, Stuttgarter Biblische Monographien
9 (Stuttgart: Katholisches Bibelwerk, 1969), 30–35.

history more over the scandal of the cross than over the miracle of the resurrection. The disciples in Mk may thus represent a particular type of Christian faith which, from Mk's perspective, failed to take sufficient account of the cross of Jesus. Resistance to a suffering Christ may have involved the adoption of, or identification with, a resurrected, exalted Lord.[45] Acceptance of this present resurrected Christ may have been perceived as the realization of the Kingdom.[46] Principally, this non-Mkan faith reflects an affirmation of unbroken power and a vital need for personal prestige (10:35–37). Mk's choice of the disciples as Jesus' chief opponents would seem natural if they symbolize anti-passion Christians in Mk's time who had based their prestige on the authority of the twelve under the primacy of Peter.[47]

When read in this light, Gethsemane discloses a more sharply focused relevance. On the threshold of his own passion Jesus deals in exemplary fashion with the Christians' crisis of the cross, because the kind of testing he undergoes at Gethsemane may be the very one Christians are exposed to in the Mkan setting. As they are tempted to shortcut the way to the Kingdom by avoiding the cup, so is Jesus at Gethsemane. To define Gethsemane, therefore, as a testing which prepares Jesus for his passion is to describe only one dimension of the story. The Jesus of Gethsemane also suffers in the place of and as a model for Christians. Mk forces Jesus to the brink of recanting his passion identity because the Evangelist deals with Christians who are indifferent or hostile toward a suffering Messiah. The Mkan Jesus identifies with the "weakness of the flesh" of these Christians to the point of suffering their temptation to circumvent suffering. His struggle at Gethsemane is thus designed to overcome vicariously a Christian objection to a suffering Messiah.

By setting standards over and against the three leading disciples the

45. See V. Robbin's essay, "Last Meal: Preparation, Betrayal, and Absence," in the present volume.

46. Mk 13 is designed to oppose the concept of realized eschatology, cf. R. Pesch, *Naherwartungen: Tradition und Redaktion in Mk 13* (Düsseldorf: Patmos Verlag, 1968).

47. Still very much under way is an investigation of the opposition characters in Mk (disciples, family, false prophets, mockers, etc.) as representatives of a coherent challenge to Mkan theology. The above offers only a sketchy profile. As for the opponents' inclination to identify with the resurrected Lord, see WEEDEN, 59–81; for realized eschatology, see KELBER, 109–28; for the representational function of the disciples, see WEEDEN, 70–100, and J. B. Tyson, "The Blindness of the Disciples in Mark," *JBL* 80 (1961), 265–67.

Mkan Jesus discredits the notions of apostolic leadership and succession. Those Christians whose identity was linked with Peter, the three, and the twelve are challenged by the impact of Gethsemane. They find themselves disestablished from their apostolic base of power and reoriented toward Jesus' precarious path of suffering and death. True life is offered in following Jesus to the cross, and not by joining the disciples in flight and denial. Gethsemane invites community with the Crucified One, and by implication discourages immediate communion with the resurrected, exalted one. Christians are taken out of a falsely assumed realization of the Kingdom and confronted with the material and soteriological reality of suffering. To drink "the cup" and to wake "the hour" is to walk the way toward the Kingdom. For the clue to the Kingdom lies in "the hour" of the cross.

IV.

Temple, Trial, and Royal Christology

(Mark 14:53–65)

John R. Donahue, S.J.

The appearance of Jesus before the Sanhedrin (14:53–65) has been the object of intense historical and literary critical research in recent years.[1] One facet of the debate concerns discrepancies between Mk's account and the Rabbinic prescriptions for a valid trial. Capital trials were to be held only by day (Sanh 4:1), but Jesus was tried at night (cf. Mk 14:53; 15:1); no legal procedures were to take place on a Sabbath or feast day (Sanh 4:1; cf. Mk 14:1, 12); the sentence of death could not be pronounced on the same day as the trial (Sanh 4:1; cf. Mk 14:64); the charge of blasphemy required the pronouncing of the divine name (Sanh 7:5; cf. Mk 14:62); trials were to be held in the official chamber, not in the house of the High Priest (Sanh 11:2; cf. Mk 14:54); prior examination of witnesses, as well as independent agreement of their testimony, was required (Deut 19:15–18; Sanh 4:5; cf. Mk 14:56–59).[2] The fact that Jesus was executed by a Roman official by a method reserved for those considered a threat to the public

1. E. Bammel, ed., *The Trial of Jesus*, SBT, 2d Ser. 13 (Naperville, Ill.: Allenson, 1970); J. Blinzler, *The Trial of Jesus*, trans. I. and F. McHugh (Westminster, Md.: Newman, 1959); S. G. F. Brandon, *The Trial of Jesus of Nazareth* (New York: Stein and Day, 1968); D. R. Catchpole, *The Trial of Jesus*, Studia Post-Biblica 18 (Leiden: E. J. Brill, 1971); H. H. Cohn, *The Trial and Death of Jesus* (New York: Harper & Row, 1971); G. S. Sloyan, *Jesus on Trial* (Philadelphia: Fortress Press, 1973); P. Winter, *On the Trial of Jesus*, 2d ed. rev. by T. A. Burkill and G. Vermes (Berlin: W. de Gruyter, 1974).
2. E. Lohse, *"synedrion,"* TDNT VII, 867–68; Blinzler, *Trial*, 149–63.

order raises two additional problems: the competence of the Sanhedrin to pronounce and execute the death sentence and the nature and extent of Jewish involvement in the death of Jesus.[3]

Attempts have been made to save the historicity of Mk, ranging from the "traditional" two trial theory (one religious but illegal, the other [15:1–5] civil, but legal) to the view that, prior to A.D. 70, the Sanhedrin was dominated by Sadducees, and therefore not bound by the later Rabbinic code.[4]   When, however, these historical problems are coupled with the observations that the Mkan version of the "trial" is the end product of a growth of tradition and mirrors the theological purposes of the Evangelist more than the desire to preserve historical tradition, the Mkan narrative of Jesus before the Sanhedrin must be bypassed as a primary source for historical reconstruction.[5]   The thrust of the present essay is to show that Mk has constructed the trial narrative in such a way that it embodies major theological concerns of his Gospel. The trial itself is considered an entree to Mk's theology.

1. THE GROWTH OF THE TRADITION

Concurrent with studies of the historicity of the trial, there has been extensive research into the stages of the growth of the narrative.   Although the narrative seems to flow smoothly, there are incongruities which suggest a growth of the tradition: (1) in 14:53a, 60, 61, 63 there is mention of a single High Priest, while in 14:53b and 14:55 several high priests are mentioned whose relation to the single High Priest is not clarified; (2) there is a double introduction to the narrative (14:53, 55); (3) there is excessive repetition of the inadequacy or falseness of the witnesses (14:55, 56a, 57, 59); (4) since the charge in 14:58 plays no further role in the narrative, its function is not clear; (5) after Jesus' silence in 14:61, his confession in 14:62 is surprising; (6) the trial's intercalation into the story of Peter's denial calls for an explanation; (7)

---

3. Winter, *Trial*, 90–96.

4. For a restatement of the "traditional" view, see W. L. Lane, *The Gospel According to Mark*, The New International Commentary on the New Testament 2 (Grand Rapids, Mich.: Eerdmans, 1974), 528–30. Blinzler, *Trial*, is the most consistent advocate of the Sadducean Sanhedrin.

5. Sloyan (*Trial*, 89–109) and Catchpole (*Trial*, 220) hold that the Lkan trial (Lk 22:66–71) is a better locus for historical inquiry.

the accumulation of christological titles in 14:61–62 demands investigation.[6] Also, the insertion of the narrative of Peter's denial (14:54, 66–72) and the similarity in structure between the Sanhedrin trial and the Roman trial suggest that the Sanhedrin trial is both secondary to its context and modeled on the Roman trial.[7]

These problems have led different authors to suggest a variety of decompositions of the narrative into tradition and redaction. M. Dibelius holds that the narrative grew out of the Temple charge in 14:58. He also claims that the addition of 14:62, the Messianic confession, was the motive which determined the presence of the trial in the Passion Narrative.[8] For R. Bultmann the trial belongs to the latest stage of the Passion Narrative and seems to have developed from the brief statement in 15:1. He sees different motives at work in the formation of the narrative. The christological material of 14:62 is a first expansion; the mention of the witnesses and the Temple saying (14:57–59) are awkward insertions, and the mocking (14:65) is "in a peculiarly unfortunate place."[9] More recently E. Linnemann suggests that the pericope developed out of two independent narratives: pericope A, which is modeled on 15:1–5, comprises 14:53b, 57, 58, 61b, 60a, 61a (in this sequence) and is influenced by the image of Jesus as the silent sufferer (Isa 53:7); pericope B is a later narrative of the Messianic claim, 14:55a, 56, 60a, 61c, 62, 63, 64. While Linnemann's observations are helpful in pointing to difficulties in the narrative, her deconstruction into partial verses and her reconstruction of two independent pericopes rests more on the laws of modern logic than on a study of the ways in which traditions develop.[10] Authors subsequent to Linnemann, while less sanguine about discovering the exact limits of the tradition, still postulate a developing tradition. G. Schneider holds that Mk created the trial scene as a diptych to the denial of Peter. Each has a threefold accusation (14:56, 66–69; 57–59, 69–70a; 60–64, 70b–71) which serves to contrast the confessing Jesus to the denying Peter. The nucleus of

6. DONAHUE, 9–10; LINNEMANN, 109–10.

7. G. Braumann, "Markus 15, 2–5 und Markus 14, 55–64," *ZNW* 52 (1961), 273–78.

8. M. Dibelius, *From Tradition to Gospel*, trans. B. L. Woolf, rev. 2d ed. (New York: Scribner's, n.d.), 182–83, 192–93.

9. BULTMANN, 271; cf. also 270, 281.

10. LINNEMANN, 109–35.

the pre-Mkan tradition is a reference to an appearance before a high priest (sing.), the Messianic question of 14:61b, and a charge of blasphemy (14:64). The pre-Mkan tradition looks therefore very much like the Lkan trial.[11] L. Schenke has perceptively analyzed the difficulties in the trial scene and suggested that 14:53a (the High Priest in the singular), 55–56, 60–61, 63–65 formed an original nucleus to which Mk added 14:53b, 57–59 and 62.[12] Finally, as part of a comprehensive survey of the whole Passion Narrative, D. Dormeyer uncovers three overlapping strains in the trial narrative: T, part of a primitive Acts of a Martyr (14:55); Rs, a secondary redaction of this stratum in the direction of Christology (14:56, 61b, 62a, 63, 64, 65b), and a final redaction, Rmk, where Jesus, the suffering Son of God, is proposed as a model of conduct (14:53b, 57–61a, 62ab to end of 65ac).[13]

These recent attempts to separate tradition and redaction in the trial narrative reveal a growing consensus that the Temple material of 14:57–59 and the christological confession of 14:61–62 are either "secondary" to the oldest tradition or due to Mk himself. Such attempts, however, show the characteristic of German redaction criticism to demarcate exactly the traditional (pre-Mkan) material from Mk's redaction and to derive Mk's theology primarily from the redactional material. There is also the tendency to see the theology of the trial in isolation from the theology of the rest of the Gospel.

In the following we will suggest a history of tradition of the trial, but with the caution that the whole pericope in its final form is due to Mk. Mk works less in dialectical opposition to the tradition and more by adaptation of the tradition to his own purposes. When verses are described as "traditional," it is not claimed that the language of the verse represents the actual wording of the tradition, but that it is possible to isolate places where Mk is working with the tradition in contrast to those places where he is composing or inserting new material. We will also attempt to indicate a setting in life for the various stages of the tradition.

11. G. Schneider, "Jesus vor dem Sanhedrium," *BiLe* 11 (1970), 1–15; "Gab es eine vorsynoptische Szene 'Jesus vor dem Sanhedrium?'" *NovTest* 12 (1970), 22–39; *Die Passion Jesu nach den drei älteren Evangelien* (Munich: Kösel, 1973), 55–64.
12. L. Schenke, *Der gekreuzigte Christus*, Stuttgarter Bibelstudien 69 (Stuttgart: Katholisches Bibelwerk, 1974), 26–46.
13. DORMEYER, 149–50, 157–74, 288–90.

Nature of the Mkan Composition: The initial verse (14:53) affirms two things: (a) the leading away (*apēgagon*) of Jesus, and (b) the gathering of the high priests. Elements suggesting Mkan redaction of a tradition are the Mkan custom of indicating a new stage of action by a change of place, the introduction of new sections by the use of the third impersonal plural, "they," and the naming of Jesus in introductory sections.[14] However, the use of *apagein*, a technical term for leading people to trial, the mention of the High Priest in the singular, and the similarity with 15:1 (Lk 22:66 and Jn 18:13) suggest that Mk expresses the traditional view that Jesus was led before some Jewish official and expanded it into a full-blown trial. The assembly of the requisite members of the Sanhedrin (14:53b), their desire to find testimony "to put him to death" (cf. 3:6; 11:18; 12:12; 14:1), the specific charge of the witnesses (14:57–59), and the accumulation of christological titles (14:61–62), which provides the specification for the condemnation, are not only those verses which betray the heaviest concentration of Mkan literary characteristics, but those very verses which make an informal hearing into a "trial."[15]

The second stage of reflection is rooted in the apologetic use of the Old Testament by the early Church. J. Jeremias and C. Maurer tended to see the suffering servant of Deutero-Isaiah as the prototype for the suffering of Jesus.[16] The recent work of L. Ruppert suggests that a more basic prototype is the "suffering Just One," the picture of a righteous man surrounded by false accusers, but faithful to God.[17] This type of suffering Just One extends from the psalms of lamentation through the figure of the suffering prophet and reaches its final stage of

14. DONAHUE, 64–65.

15. Ibid., 53–102 for detailed evidence. Some of the Mkan characteristics which appear in other redactional sections of Mk as well as in the trial are the use of *kai* parataxis to link pericopes; a fondness for *erchesthai* and its compounds; a tendency to "universalize scenes" (14:53b, cf. 1:32; 2:12; 6:33; 9:15; 11:17); the Mkan insertion of 14:57–59; a fondness for *pas* and *holos* in redactional sections (see E. Schweizer, "Anmerkungen zur Theologie des Markus," *Neotestamentica* [Zurich: Zwingli Verlag, 1963], 93–104). Also it should be noted that outside of Mk and Mt the other references to the death of Jesus in the New Testament do not mention a formal Jewish trial. See Blinzler, *Trial*, 271–89, for texts.

16. J. Jeremias and W. Zimmerli, *The Servant of God*, SBT 20 (London: SCM Press, 1965); C. Maurer, "Knecht Gottes und Sohn Gottes im Passionsbericht des Markusevangeliums," *ZTK* 50 (1953), 1–38.

17. L. Ruppert, *Jesus als der leidende Gerechte?*, Stuttgarter Bibelstudien 59 (Stuttgart: Katholisches Bibelwerk, 1972). This is a summary of Ruppert's massive two-volume work, *Der Leidende Gerechte*, Forschung zur Bibel 5 und 6 (Würzburg: Echter Verlag, 1972–73). See also DORMEYER, 248–49.

development in the diptych of the Wisdom of Solomon (Wis 2:12–20; 5:1–7). The parallels between the Wisdom of Solomon and the Passion Narrative are striking. In Wisdom of Solomon the enemies lie in wait for the righteous man (2:12) whose ways are strange (2:15); he boasts that God is his father (2:16); he is tested with insults and torture (2:19) and condemned to a shameful death (2:20). Nonetheless, the righteous sufferer will stand with great confidence in the presence of those who accuse him (5:1–2); when they see him (cf. Mk 14:62) they will be shaken with fear and amazed (cf. Mk 15:5; 16:6, 8); at his death he will be numbered among the sons of God (Wis 5:5; cf. Mk 15:39).

These observations provide the key for viewing the pre-Mkan trial traditions as an apologetic historicization arising out of complex reflections on a variety of Old Testament texts. As we will see, the puzzling material concerning the false witnesses mirrors Pss 27 and 35, psalms of the suffering Just One, and the whole trial context is like the picture in the Wisdom of Solomon. Such a process fits in well with the needs of the nascent Church to affirm two things: that the death of Jesus was according to the scriptures (1 Cor 15:3), and that, though dying a criminal's death, Jesus was still innocent. Jesus, too, is charged by enemies who seek his life (Mk 14:55); false witnesses rise up (14:57–59); he is challenged as to whether he is a son of God (14:61), and mocked as a suffering prophet (14:65). Upon this substructure Mk builds his theology of the trial narrative by the addition of the Temple saying of 14:58 and the christological tableau of 14:61–62, and thus the trial narrative expresses a theology coherent with that of the Gospel as a whole.

2. THE TEMPLE SAYING 14:58

The charge against Jesus, "I will destroy this temple that is made with hands, and in three days, I will build another not made with hands" (14:58) evokes major questions: is the saying for Mk a true representation of Jesus' activity, and, if so, why is it alleged by false witnesses, and, what is the origin and meaning of the saying? The first question has been answered in various ways. The witnesses are false not because of the content of what they say, but because they attack Jesus (Bertram); the statement is true, but attributed to false witnesses because it caused embarrassment to the Christian community (Taylor), and the charge is simply false (Weeden) because for Mk it represents a false Christology and false eschatology.[18]

A suggested resolution of the question of the "falseness" of the charge is found in the Old Testament setting of this motif. This motif of the "false witnesses rising up" is part of the pre-Mkan tradition of the suffering Just One, directly influenced by the psalms:

> . . . for unjust witnesses have risen against me and their injustice is false. (Ps 27:12)
> Unjust witnesses rise up; they ask me of things that I know not. (Ps 35:11)

When taking over these traditions Mk subtly changes the "falseness" of the witness to their lack of agreement. The repetition of the lack of agreement (14:56b, 59) constitutes the frame for a Mkan insertion—a recognized technique whereby Mk calls attention to material important to his purpose by bracketing the material with two almost identical verses or phrases.[19] Therefore it is not clear that in content the charge is false for Mk. It simply evokes a reaction of incomprehension by the witnesses much like other sayings and deeds of Jesus throughout the Gospel.[20]

Analysis of the Temple saying sheds light on its origin and function. This saying, or some variation of it, appears in different traditions in the New Testament (Mk 14:58 = Mt 26:61; Mk 15:29 = Mt 27:39; Acts 6:14; Jn 2:19). In each instance the first part of the saying contains a statement about the destruction of the Temple using some form of the verb *lyein* (cf. Mk 13:2). The second part of the saying is more freely

---

18. BERTRAM, 56; TAYLOR, 566. T. J. Weeden, in his essay in the present volume, "The Cross as Power in Weakness," makes the interesting observation that the statement is false because it attributes to Jesus a divine man Christology and eschatology which Mk rejects. Although I hold that the content of the statement is true for Mk, I am willing to admit that the form is "false" because it is uttered by Jesus, according to Mk at the wrong time, i.e., before his enthronement and coming. Apropos of Weeden's position is the problem of the evidence for associating divine man with Temple building and Temple destroying.

19. DONAHUE, 71–84, 241–43.

20. Throughout the Gospel the reaction to Jesus' teaching and actions is either amazement (cf. 1:22, 27; 2:12; 4:41; 5:20) or misunderstanding (2:16–18; 3:21; 4:11–12; 6:51–52; 8:17–19; 8:31–32; 9:10, 32; 10:10; 10:35, 37). Mt (26:60–61) does not record the charge as false but separates it from the appearance of the false witnesses.

adapted to the purposes of the individual authors. In Acts 6:14 the second part refers to changing the customs of Moses, and in Jn 2:19 the second part is given a resurrection reference (Jn 2:21–22). Since Mk uses *hieron* for Temple in those places which are redactional (11:11, 15–16, 27; 12:35; 13:1, 3; 14:49), it is clear that in 14:58 Mk uses traditions to build a two-part saying. One part "I will destroy" builds on the tradition of sayings in which Jesus prophesies destruction of the Temple (13:2; Mt 23:37–39; Lk 13:34–35). The second part as well as the distinction between "made with hands" and "not made with hands" is a Mkan creation.

To grasp fully the import of 14:58, its meaning and function both in the trial narrative and in the Gospel as a whole must be explained. A number of scholars hold that Mk is appropriating a current Jewish expectation that the Messiah was expected to destroy the old Temple and build a new one. Hence, the statement is considered a veiled claim that Jesus is Messiah.[21] However, this "expectation" is more a creation of contemporary scholarship than a motif of first century Jewish thought. The Jewish background reveals a variety of expectations concerning the Temple: (a) opposition to a defiled Temple and a call for its purification; (b) the hope—as in the 4Q Florilegium of Qumran—that Yahweh will build a house in the last days; (c) the anticipation of a new Jerusalem; (d) the expectation in the later Targums that the Messiah would build the Temple.[22] What is lacking prior to Mk is the definite conjunction of destruction and rebuilding of the Temple which is attributed to a person other than Yahweh. We affirm that in 14:58 Mk creates a Christian exegesis of Temple expectations which function within his overall theological purpose.

By attributing to Jesus a statement that he would destroy the Temple, Mk brings to a culmination the anti-Jerusalem and anti-Temple polemic

21. Cf. H. L. Strack and P. Billerbeck, *Kommentar zum Neuen Testament aus Talmud und Midrasch* (Munich: C. H. Beck, 1922–28), I, 1003–1005; BULTMANN, 120; E. Lohmeyer, *Das Evangelium des Markus*, 17th ed. (Göttingen: Vandenhoeck & Ruprecht, 1967), 327.

22. L. Gaston, *No Stone on Another*, NTSup 23 (Leiden: E. J. Brill, 1970), 102–12. For the most recent and thorough investigation of the background of the Temple saying, see D. H. Juel, "The Messiah and the Temple: A Study of Jesus' Trial before the Sanhedrin in the Gospel of Mark," (Ph.D. dissertation, Yale University, 1973), 177–305. 4Q Florilegium is a pesher-type commentary on 2 Sam 7:10–14 and on other Old Testament texts, see J. M. Allegro, ed., *Discoveries in the Judaean Desert of Jordan V: Qumran Cave 4* (Oxford: Clarendon Press, 1968), 53–55.

which runs through the Gospel. Early in the ministry scribes "from
Jerusalem" charge Jesus with demonic possession (3:22). Pharisees
and scribes "from Jerusalem" engage him in a dispute over the issue of
ceremonial cleanliness (7:1–13). His "way" to Jerusalem is a journey
to the place of opposition and suffering (8:27–10:52), and his final
discourse predicts destruction of the city (Mk 13).[23] From Mk 11
onward the opposition is directed clearly at the Temple. Jesus' initial
action in entering Jerusalem is to declare the Temple as no longer a
valid place of worship (11:15–18); the withered fig tree narrative,
which frames the Temple cleansing, symbolizes the unfruitfulness of the
Temple.[24] The debate on the *exousia* of Jesus is with Temple authorities (11:27–33), and Mk directs the parable of the Vineyard Workers
against these same authorities (12:10; cf. 11:27), Jesus delivers his
final discourse on the Mount of Olives "while enthroned upon the
eschatological counter mountain and looking upon the Temple whose
downfall he has in mind."[25] The gathering of the elect (13:26–37)
will take place only after the Temple has been destroyed (13:14).
Each major anti-Temple section of Mk is followed by a notation that the
Temple leaders sought to kill Jesus (11:18; 12:12; 14:1).

The second part of the saying pictures Jesus as the builder of another
Temple "not made with hands." In this saying Mk is playing on the
varied meanings of *naos*, which in the New Testament connotes (a) the
physical Temple (Mk 14:58a); (b) the body of the individual Christian
or the community as a whole (1 Cor 3:16–17; 2 Cor 6:16; Eph 2:21),
and (c) the heavenly eschatological Temple (2 Thess 2:4; Rev 11:19,
14:15–17). The community of Qumran also felt itself living in the
end time and in opposition to the Jerusalem Temple, and it too applied
Temple images and symbols to its communal life.[26] For Mk, then, the
community is the other Temple which Jesus will build. The meaning of
"not made with hands" is debated. Drawing on the use in the LXX

---

23. E. Lohmeyer, *Galiläa und Jerusalem* (Göttingen: Vandenhoeck & Ruprecht, 1936);
R. H. Lightfoot, *Locality and Doctrine in the Gospels* (New York: Harper and
Brothers, 1938), 111–26.

24. KELBER, 98–102.

25. Ibid., 112.

26. B. Gärtner, *The Temple and the Community in Qumran and the New Testament*,
NTSMS 1 (Cambridge: Cambridge University Press, 1965), 22–42; Juel, "Jesus'
Trial," 242–57; R. J. McKelvey, *The New Temple* (Oxford: Oxford University Press,
1969), 50–70. The Qumran texts most often discussed are 1QS 5:4–7; 8:4–10; 9:3–6.

where the term "made with hands" refers to idols, E. Lohse suggests that in 14:58 the contrast is between a reality which is accomplished by men and one accomplished by God.[27] Juel, after an exhaustive survey, concludes that the contrast is between realities of a different order, so that "not made with hands" is akin to "spiritual."[28]

The second part of the saying thus brings to a culmination the activity of Jesus throughout the Gospel in calling and forming disciples into the nucleus of a new community. The first public act of Jesus is to call disciples (1:16–20). Those initially called are expanded into a group of the twelve who share in the same ministry and power as Jesus (3:13–19). Although the disciples misunderstand Jesus' ministry and teaching and abandon him in the Passion Narrative, they are given a promise that Jesus will again be their leader after the resurrection (14:28), while the women are told to announce to "his disciples and Peter" that they will see him in Galilee (16:7).[29]

Mk intends the Temple saying to be read on two levels. One level pictures Jesus' ministry as bringing an end to the Temple of this order and preparing for a Temple of a different order. The repetition of the Temple charge in the crucifixion narrative (15:29), as well as the splitting of the Temple veil which symbolizes the destruction of the Temple, shows that for Mk the Temple has lost its meaning to Christians. Jesus is tried and put to death for his opposition to the Temple, but at the same time his death is the end of the Temple. On a second level Mk addresses a community which has experienced the horrors of war (Roman-Jewish War) and the destruction of the Temple. As this community becomes estranged from Judaism, it too undergoes trial and persecution (13:9–13) as Jesus did.[30] In his ministry and trial Jesus is the prophetic model of the experiences his community must undergo, but at the same time he voices the prophetic hope that this community is to be the new *naos*, a substitute for the Temple destroyed proleptically

27. E. Lohse, "*cheiropoiētos*," TDNT IX, 436–37.

28. Juel, "Jesus' Trial," 228–41.

29. WEEDEN, 20–51; C. F. Evans, "'I Will Go before You into Galilee,'" *JTS* 5 (1954), 3–18.

30. There is a growing consensus that Mk is written after A.D. 70 and in response to the destruction of the Temple. S. G. F. Brandon, "The Date of the Markan Gospel," *NTS* 7 (1961), 126–41; N. Q. Hamilton, "Resurrection Tradition and the Composition of Mark," *JBL* 84 (1965), 419; KELBER, 112–13; R. Pesch, *Naherwartungen: Tradition und Redaktion in Mk 13* (Düsseldorf: Patmos Verlag, 1968), 93–96.

in the ministry of Jesus and historically in the events of the Roman-Jewish War.[31]

3. THE CHRISTOLOGICAL TABLEAU 14:61–62

Literary criticism reveals that the full christological question of 14:61 and the answer of Jesus in 14:62 are the work of Mk. In the question, "Are you the Christ, the Son of the Blessed?" Mk has the High Priest ironically attribute to Jesus the major titles of the Gospel.[32] Jesus' answer, "I am" (which serves as a transition to the citation of Ps 110:1 and Dan 7:13), unveils the Messianic Secret by defining in what sense Jesus is the Son of the Blessed. Only as the enthroned (Ps 110:1) and coming (Dan 7:13) Son of Man will the full identity of Jesus be revealed. Jesus' confession in 14:62 forms a culmination of Mkan Christology. The earthly ministry is a secret epiphany of the Son of Man (2:10; 2:28); it is also a call to follow him in suffering (8:31; 9:31; 10:33–34). The future revelation of the Son of Man (8:38; 13:26; 14:62) will be a vindication of this suffering as well as a final revelation of Jesus.[33] Son of Man thus functions as a prism through which the titles Messiah and Son of the Blessed (God) are to be viewed. Since in 14:62 Mk has made a definitive christological statement, the titles which dominate the latter part of the Passion Narrative, King and Son of God (Mk 15), are to be seen as already having been given a meaning in the trial narrative.[34] The trial is really the trial of him who will be enthroned as King and hailed as Son of God.

This understanding of the function of 14:61–62, however, leaves unanswered the question of the relation of the Christology to the Temple saying (14:58), as well as to the theology of the Kingdom. It will be

---

31. Among those who see the Temple imagery in Mark as a reference to the Christian community are: E. Lohmeyer, *Markus*, 566; O. Michel, *"naos,"* TDNT IV, 883; TAYLOR, 566; E. Schweizer, *The Good News According to Mark*, trans. D. H. Madvig (Atlanta, Ga.: John Knox Press, 1970), 329.

32. DONAHUE, 88–95, 177–80; N. Perrin, *A Modern Pilgrimage in New Testament Christology* (Philadelphia: Fortress Press, 1974), 84–93, 104–21; see also N. Perrin's essay, "The High Priest's Question and Jesus' Answer," in the present volume.

33. K. Berger ("Die königlichen Messiastraditionen des Neuen Testaments," NTS 20 [1973], 19) describes the answer of Jesus (14:62) as a prophetic threat.

34. Perrin, "The High Priest's Question," in this volume, develops this prospective function of 14:61–62. DONAHUE, 209, calls the trial narrative an "anticipatory commentary" on the crucifixion narrative.

the focus of the following sections of this essay to show how Mk constructs a royal Christology which throws light on the above relationships.

4. MARK'S ROYAL CHRISTOLOGY

The understanding of Mark's royal Christology is furthered by the
publication of a text from Cave IV at Qumran which illustrates how Son
of God and Son of the Most High were used in pre-Christian Judaism.
The text (4QpsDan A^a = 4Q243) as reconstructed and translated by
J. A. Fitzmyer reads as follows:

> [But your son] 7 shall be great upon the earth, 8 [O King! All (men)
> shall] make [peace], and all shall serve 9 [him. He shall be called the
> son of] the [G]reat [God], and by his name shall he be named. (Col.
> II) 1 He shall be hailed (as) the Son of God, and they shall call him
> Son of the Most High. As comets (flash) 2 to the sight, so shall be
> their kingdom. (For some) year[s] they shall rule upon 3 the earth
> and shall trample everything (under foot); people shall trample upon
> people, city upon ci[t]y, 4 (*vacat*) until there arises the people of God,
> and everyone rests from the sword.[35]

Since, as Fitzmyer notes, "The text will long be debated because of its
fragmentary nature,"[36] and since the whole fragment has not been published, our discussion will be more suggestive than definitive.

Contextually, this Qumran text appears to refer to an event which will
cause someone to fall before a throne. The enthroned king is shaken by
evils. A change could be alluded to in line 7 where a royal figure (the
king's son?) will be great and given lofty titles, Son of God and Son of
the Most High (col II.1). The reign of the enemies will continue until
the people of God arise and everyone rests from the sword. Fitzmyer
notes that the fragment is in a clear apocalyptic context and states that
one problem of the text is the identification of the person referred to.
He asks:

---

35. This text in the possession of J. T. Milik has often been alluded to in recent years.
Milik made it public in a lecture at Harvard in December 1972. J. A. Fitzmyer ("The
Contribution of Qumran Aramaic to the Study of the New Testament," *NTS* 20
[1974], 382–407; cf. 393) has published and commented on an important section of
the text. The section cited above (I.7–9—II.1–4) follows Fitzmyer's translation. The
comments in the following paragraphs are based on Fitzmyer's discussion.

36. Ibid., 393.

To whom does the third singular masculine refer? Is it "the people of God" (II.4)? Is it an individual person? Or is it a person representing a collectivity (in the manner of the "one like a son of man" in Dan. VII. 13 representing the "holy ones of the Most High" in Dan. VII.18)?[37]

While it would be fascinating to speculate whether in this text Son of God and Son of the Most High are further interpreted by a veiled allusion to Dan 7:13, so that the parallels to Mk 14:61–62 would be clear, at the present time there is not enough evidence to prove this. Nonetheless, despite the problems associated with the text, two things are critical for throwing light on Mk's use of Son of God, Son of the Most High God, and Son of the Blessed: (1) the appellations Son of God and Son of the Most High are given to a royal figure and (2) they are given in an apocalyptic context which anticipates a period of struggle before the final victory.

The appellation of Son of God to an enthroned one or his son raises questions about the way prevailing scholarship has viewed Son of God and its synonyms (Son of the Most High, Son of the Blessed) in Mk. Direct Mkan parallels to the Qumran usage are found in 1:1; 3:11; 15:39 (Son of God) and in 5:7 (Son of the Most High God). Contemporary scholarship tends to see the use of Son of God and Son of the Most High in 3:11 and 5:7 (both on the lips of demons) as representing primarily a Hellenistic *theios anēr* or divine man Christology which Mk rejects or reinterprets in his Gospel.[38] In light of the Qumran text where in a Jewish setting the title is applied to a human royal figure and not to a Hellenistic demigod, it is problematic whether Son of God can without questioning be called "Hellenistic." A further observation likewise casts doubt upon the Hellenistic interpretation of Mk's Son of God. In intertestamental Judaism and in Judaism concurrent with early Christianity royal figures such as Solomon were viewed as exorcists and exorcisms were done in the name of Solomon.[39] Therefore when the demons address Jesus as Son of God and Son of the Most High God

---

37. Ibid., 392.
38. WEEDEN, 154: "He [Mk's Jesus] muzzles those confessions to his christological nature whose connotation or meaning is solely an identification of Jesus as a *theios aner* Christ." See also H. D. Betz, "Jesus as Divine Man," *Jesus and the Historian*, ed. F. T. Trotter (Philadelphia: Westminster Press, 1968), 114–33.
39. Josephus, *Ant* 8, 46–47; Berger, "Messiastraditionen," 9; G. Vermes, *Jesus the Jew* (New York: Macmillan, 1973), 62–65.

(3:11; 5:7), he is announced as King whose Kingdom (1:14–15)
spells the downfall of the kingdom of evil. The Messianic Secret which
follows the appellations (3:12) is Mk's way of indicating that just as
the Kingdom demands "a new time and a new place," so too does the
revelation of Jesus as enthroned King, Son of God, demand a new time
and a new place.[40]

In the trial narrative the royal Messianic Secret is revealed. Not only
is the appellation Son of the Blessed a surrogate for Son of God, but
there is an interesting structural similarity between the Qumran text and
Mk.[41] In both cases the context is apocalyptic, and in both cases the
appellation is followed by a reference to eschatological time—at
Qumran, the time when the people of God will arise, and in Mk, the
time when the Son of Man will come with the clouds of heaven. Therefore Mk has the High Priest ironically affirm the Kingship of Jesus,
while he makes Jesus' confession point to the future and final revelation
of this Kingship. Jesus, anointed Son of the Blessed, is King as the
coming Son of Man.

Son of God as used by Mark to picture Jesus as anointed King of the
end time fits in with the other uses of the royal motif in Mk. For a
variety of reasons the royal Christology of Mk has been played down
and seen as a residue of a Christology which Mk does not adopt. S. E.
Johnson states a common view when he writes:

> The Gospel of Mark represents the culmination of a process whereby
> messianism is so transformed that it is practically rejected. The Evan-
> gelist's interest, as everyone knows, is to show Jesus as suffering Son of
> Man and son of God. For him this is the true messianic secret, while
> the concept of Davidic messiahship is external and a misunderstanding
> of the true situation.[42]

F. Hahn feels that royal Messianism, with its political overtones, is
played down in the growth of the Synoptic tradition.[43] It is our con-

40. KELBER, *passim*, esp. 138–44.

41. There is no discovered Jewish text where "the Blessed" is used as a surrogate for
the divine name. Mk has most likely constructed this surrogate himself and put it on
the lips of the High Priest, DONAHUE, 90; Juel, "Jesus' Trial," 109–14.

42. S. E. Johnson, "The Davidic-Royal Motif in the Gospels," *JBL* 87 (1968), 136.
Despite his reservations Johnson gives many clues for the presence of the royal motifs
in Mark.

43. F. Hahn, *The Titles of Jesus in Christology*, trans. H. Knight and G. Ogg (London: Lutterworth, 1969), 136–93.

tention that such views are overly influenced by the modern conception of a split between political and religious Messianism. The 4Q Qumran text where a royal figure is addressed in an apocalyptic context as Son of God as well as the mixture of political and religious ideology in the Zealot movement indicate that a distinction between "religious" and "political" is not applicable to first century Judaism.[44] There is also the hidden presupposition that when a christological view in the tradition is modified by Mk, he is rejecting the earlier Christology. It is our contention that Mk has taken elements of royal Messianism from the tradition and modified them to create his own royal Christology.

A survey of aspects of royal Christology built on motifs from the Old Testament story of David and from Davidic expectations supports this view.[45] We have already noted that exorcism distinguishes a person as possessor of royal power in David's line. Mk's first miracle after the proclamation of the Kingdom is an exorcism (1:21–28). In the controversy of the plucking of the grain on Sabbath (2:23–28), Jesus, like David, is pictured as one who takes food "when he was wandering and had not yet established his kingdom" (cf. 1 Sam 21:1–6).[46] As noted, the demoniacs address Jesus with the royal titles, Son of God and Son of the Most High God (3:11; 5:7). The allusion in 6:34 to the people being like a sheep without a shepherd recalls the frequent allusion in the Old Testament to the king as shepherd.[47] At the conclusion of the middle section of Mk, two pericopes stress the royal motif. James and John in asking to sit at the left and right of Jesus are pictured as asking for a place in a royal cabinet (10:37–38), and blind Bartimaeus hails Jesus as Son of David in a way which prepares for the ministry of Jesus in Jerusalem, the city of David.[48] Mk views the entry

---

44. Josephus, *Wars* 2, 434; 4, 566–76. M. Hengel, *Die Zeloten*, Arbeiten zur Geschichte des Spätjudentums und Urchristentums 1 (Leiden: E. J. Brill, 1961), 299–304.

45. W. Brueggemann ("David and His Theologian," *CBQ* 30 [1968], 156–81, and "From Dust to Kingship," *ZAW* 84 [1972], 1–18) has shown that Israel's early traditions were redacted in light of the David story. W. Wifall ("David—Prototype of Israel's Future," *BibTB* 4 [1974], 92–107) demonstrates how these same traditions influence Ezekiel and Deutero-Zechariah, and suggests that they are projected into the New Testament. In what follows I build on their insights.

46. Johnson, "Davidic-Royal Motif," 139.

47. Jn 6:15 concludes his version of the feeding with the statement that the crowds wanted to make Jesus King.

48. V. Robbins, "The Healing of Blind Bartimaeus (10:46–52) in the Marcan Theology," *JBL* 92 (1973), 224–43; cf. also 2 Sam 5:6 where the blind and the lame are to appear before David outside of Jerusalem.

as an anticipation of the coming Kingdom of David (11:10).[49] In the
Jerusalem ministry Jesus takes possession of the Temple, teaches with
royal authority, and asserts his superiority to David. Furthermore, he
vindicates the rights of a poor widow (12:41–44) in the manner of
faithful kings of Israel (cf. Isa. 11:4).

In the Passion Narrative there are events which parallel the story of
David's trials as he tries to regain his royal power. Like David, Jesus
makes a sorrowful ascent to the Mount of Olives (14:26, 33; 2 Sam
15:30). In his hour of trial Jesus is accompanied by three followers
(14:33), as David in his trial is accompanied by three commanders,
Joab and Abishai, sons of the same father, and Ittai of Gath (2 Sam
15:19–24), who like Peter protests his enduring fidelity to his Lord
(14:29; 2 Sam 15:19–21). One of David's followers wants to strike
with the sword when David is attacked (14:47; 2 Sam 16:9–11). The
prophecy of the striking of the shepherd and the scattering of the flock
(14:27), an allusion to Zech 13:7b, concerns a royal figure. Just as
David is betrayed by one of his trusted followers, Ahithophel, Jesus is
betrayed by Judas (14:42; 2 Sam 15:31).[50] The trial before Pilate
and the crucifixion are dominated by the description of Jesus as King.[51]
Just as Mk begins his Gospel by the proclamation of Jesus as Son of
God (1:1) and then announces the arrival of the Kingdom (1:14–15),
he concludes it with the proclamation of Jesus as King interpreted by the
final use of Son of God in the Gospel (15:39). Finally, as B. Lindars
has noted, the crucifixion narrative is formed by reflection on Ps 22
which, whatever modern scholarship tells us of the original date and
setting of the psalm, in Mk's time was thought to be a psalm of
David.[52]

Not only do these individual elements support a Mkan use of motifs
from the David story to structure his narrative, but there is a strong

49. KELBER, 92–97, shows Mk's redaction here.
50. The parallels with the David story suggest that, while in earlier stages of the
formation of the Passion Narrative, the psalms and prophetic literature influenced the
material, in the final narrative, the Old Testament narrative form provided a model.
51. Berger ("Messiastraditionen," 22) shows that king and Son of God are often
interchangeable. N. Perrin ("The High Priest's Question," in this volume) calls
attention to the king motif in Mk 15. In Jn 1:49 the two titles, king and Son of God,
have become merged.
52. B. Lindars (*New Testament Apologetic* [Philadelphia: Westminster Press, 1961],
90) calls Ps 22 "a quarry for pictorial detail in writing the story of the Passion."

internal similarity between David's history and the passion of Jesus. David is pictured (2 Sam 15–19) as the anointed King who is being kept from full possession of his Kingdom and locked in a struggle to obtain it. In Mk Jesus is anointed King at his baptism, and proclaimed so at his transfiguration; his ministry brings about the arrival of the Kingdom, but an arrival which precipitates a struggle to obtain full possession.[53] For Mk the final assumption of total power and the handing on of royal authority will take place when Jesus returns as Son of Man. Mk uses Son of Man as an interpretative symbol for these royal traditions as he does for others. Son of Man sayings come at critical places in the development of the royal imagery. In 2:28 after the picture of Jesus' Davidic Sabbath breaking, the Son of Man emerges as lord of the Sabbath. After the request of the disciples to share in the power of Jesus (10:35–37), Jesus affirms that the Son of Man came to give his life as a ransom in a saying (10:45) which summarizes the theology of 8:27–10:52. After the royal designation, Son of the Blessed in 14:61, a future Son of Man saying is used (14:62). These three Son of Man sayings (2:28; 10:45; 14:62), therefore, occur at critical places in the Gospel, and one of their functions is to interpret preceding Davidic traditions.

Mk's use of the royal Christology motifs in 14:62 provides the bridge between the Temple saying and the Christology of the trial. In Jewish thought the influence of the dynastic oracle of 2 Sam 7:11–14 that the scion of David would "build a house for my name" fostered the view that Temple building was a royal function of one designated by Yahweh.[54] Mk applies this function to Jesus, but in the transformed sense that the Temple is the future community. Royal Christology also provides the bridge between the Passion Narrative and the other major theme of the Gospel, the proclamation of the Kingdom. W. Kelber has shown that Mk may be countering a false kingdom theology by orienting the Kingdom to a new time (the parousia) and a new place (Galilee).[55] The bringer of the Kingdom, Jesus, is like the Kingdom, hidden, and he points to his assumption of Kingly rule to a new time (the

---

53. P. Vielhauer, "Erwägungen zur Christologie des Markusevangeliums," *Aufsätze zum Neuen Testament* (Munich: Chr. Kaiser, 1965), 199–214.
54. Juel, "Jesus' Trial," 258–304.
55. KELBER, 138–45.

parousia, 14:62) and at a new place (Galilee, 14:28; 16:7) where those who are gathered to see him will be the nucleus of the Temple not made with hands.

5. CONCLUSION

Mk is the creator of the final form of the trial narrative. He takes over a tradition of an appearance of Jesus before a Jewish official and merges this with the Christian apologetic of Jesus as the suffering Just One. In this latter tradition there is present the situation and juridical language which enables Mk to expand the narrative into a full-blown trial. In so doing he brings to culmination major themes of his Gospel—discipleship, the contrast between the confessing Lord and the denying Peter, the opposition between Jesus and the Temple, the ministry of Jesus as the beginning of the new place for the revelation of the Kingdom of God, and the christological identification of Jesus, the royal bringer of this Kingdom, as the hidden and suffering Son of Man in his ministry and the future enthroned Son of Man. In the trial narrative Mk uses the royal Christology to interpret the trial and death of Jesus as the suffering of the crucified King. By having Jesus point to the new Temple, and picturing Jesus as the builder of this Temple Mk also creates a definite eschatological timetable for his Gospel. Jesus is King, but he will be revealed as such only at the parousia when the community will see him (14:62; 16:7).

Mk writes as a theologian. He takes traditions from various sources and adapts them to the needs of his community. He writes as a theologian in an apocalyptic context where a figure from the past is made to speak directly to the needs of a community, a community shaken by the horrors of the Roman-Jewish War and wary of the power of Rome. The Evangelist proclaims a message of faith. His readers are to have a change of heart and believe in the Gospel (1:15). Belief for Mk is rooted in irony and paradox. Jesus' way to his death is really his way to being raised up. In condemning him the Jewish officials are judging themselves. Jesus is mocked as a false prophet at the very moment when his prophecy about Peter is being fulfilled.[56]   Pilate and the

56. Juel, "Jesus' Trial," 104.

mockers call him King, while a centurion proclaims the real meaning of his Kingship. Irony is the rhetorical medium through which Mk conveys his message of faith. Mk also proclaims a message of hope. Just as the trial of Jesus is paradoxically his proclamation as enthroned King, so too will the trials of Christians be the means by which the Gospel of the Kingdom is proclaimed (13:9–13). Suffering and death were not the end for Jesus, nor are they the end for the Christian. Mk's call to radical faith and radical hope remains the good news to a Christian of any age who must always suffer the trial of living between promise and vision, between the good news proclaimed and the good news realized.

V.

The High Priest's Question and Jesus' Answer

(Mark 14:61–62)

Norman Perrin

It is a feature of the Gospel of Mk that at key points in the narrative we have passages which serve a retrospective and prospective function: they summarize and interpret what has gone before, and they anticipate and interpret what is to come after. One such passage is the redactional transitional unit 1:14–15. This interprets the significance of the Baptist in the divine-human drama with which the Evangelist is concerned:[1] "Now after John the Baptist *was delivered up* (*paradothēnai*). . . ." It also anticipates and interprets the ministry of Jesus in Galilee: "Jesus came into Galilee, *preaching* (*kēryssōn*) the gospel of God. . . ." Another good example is the redactional summary, 3:7–12, which interprets the ministry of Jesus, already begun and to continue, as a ministry in which he exercises his authority as Son of God (important as a complement to the authority of Jesus as Son of Man in 2:10 and 2:28), and which sounds the note of the Messianic Secret, a theme anticipated in 1:34 and to be developed strongly in what is to come after 3:7–12.

---

1. On Mk's concern for the divine-human drama which begins with the Baptist "preaching" and being "delivered up," continues with Jesus "preaching" and being "delivered up," and with the Christians "preaching" and being "delivered up," and which is shortly to reach its climax in the coming of Jesus as Son of Man, see N. Perrin, *The New Testament: An Introduction* (New York: Harcourt Brace Jovanovich, 1974), 144–45.

It is my concern in this essay to argue that 14:61–62, the High Priest's Question and Jesus' Answer, serves this combination of retrospective and prospective purpose. Retrospectively, it functions as the climax to the christological themes of the Gospel, and it marks the formal disclosure by Jesus of the Messianic Secret. Prospectively, it looks forward to the further christological climax of the centurion's confession in 15:39, it anticipates and interprets the crucifixion/resurrection of Jesus, and it anticipates the parousia.[2]

1. THE RETROSPECTIVE FUNCTION OF 14:61-62 IN THE GOSPEL

CHRISTOLOGY AND THE MESSIANIC SECRET

There are four elements in the question and answer which concern us in this connection. The High Priest asks, "Are you the *Christ*, the *Son of the Blessed?*" and Jesus answers, "I am (*egō eimi*); and you will see the *Son of Man* sitting at the right hand of Power and coming with the clouds of heaven." We have therefore three christological designations —Christ, Son of the Blessed, i.e., Son of God, and Son of Man—and the formula-like acceptance of the designations Christ and Son of God, *egō eimi*. We will investigate each of these as to their meaning for the Evangelist and their function in the Gospel.

1. Egō eimi

The meaning of this phrase for Mk must be seen in the light of the meaning and function of the same phrase in 13:6, "Many will come in my name, saying *egō eimi*, and they will lead many astray." This reflects the situation also envisaged in 13:21–22: "And then if any one

---

2. This is the third time I have addressed myself to these verses. The first time was in N. Perrin, "Mark XIV.62: The End Product of a Christian Pesher Tradition?" *NTS* 12 (1965/66), 150–55; reprinted in *A Modern Pilgrimage in New Testament Christology* (Philadelphia: Fortress Press, 1974), 10–22. The second time was in "The Christology of Mark: A Study in Methodology," *JR* 51 (1971), 173–87; reprinted in *Pilgrimage*, 104–21. On the first occasion I was concerned with the way in which the verses exhibited early Christian *pesher* traditions, a form critical concern. On the second I was concerned with the way they exhibited the Evangelist's Christology, a redaction critical concern. On this occasion I am concerned with their function in the structure of the Gospel as a whole, a literary critical concern. My own work on these verses reflects the development of method in the study of the Gospel. On the Christology of Mk 14:61–62, cf. also DONAHUE, 88–95, 138–42, *passim*.

says to you, 'Look, there is the Christ!' or 'Look, there he is!' do not believe it. False Christs and false prophets will arise and show signs and wonders, to lead astray, if possible, the elect." *Egō eimi* is, for Mk, a Messianic claim formula, a meaning Mt recognizes when he makes the *egō eimi* of Mk 13:6 explicit, "I am the Christ" (Mt 24:5).[3] In Mk 14:62 therefore Jesus is making an explicit Messianic claim, the Messianic Secret is being formally disclosed.[4]

The Messianic Secret is a major theme in Mk, and a very much discussed one. The essential clues to understanding it are (a) the recognition that not all the commands to secrecy are of the same type in the Gospel, and (b) the further recognition that the secrecy motif functions as part of Mk's overall christological purpose.[5] The commands to secrecy which concern us are the following:

> 1:34: ". . . he would not permit the demons to speak, because they knew him."

This is the first statement of the theme.

> 3:11–12: "And whenever the unclean spirits beheld him, they fell down before him and cried out, 'You are the Son of God.' And he strictly ordered them not to make him known."

This is the retrospective/prospective statement of the theme mentioned above.

> 8:30: "And he charged them to tell no one about him."

This is Jesus' immediate response to Peter's confession at Caesarea Philippi.

> 9:9: "And as they were coming down from the mountain, he charged them to tell no one what they had seen, until the Son of man should have risen from the dead."

This is the descent from the mountain of the transfiguration.

---

3. In his version of Mk 14:62 Mt redacts the claim formula to "You say that I am" (Mt 26:64) in the interest of his own presentation of the relationship between Jesus and the Jewish people and their representatives.

4. DONAHUE, 93, 95, 181, *passim*.

5. I am now developing a thesis which I first presented in PERRIN, 46–50.

9:30–31: "They went on from there and passed through Galilee. And he would not have any one know it; for he was teaching his disciples, saying to them, 'The Son of man will be delivered into the hands of men. . . . ' "

This is the introduction to the second passion prediction, and it is the last command to secrecy before the Secret is disclosed in the *egō eimi* of 14:62.

If we consider these commands to secrecy in the context of Mk's overall christological purpose, then their function becomes clear: Mk is creating a dramatic interval of time in which the true meaning of "You are the Son of God" or "You are the Christ" can be taught. Only after this teaching is complete, only after the passion predictions and the full development of the Mkan Christology through the use of Son of Man, only then does the Jesus of Mk's Gospel accept without qualification or command to secrecy the designation as the Christ, the Son of God, by means of the *egō eimi* of 14:62. I shall return to this point further below after I have discussed the function of the various forms of Son of God in the Gospel. Only when we have done that can we account for the conspicuous absence of a command to secrecy in the case of the Gerasene demoniac (5:1–20), especially 5:7.

2. Christ (Christos)

Christ is used as a designation for Jesus six times in Mk (1:1; 8:29; 9:41; 12:35; 14:61; 15:32), but only in four of these instances is it titular (1:1; 8:29; 14:62; 15:32). In addition to this it is used of the false Christs in 13:21.

1:1: "The beginning of the gospel of Jesus Christ, the Son of God."

The superscription of the Gospel. Son of God is omitted by some manuscripts, but in view of the structure of the Gospel as a whole it should certainly be read.

8:29: "And he asked them, 'But who do you say that I am?' Peter answered him, 'You are the Christ.' "

The confession at Caesarea Philippi, the watershed of the Gospel.

14:62: "Are you the Christ, the Son of the Blessed?"

The High Priest's question.

> 15:32: "Let the Christ, the King of Israel, come down from the cross, that we may see and believe."

Part of the mocking at the cross.

The exact status of Messiah (Christ, the Anointed One) as a title in pre-Christian Judaism is not clear. In an important recent discussion of the matter G. Vermes[6] differentiates between Messianic *expectation* and Messianic *speculation*. So far as expectation was concerned Vermes concludes that "if in the inter-Testamental era a man claimed, or was proclaimed, to be 'the Messiah,' his listeners would as a matter of course have assumed that he was referring to the Davidic Redeemer and would have expected to find before them a person endowed with the combined talents of soldierly prowess, righteousness and holiness."[7]

That the early Christians, proclaiming Jesus to have been the Messiah, ran into this kind of expectation is evident from the dispute in Mk 12:35–37, and it is possible that the emphasis upon Jesus as a *healing* Son of David in Mk 10:46–52 is part of an attempt to emphasize a rather different aspect of the Son of David expectation in connection with Jesus than the "soldierly prowess" normally associated with the expectation.

But it is the insight with regard to *speculation* that is most important to our understanding of the use of *Christos* in early Christianity and the Gospel of Mk. Vermes points out that "certain learned and/or esoterical minorities" within "Palestinian Jewry" developed particular Messianic speculations. He traces the development of speculation concerning "the Priest Messiah" from its inception in connection with Simon, the first Hasmonean to be invested with dynastic leadership, through the Testament of Levi, to the Qumran speculation concerning "the Messiahs of Aaron and Israel," where a priestly Messiah is expected as well as the Davidic Redeemer. He traces, further, the developing speculation (growing out of Deut 18:18–19) concerning a prophetic Precursor of the Messiah (or Messiahs). From the first century A.D. onward, he shows there was speculation concerning "the hid-

---

6. G. Vermes, *Jesus the Jew* (New York: Macmillan, 1973), 129–56.
7. Ibid., 134.

den and revealed Messiah." The Messiah would be revealed after a period of concealment, either on earth or in heaven; according to one version of this speculation the concealment began with the destruction of the Temple in A.D. 70. Finally, he points to speculation concerning "the slain Messiah," where it is thought that the Messiah could be slain on the eschatological battlefield. This strand of speculation is connected with Zech 12:10–12: "They shall look on me, on him whom they have pierced . . . they shall wail . . . ,"[8] and Vermes infers that it was caused by the tragic fate of Simeon Ben Kosiba, slain in A.D. 135.

Vermes traces four forms of Messianic speculation in Palestinian Jewry; we may add a fifth: early Christian speculation concerning Jesus. At the beginning Christians are an esoteric minority in Palestinian Jewry and they develop their speculation, which in turn develops into a confession.

In Mk the confessional element is dominant. At Caesarea Philippi Jesus is formally confessed as "the Christ"; he is mocked at the cross as "the Christ, the King of Israel"; the superscription of the Gospel identifies him as "Jesus Christ, the Son of God"; and he formally accepts the designation "Christ, the Son of the Blessed" by means of the *egō eimi* of 14:62. The Christians, as an esoteric minority in Palestinian Jewry, have developed their own speculation with regard to the Messiah, and they now confess Jesus as *that* Messiah. Mk is following that practice and structuring major elements of his Gospel around the watershed confession, with its command to secrecy, and the climactic response to the High Priest's question, with its disclosure of the secret.

3. The Son of the Blessed

Son of God, or Son of the Blessed, is found eight times in Mk, as follows:

1:1:   The superscription, "Jesus Christ, the Son of God."
1:11:   The heavenly voice at the baptism, "Thou art my beloved Son. . . ."
1:24:   The demoniac's identification of Jesus, "I know who you are, the Holy One of God."

---

8. Ibid., 139 (Vermes's translation). The Christians also made use of this text in connection with Jesus, cf. Rev 1:7.

3:11:   In a redactional summary it is said that whenever unclean
        spirits beheld Jesus they cried out, "You are the Son of God."

5:7:   The Gerasene demoniac identifies Jesus as "Son of the Most
        High God."

9:7:   The heavenly voice at the transfiguration, "This is my beloved
        Son . . ."

14:61: The High Priest's question, "Are you the Christ, the Son of the
        Blessed?"

15:39: The testimony of the centurion, "Truly this man was a Son of
        God!"

There is a ninth use (13:32), "But of that day or that hour no one
knows, not even . . . the Son, but only the Father." This is not related
to the other uses but is rather part of a sayings tradition using "Son"
absolutely, of which Mt 11:25–27 (=Lk 10:21–22) is the most striking example.[9] We shall not consider it further.

We need to reflect on these eight references in terms of their *function*
in the Gospel. It is my contention that they fall into three groups: a
confessional group (1:1; 14:61; 15:39); a group of *testimonies* (1:11;
3:11; 9:7); and a group exhibiting an *exorcism recognition motif*[10]
(1:24; 5:7).

The Confessional Use of Son of God: 1:1; 14:61; 15:39

The superscription clearly reflects the confession of Jesus as "the
Christ, the Son of God," and it is evident that the Evangelist is defining
his whole work in terms of "Jesus Christ, the Son of God." In the
combination we are to understand "Son of God" as a further definition
of "Christ." The fact that the confession at Caesarea Philippi is "You
are the Christ" (8:29) shows that this is the key designation; "Son of
God" in 1:1 further defines it.

The use of "Son of God" in this formal confessional sense is a specifically *Christian* use. Even if an eschatological use of Son of God has

---

9. For a discussion of this tradition see M. J. Suggs, *Wisdom, Christology, and Law
in Matthew's Gospel* (Cambridge, Mass.: Harvard University Press, 1970), 71–97.
10. I owe this insight to D. H. Juel, "The Messiah and the Temple: A Study of Jesus'
Trial before the Sanhedrin in the Gospel of Mark" (Ph.D dissertation, Yale University, 1973), 117.

now been found in the Qumran texts,[11] this does not change the fact that Son of God is not used in Judaism as a formal Messianic designation in the manner represented by Mk 1:1.

"Christ, the Son of the Blessed," in 14:61 is a variation on the theme "Christ, the Son of God" in 1:1. That this is a Christian use, perhaps even distinctively Mkan use, is shown by the fact that "Son of the Blessed" is unique in the New Testament and in all extant Jewish literature.[12] As Mk uses it, "Son of the Blessed" further defines "Christ"; for Mk it clearly is an equivalent to "Son of God," and a full-fledged Messianic designation.

In 15:39 Mk makes the centurion say, "Truly this man was a Son of God!" In itself "a son of God" is ambiguous; it is anarthrous and it could mean simply "a righteous man" as indeed Lk 23:47 renders it. But in 1:1, where "Son of God" is certainly a christological title, it is also anarthrous. Furthermore, the sequence of texts 1:1 "Christ, Son of God," 8:29 "Christ," 14:61 "Christ, Son of the Blessed," 15:39 "Son of God," demands that Son of God be taken in its full christological sense in 15:39. Lastly, the confession "is clearly of profound importance to Mk: it is one of the two results of Jesus' death Mk reports."[13] So *pace* RSV we should read 15:39 as, "Truly this man was Son of God!"

The Use of Son of God in Testimonies to Jesus: 1:11; 3:11; 9:7

This group of texts can be viewed in a new light since G. Vermes's discussion of "Supplementary Evidence" with regard to the use of Son of God in Judaism in New Testament times.[14] He is particularly concerned with charismatic Judaism, and with a small group of Jewish charismatics who were associated with Galilee and who were approximately contemporary with Jesus. He considers especially Hanina ben Dosa in connection with the use of Son of God, and he shows that, in

---

11. Professor J. A. Fitzmyer has assured me verbally that he has seen it, but it is not yet published. Apparently it represents the natural next step from the use of 2 Sam 7 in 4Q Florilegium (ibid., 198). Editor's note: the text has now been published: J. A. Fitzmyer, "The Contribution of Qumran Aramaic to the Study of the New Testament," *NTS* (1974), 382–407.
12. Juel, "Jesus' Trial," 112–15, for a full discussion.
13. Ibid., 119. The other is, of course, the tearing of the Temple curtain.
14. Vermes, *Jesus the Jew*, 206–10.

striking parallelism to Jesus in the Gospel of Mk, Hanina ben Dosa was believed to have been called "my son" by a heavenly voice, and that demons were regarded as having heard this testimony. G. Vermes's conclusion is worth quoting in full:

> Taken together, the various elements of the Hanina tale coalesce to form a picture closely resembling that included in the gospels. Like Jesus, he is commended by the heavenly voice and proclaimed *Son of God*. And, as in the case of Jesus, this commendation is heard by the demons who, in consequence, know, fear, and obey him.[15]

The understanding of the Evangelist Mk is similar to this: the voice testifies at the baptism (1:11) and at the transfiguration (9:7); the unclean spirits have heard this testimony and they echo it (3:11). But Mk understands Son of God in its full *Christian* Messianic significance, so the unclean spirits are commanded to keep the Messianic status of Jesus secret (3:12).

Son of God or Its Equivalent, in Exorcism Recognition Scenes: 1:24; 5:7

In 1:24 an unclean spirit recognizes Jesus, "I know who you are, the Holy One of God," and in 5:7 an unclean spirit cries out, "What have you to do with me, Jesus, Son of the Most High God." The two titles are equivalent, and these are recognition scenes common in accounts of exorcisms.[16] They are part of the account of the exorcism, and it is evident that Mk does not regard them as significant at the level of Jesus' Messiahship, as he does the testimony usage, *because there is no Messianic secrecy command* in 1:24[17] or 5:7, as there is in 3:12.

It can be seen, then, that "Son of the Blessed" in 14:61 is a deliberate echo of the "Son of God" in 1:1, and preparation for the final use of "Son of God" in 15:39. Moreover, between the first and the second of these confessional uses of the title, i.e., between 1:1 and 14:61, there is a series of uses of the title or its equivalent in testimonies from the heavenly voice and from an unclean spirit, and a further series of uses of the title or its equivalent in exorcism recognition scenes.

---

15. Ibid., 209. Son of God is not here a Messianic title, but an honorific title for a specially charismatic individual.

16. Juel, "Jesus' Trial," 117.

17. The command "Be silent" in 1:25 is part of the exorcism, not a Messianic secrecy command. The same command is addressed to the sea in 4:39 (*pephimōso*).

We are now in a position to return to 14:61–62 as the formal disclosure of the Messianic Secret. If we review the secrecy commands that concern us in light of the factors argued above, then 1:34 is part of the theme of the demonic testimony to Jesus, as is 3:11–12. 8:30 is connected to the confession in 8:29, and 9:9 returns to the testimony motif; the disciples are to keep secret the testimony of the heavenly voices.[18] 9:30–31 is the key to the function of the Secret in Mk's literary scheme, a point made above. In other words the Messianic Secret is a literary device of the Evangelist, designed to emphasize the importance of a correct understanding of christological confession and christological testimony—the confession and testimony are to be kept secret until they can be properly understood—and to create the narrative opportunity for the teaching of that correct understanding. The conditions necessary for the correct understanding of Jesus as the Christ, the Son of God, only come into being during and in light of the passion, the point made in 9:30–31.[19] This suggested solution to the problem of the Secret accounts for all the data, including the spectacular omission of the motif in 5:1–20.

4. The Son of Man

I have devoted more than a decade of constant inquiry into the many facets of the problem of the Son of Man, and the results of this inquiry have now been collected and published.[20] So far as the use of Son of Man by Mk is concerned, a most obvious feature of my work has been the way it has followed the methodological shift from form criticism through redaction criticism to literary criticism. My first interest in Mk in connection with the Son of Man was in his redaction and use of existing tradition, in an article appropriately entitled "The Creative Use of the Son of Man Traditions by Mark."[21] In that article I distinguished between Son of Man sayings "which show little or no trace of Markan redaction or composition: 9:12, 13:26, 14:21 (two), 14:41, 14:62"[22] and those which showed "a characteristically Markan usage,"[23]

18. In 1:11 only Jesus hears the voice; there is no public testimony.
19. Verses 9:30–31 also address Mk's readers directly, helping them to identify themselves and their situation in relationship to the situation depicted in the narrative.
20. N. Perrin, *Pilgrimage*, cf. note 2.
21. First published in *USQR* 23 (1968), 237–65; reprinted in *Pilgrimage*, 84–93.
22. *Pilgrimage*, 86.
23. Ibid., 87.

i.e., those between 2:10 and 10:45. When I turned to "The Christology
of Mark: A Study in Methodology,"[24] I had moved from this only to the
point of recognizing 14:62 as "the climactic element in Mark's Christological statement."[25] But now I have reached the methodological point
of recognizing that so far as the interpretation of Mk is concerned questions of tradition and redaction are comparatively unimportant: what
matters is the *function* of the text concerned in the Gospel as a whole.
For this reason I shall now review the matter of the Son of Man in Mk
again, this time from the literary critical perspective of the *function* of the
relevant texts in the Gospel as a whole.

Verses 2:10 and 2:28, the references to Jesus as Son of Man with
exousia to forgive sins and to abrogate the Sabbath law, serve the function of equating the authority of Jesus with that of the Son of Man.
They are juxtaposed with the two references to Jesus as Son of God in
3:11 and 5:7. Mk shows that Jesus has authority both as Son of Man
and as Son of God.

The references in 8:27–10:45 remain the key to the Mkan use of
Son of Man because this section *functions* as the central interpretative
section of the Gospel. Here we find the *apocalyptic* authority of Jesus
as Son of Man (8:38), the *necessity* for the passion of Jesus as the
passion of the Son of Man (8:31; 9:31; 10:33, the last two using the
key verb *paradidonai*), and the interpretation of the passion of the Son
of Man as a *ransom* (10:45).

After the central interpretative section of the Gospel we move to the
apocalyptic discourse, where there is a restatement of the theme of the
apocalyptic Son of Man (13:26), and to the Passion Narrative. In it
Son of Man is used three times.[26] Twice in the Last Supper scene,
14:21: "the Son of Man goes as it is written of him . . . the Son of Man
is 'delivered up' (*paradidotai*)," and once in the Gethsemane scene,
14:41: "the Son of Man is 'delivered up' (*paradidotai*)." These references pick up the use of *paradidonai* in 9:31 and 10:33, and they
carefully set the stage for the passion of Jesus as the passion of the Son

24. First published in *JR* 51 (1971), 173–87; reprinted in *Pilgrimage*, 104–21.
25. *Pilgrimage*, 118.
26. I am now treading on what is for me new ground, and I am indebted to the
stimulus of D. H. Juel ("Jesus' Trial"), and also to H. Boers, "Where Christology Is
Real: A Survey of Recent Research on New Testament Christology," *Interpr* 26 (1972),
300–27.

of Man[27] and as ordained by God. In connection with 14:41 Boers makes an important point in noting that from this moment forward Jesus becomes a very passive figure in the Narrative.[28] This is a striking change from the authority, power, and initiative he has been portrayed as exhibiting throughout the previous narrative, but in chapters 15 and 16 he is the passive object of the handling of others. Note, for example, the constant repetition: "they led Jesus"; "they bound Jesus and led him away"; "the soldiers led him away"; "they brought him to the place," and so on. Almost the only moment when Jesus asserts himself is in the reply to the High Priest's question.[29]

After 14:41 the next and final use of Son of Man by Mk is 14:62: "You will see the Son of man sitting at the right hand of Power, and coming with the clouds of heaven." Now the identification of Jesus as the *suffering* Son of Man is complete and here, in the midst of the Passion Narrative, Mk directs the attention of his readers forward to that which is still to take place in the Narrative, and we reach, therefore, the prospective function of 14:62 in the Gospel.

2. THE PROSPECTIVE FUNCTION OF 14:61–62 IN THE GOSPEL

Interpretation of the Crucifixion/Resurrection and Anticipation of the Parousia

Insofar as 14:62 is prospective of the centurion's confession, we have discussed it above. We are therefore concerned now with the following three elements in Jesus' answer: *"You will see the Son of man sitting at the right hand of Power and coming with the clouds of heaven."* My claim is that the "you" in "you will see" appeals to the readers of the Gospel, that "sitting at the right hand of Power" views the crucifixion-burial-resurrection as one continuous event and interprets it as an en-

---

27. In this connection it is interesting that *paradidonai* is also used in 1 Cor 11:23, "on the night when he was betrayed" ("delivered up": *paredideto*), i.e., on the night when the passion began.

28. Boers, "Christology," 316–27. Cf. also Perrin, *Pilgrimage*, 131–32.

29. The portrayal of Jesus in this very passive manner will have been Mk's way of dramatizing the element of divine necessity in the passion. He portrays Christians as becoming similarly passive as they in turn are "delivered up" (13:9–13).

thronement, and that "coming with the clouds of heaven" anticipates the parousia.

1. *You will see . . .*

A feature of the Gospel of Mk is the way in which the Evangelist addresses his readers directly out of the narrative. A good example of this is to be found in 2:10, which is the first Son of Man saying in the Gospel as 14:62 is the last. In 2:9–11 we have a tautologous command to the paralytic, "Rise, take up your pallet and walk [go home]." This command surrounds the Son of Man saying, "But that *you may know* that the Son of man has authority on earth to forgive sins," and hence calls special attention to it.[30] This observation, together with the well-known syntactical problems of these verses, suggests that the Son of Man saying is an aside by the Evangelist to his readers.[31] It is the readers of the Gospel to whom the Son of Man teaching is particularly addressed, and in 2:10 the Evangelist makes this explicit.

But if the "you" to whom the first Son of Man saying in the Gospel is addressed may be considered to be the readers of the Gospel, then the "you" of the last such saying may also be those same readers. By the very nature of the case nothing can be proven. Understanding that the readers of the Gospel are the ones addressed by these sayings, however, might make real sense of 2:9–11, of the function of 2:10 and 14:62 in the Gospel, and of the function of the Son of Man saying altogether.

2. *. . . the Son of Man sitting at the right hand of Power*

If this saying is addressed to the readers of the Gospel, then it makes very real sense—as it does not, incidentally, if it is addressed to the High Priest. Mk certainly believed that he and his readers could "see," i.e., "know" Jesus as ascended to the right hand of God. But if we observe a *prospective* function for 14:62 in the Gospel narrative then it may well be that we should consider the possibility that this is a Mkan interpretation of the crucifixion/resurrection of Jesus, the narrative of

---

30. DONAHUE, 77–84, 241–43. The author has shown that this kind of tautologous speech is a "very important compositional technique used by Mk for a variety of functions" (241).

31. Professor J. A. Fitzmyer has suggested this possibility to me verbally.

which follows immediately. In support of this possibility I offer the following two arguments.

The first point to be argued here is that Mk himself views the crucifixion-burial-resurrection of Jesus as one unit; that so far as Mk is concerned it is wholly legitimate to speak of the crucifixion/resurrection of Jesus. Actually we can go even further than that because the fact is that Mk views the passion of Jesus as one continuous event, an event which begins with Jesus being "delivered up" and ends with the discovery by the women of the empty tomb. The careful sequential time references in the Passion Narrative are evidence for this. These begin in 14:1, "It was now two days before the Passover and the feast of Unleavened Bread," but they become continuous only with the account of Jesus being "delivered up": "on the first day of Unleavened Bread" (14:12; 14:11: *paradoi*), "evening" (14:17), "as soon as it was morning" (15:1), "the third hour" (15:25), "the sixth hour" (15:33), "the ninth hour" (15:34), "when evening had come" (15:42), "when the Sabbath was past" (16:1), "very early on the first day of the week" (16:2). The narrative effect of these careful time references is unmistakable. From the "delivering up" of Jesus to the discovery of the empty tomb by the women Mk intends us to read one continuous unit of narrative. For the Evangelist the passion includes the resurrection.

In this connection the absence of appearance stories in Mk becomes significant.[32] Appearance stories would interfere with the smooth flow of arrest-trial-crucifixion-burial-resurrection-discovery of the empty tomb, and, in addition, they would put the emphasis upon the risen Jesus appearing again on earth *before* the parousia. But Mk envisages Jesus as risen to be with God in the heavens, whence he will appear again only *at* the parousia, hence proleptic appearance stories are rigorously suppressed.

The second point to be argued in this connection is that Mk presents the crucifixion of Jesus as itself an enthronement.[33] From 15:1 on-

---

32. The work of R. H. Lightfoot and his pupils has convinced me that the Gospel always ended at 16:8.

33. Cf. P. Vielhauer, "Erwägungen zur Christologie des Markusevangeliums," *Aufsätze zum Neuen Testament* (Munich: Kaiser Verlag, 1965), 199–214. The author argued the crucifixion/enthronement thesis on the basis that baptism, transfiguration, and crucifixion represented three stages of an enthronement ritual wherein *"die Kreuzigung entspricht der eigentlichen Inthronisation"* (213). I am concerned to argue this point about the crucifixion narrative from the text of Mk 15.

ward Mk misses no possible opportunity to refer to Jesus as "King." In
15:2 Pilate asks, "Are you the King of the Jews?" and Jesus accepts the
designation.[34] Then Mk has Pilate accept this designation of Jesus in
15:9, "Do you want me to release for you the King of the Jews?"
Furthermore, Mk has Pilate attribute it to the Jews in 15:12, "the man
whom *you call* the King of the Jews." Then the soldiers salute Jesus,
however ironically, as "King of the Jews" (15:18), the inscription on
the cross reads "The King of the Jews" (15:26), and the crowds mock
Jesus as "Christ, the King of Israel" (15:32). If there is a single place
in Mk 15 where the Evangelist could have used "King" in reference to
Jesus and has failed to do so, then I cannot imagine where it might be.
For Mk the crucifixion narrative is the narrative of the enthronement of
Christ as King.

In light of these considerations it is not too much to suggest that the
Son of Man saying we are considering is the Evangelist's prospective
interpretation for his readers of the crucifixion/resurrection of Jesus as
his enthronement/ascension as Christ and Son of Man.

3. . . . and coming with the clouds of heaven

The interpretation I have suggested of the "you will see" and the first
part of the Son of Man saying is necessarily tentative. However, no
such reservation need be expressed about the interpretation of the second part of the Son of Man saying: this is obviously and deliberately
prospective of the parousia. Throughout the Gospel Mk deliberately
directs the attention of his readers toward the coming of Jesus as Son of
Man. This is the climax of the divine-human drama which begins with
the "preaching" and being "delivered up" of John the Baptist; there is
no pericope in the Gospel which should not be read in light of it, and
there are many which explicitly anticipate it.[35] It is therefore only to
be expected that the last Son of Man saying in the Gospel should end on
a note prospective of the parousia, as it does. But the saying is not only
prospective of the parousia itself; it also alerts the reader to the further
anticipation of the parousia to be found in the subsequent narrative at

34. Although not with the formal *egō eimi* because this is not the disclosure of the
Messianic Secret.
35. For details of the constant thrust toward the parousia in the Gospel, cf. PERRIN,
31–45.

16:7, ". . . he is going before you into Galilee; there you will see him.
. . ." I need not stay to argue this point; it is not one that would be
disputed.

My concern in this essay has been to argue that 14:61–62 *functions*
both retrospectively and prospectively in Mk. Retrospectively, it is
the climax of the christological concerns of the Evangelist, and it marks
the formal disclosure of the Messianic Secret. Prospectively, it prepares the
way for the christological climax of the centurion's confession; it interprets the crucifixion/resurrection of Jesus as the enthronement/ascen-
sion of Jesus as Christ and Son of Man; and it anticipates the parousia.
These verses take on a new significance as they are examined from the
literary-critical standpoint of their function in the Gospel.

VI.

Peter's Curse and Cursed Peter

(Mark 14:53–54, 66–72)

Kim E. Dewey

The need to deal with or in some way account for the story of Peter's denial of Jesus lingers not only through the Gospel tradition but even on into later apocrypha and folktale. That so negative a story about Peter is not shaken from the tradition is surprising; rather, it appears to be an enduring strand in a developing Petrine trajectory in early Christianity.

Mk plays a key role by bringing the story into the Gospel tradition. And this raises the questions with which we must deal. How did the story look and what was its character prior to Mk? How much has Mk embellished the story? And how does it serve Mkan themes and interests within the plot of the Gospel?

1. TRADITION AND REDACTION

Exegetes have long sought to determine the pre-Gospel appearance of a denial story.[1] Our intention in this section is to show that by observing the confluence of generally recognized characteristics of Mkan language, style, compositional techniques, and literary themes we can at the same time discern definite traces of an earlier tradition underlying Mk's

1. M. Goguel, "Did Peter Deny His Lord? A Conjecture," *HTR* 25 (1932), 1–27; G. Klein, "Die Verleugnung des Petrus," *ZTK* 58 (1961), 285–328; LINNEMANN, 70–108; M. Wilcox, "The Denial-Sequence in Mark XIV. 26–31, 66–72," *NTS* 17 (1971), 426–36; SCHENK, 215–23; DORMEYER, 150–57.

narrative: a simpler one-stage denial story, with its own language and style, and a highly formalized version of the saying predicting the denial (14:30, 72). In the process we not only gain insight into the nature and function of the traditional material but also bring into sharper focus those concerns of Mk for which the story has been adapted and redactionally expanded.

The denial story frames the narrative of Jesus' hearing before the Sanhedrin. This technique of inserting one story within another (intercalation) is recognized Mkan style.[2] Here Mk has split the denial story and inserted the hearing with the effect that these two incidents appear to serve as commentary upon each other—certainly Mk sees their relationship as important. In fact, Mk frames this whole unit (denial-hearing) with references to the assembled Sanhedrin (14:53; 15:1). Within the denial story itself, its division into three stages is noteworthy; the frequent use of series of three in arranging material is recognized Mkan technique.[3] Hence, the use of the denial story as a frame story and the threefold structure of the pericope suggest at the outset that the larger complex is a Mkan construction.

Thus, 14:53–54 serves as an introduction to both the hearing and the denial. Both verses are a mixture of Mkan and non-Mkan elements. For example, Mk's tendency to universalize scenes is responsible for bringing together the various groups in the second half of 14:53 and for creating a formal trial before the Sanhedrin.[4] However, the first half of the verse is non-Mkan. There the use of the aorist (*apagein*) and the mention of the High Priest (singular) contrast sharply with Mk's typical use of the historical present (*synerchesthai*)[5] and the mention of the high priests (plural). Verse 14:54, generally recognized as pre-Mkan tradition,[6] actually contains both Mkan and non-Mkan elements.[7] All

---

2. T. A. Burkill, *Mysterious Revelation* (Ithaca, N.Y.: Cornell University Press, 1963), 121 n. 10, 243 n. 43; D. E. Nineham, *The Gospel of St. Mark* (Baltimore, Md.: Penguin Books, 1963), 112, 370–73; NEIRYNCK, 133; DONAHUE, 42, 58–63.

3. Burkill, *Revelation*, 123–24 n. 16, 244; NEIRYNCK, 110; see W. H. Kelber's essay in the present volume, "The Hour of the Son of Man and the Temptation of the Disciples."

4. DONAHUE, 66–67; NEIRYNCK, 108–12.

5. On Mk's use of the historical present, see HAWKINS, 143–49, and DOUDNA, 40–42; on Mk's liking for *erchesthai* and its compounds, see HAWKINS, 12, 34, and NEIRYNCK, 75.

6. TAYLOR, 563; DONAHUE, 68.

7. Markan: *apo makrothen* (HAWKINS, 12; NEIRYNCK, 75–76); *akolouthein* (L. Gaston, *Horae Synopticae Electronicae* [Missoula, Mont.: SBL, 1973], 18); double parti-

of this suggests traditional material which has been slightly reworked by Mk. Then, a pre-Mkan denial story might have begun with the leading of Jesus to the High Priest and Peter's following into the courtyard, his sitting with the soldiers and warming himself by the fire. However, the surprising reintroduction of Peter into the Gospel narrative when in fact he and the other disciples had fled earlier (14:50) is Mk's handiwork. Mk wants to say something about Peter.

Verses 14:66–67a repeat information already given in 14:54 and this suggests that Mk has created these verses in order to reestablish the setting of the denial story following Jesus' hearing. Peter's location is repeated (*en tē aulē*) as is the reference to his warming himself (*thermainomenos*). Here Mk appears to be using a basic pattern of repetition, a doubling or extension technique, by reusing words and phrases found in previous verses (in some cases traditional material), incorporating them into the narrative and thereby expanding it. This technique has gone unnoticed, although Mk makes good use of it, as, for example, in the denial story.[8]

However, in 14:66 Mk may have drawn the reference to "one of the maids of the High Priest" from his source. *Paidiskē* occurs only twice in the Gospel, both in the denial story (14:66, 68), and the mention of the singular High Priest conforms to that in preceding traditional verses (14:53, 54). Therefore, having broken the flow of the original introductory verses (14:53–54), Mk has now attempted to restore the same context which bore this traditional phrase.

Following from that context, it would be logical to presume that the words spoken by this maid (14:67b) might also be traditional. The extremely rare form, *ēstha*, is a clue to their non-Mkan character.[9]

---

ciple (H. B. Swete, *The Gospel According to St. Mark* [London: Macmillan, 1898], xli; NEIRYNCK, 82–84); the use of *einai* with a participle (Swete, *St. Mark*, xli; TAYLOR, 45). Non-Markan: *hapax legomena: pros to phōs, synkathēsthai*; uncharacteristic vocabulary: *thermainesthai, hypēretēs, aulē*; aorist of *akolouthein* (DONAHUE, 67–68); careless use of prepositions (Swete, *St. Mark*, xlii).

8. While we have long been aware of Mkan repetitions (HAWKINS, 139–42, and NEIRYNCK), we have missed seeing that at least one function of repetition is purposely to enlarge a narrative in an orderly fashion. Other techniques, such as framing, intercalation and insertion (DONAHUE, 77–84, 241–43), are of a different scale and sometimes different purposes, but of a similar effect. Examples of the doubling technique might be found in 3:7–12; 14:27–31, 32–42.

9. In the entire New Testament it occurs only here and in the Mt parallel (26:69). In seven other cases Mk uses *ēs*.

Yet, the intrusive *meta tou Nazarēnou* hints that Mk has inserted the identification of Jesus as Nazarene into this verse.   In fact, Nazarene is a characteristically Mkan title,[10] appearing four times: 1:24; 10:47; 14:67; 16:6.   Mk also discloses that Nazareth is the place of Jesus' origin (1:9).   Thus at the outset of the Gospel Jesus is linked not only with Galilee,[11] but even more specifically with Nazareth.   Nazarene has a thematic import which links the denial story to the rest of the Gospel.

It is in the first miracle story (an exorcism) that Jesus is initially identified as "the Nazarene . . . the Holy One of God" by an unclean spirit (1:23–24; cf. 1:11; 3:11; 5:7; 9:7).   Prior to the exorcism is the baptism of the man from Nazareth (1:9–11), the thrust of which is not the baptism itself (of which there is no description) but an identification scene in which a heavenly voice confirms Jesus as "my beloved Son."   Then in the exorcism story (1:21–28) Jesus' identity as Nazarene is again the concern, this time receiving confirmation in near parallel expression from a demon and resulting in widespread fame (1:28; cf. 1:33; 1:45; 2:12; 3:7–8; 5:20; 6:56; 7:36.   Thus there are two early scenes in which Jesus' identity is the main concern.[12]

Nazarene next occurs in the story of blind Bartimaeus (10:46–52) where, amid a flurry of titles (Son of Man, Son of David, Rabbouni), Mk, *as narrator*, specifically identifies Jesus as the Nazarene.[13]

The last reference to the Nazarene appears in the final verses of the Gospel (16:6).   Of all the titles applied to Jesus in Mk, here Jesus rises as the Nazarene.   Mk has framed the entire Gospel and the ministry of Jesus with references to Jesus as the Nazarene (1:9, 24; 16:6) and with Jesus' traveling from Galilee and back to it.   That this framing is intentional, is indicated in the reaction of the women (16:5–6: *exethambēthēsan, mē ekthambeisthe*)

---

10. Gaston, *Horae*, 20; Lk uses the term twice: 4:34 (=Mk 1:24) and 24:19.   Mt substitutes *Nazōraios*, which Lk uses once, Acts seven times, and Jn three times.

11. The significance of which is discussed by MARXSEN, 57–58.

12. Mk avoids mentioning Nazareth or Galilee in 6:1–6 (using instead *patris*) in order to escape having Jesus discredit either place.   1:21–28 and 6:1–6 do have parallels; in both Jesus enters a place, teaches in the synagogue on the sabbath, and those who hear are astonished and respond with questions and acclamation.   In contrast, where in 1:21–28 Jesus performs an exorcism, in 6:1–6 he can do no mighty work; in the former all are amazed, in the latter they take offense; in the one Jesus is identified as a holy man, in the other a mere carpenter, son of Mary!   Jesus' identity is totally inverted (the proverb in 6:4 deprives Jesus of an identity with house and homeland).

13. Mk seems to use this miracle story to exemplify the theme of total reversal prominent in the midsection of the Gospel (8:22–10:52): that the first will be last and the last first, that the great must be a servant and the first a slave (9:35; 10:31, 43–45).   Here Jesus serves the blind man (10:51, contrast the disciples in 10:36–40).   Mk has incorporated a number of variations on this theme into this section.   And it is no accident that he has woven this reversal theme with a concern for Jesus' identity (e.g., 8:27–30; 9:2–8; 8:31; 9:31; 10:33) while casting the disciples in opposition.

which parallels the crowd's reaction to the Nazarene (1:27: *ethambēthēsan*) and in references to Peter, the first and last named disciple in the Gospel (1:16; 16:7).

In light of the above, the use of Nazarene in the denial story appears to be deliberate, for there also, as in 1:9, 1:21–28, and 16:6–7, it is linked with Jesus and Galilee (14:70).

The first denial, Peter's response to the maid (14:68), also appears to be tradition, having no strong evidence of redaction. *Arneisthai* is used only twice in the Gospel and only in the denial story (14:68, 70).[14] The neither . . . nor construction occurs only one other time in Mk (12:25), and *epistasthai* is found only here in the Gospels.

Following the denial, Peter departs from the courtyard: *kai exēlthen exō eis to proaulion* (14:68). This wording (compound verb—redundant adverb—preposition) is clumsy and contrary to Mk's careful use of prepositions. Yet this very style was found in 14:54, which seems to be part of Mk's tradition (*heōs esō eis tēn aulēn*; preposition—adverb —preposition). The similarity suggests that these verses are from the same piece of tradition.[15]

Thus, following 14:53–54, the tradition goes on to narrate the maid's questioning of Peter, his denial and exit.

The second stage of the three-denial sequence (14:69) resumes the doubling pattern, which we noticed above, with a second reference to "the maid seeing [Peter]." This doubling and other features of Mkan style and vocabulary indicate this verse to be a product of the Evangelist.[16] It also follows that the words spoken by the maid: "This man is one of them," which grow out of this context, would be Mkan.

In this second denial Peter does not speak; it is merely recorded that he again denies (14:70). Indeed, if Mk has created the maid's accusation, it is probable that he has also penned Peter's response. In fact, in what we may now claim to be a recognizable stylistic doubling pattern,

---

14. Gaston, *Horae,* 18, claims that *aparneisthai* is Mkan, but not *arneisthai*; the latter is found in Q: Lk 12:9/Mt 10:33; Lk 9:23.

15. 14:68c, *kai alektōr ephōnēsen* (Metzger-Aland text), is likely a later addition based both on the misunderstanding that cockcrow refers to a bird and on the need to make some sense of *dis* in the denial saying (14:30, 72), this being the first of two cockcrows.

16. *ērxato legein* reflects Mk's use of *archesthai* with a present infinitive, TURNER 28 (1927), 352–53; DOUDNA, 52–53. Other features: *palin*, TURNER 29 (1928), 286; HAWKINS, 13; *paristasthai*, HAWKINS, 13, 35; recitative *hoti* (contrast with its absence in traditional 14:68), TURNER 28 (1927), 9.

Mk routinely repeats *arneisthai* (here, although it is non-Mkan vocabulary, it appears in a Mkan context).

The third denial (14:70) can be established as Mkan again on the basis of the doubling pattern; the words of accusation, and the presence of the bystanders are repeated from 14:69. Moreover, "For you are a Galilean" is one of the *gar*-clauses which Mk composes and inserts at various points throughout the Gospel as thematic probes emphasizing a fact or alluding to a set of ideas relevant to a correct understanding of the context.[17] Here the clause strikes the chord of the Mkan Galilee motif, a primary concern in the Gospel.

Again, if Mk created the questioning in this third stage of the story, it is likely that he also created Peter's response: "He began to curse and vowed that 'I do not know this man of whom you are speaking'" (14:71).[18] Here the question is more one of how we are to understand the verse. Debate has centered on whether *ērxato anathematizein kai omnynai* is to be understood as Peter's cursing himself (if he lies) or his cursing Jesus.[19] In either case, however, the effect is the same: Peter utters a series of curses designed to dissociate himself publicly from Jesus. The ambiguity over the object of the curse is perhaps best understood as intentional on the part of Mk who creates the highly ironic situation in which Peter either directly curses himself or indirectly does so by cursing Jesus, and by attempting to save himself in this situation in reality loses himself and is placed in even greater jeopardy. Peter, in denying Jesus, denies his own identity and becomes subject to the curse spoken by Jesus (8:38). In effect then Jesus and Peter have cursed each other.

Thus we find that Mk has created the second and third denials, and in a progression those denials intensify from an attempt to evade an answer

---

17. C. H. Bird, "Some *gar*-clauses in St. Mark's Gospel," *JTS* n.s. 4 (1953), 171–87.

18. Note the *archesthai*-plus-infinitive construction, the recitative *hoti* (see note 16) and the doubling pattern by which, with modification, the words of denial are repeated from 14:68.

19. Most commentaries state that Peter curses himself (e.g., TAYLOR, 575; Swete, *St. Mark*, 344). H. Merkel ("Peter's Curse," *The Trial of Jesus*, ed. E. Bammel, SBT, 2d ser. 13 [Naperville, Ill.: Allenson, 1970], 66–71) concludes that Peter curses Jesus (linguistically, *anathematizein* takes a direct object and should be read that way in Mk though none is given; logically, cursing Jesus would dissuade Peter's questioners; historically, persons accused of being Christians could prove their innocence by cursing Jesus). We agree with J. Behm, "*Anathema*," TDNT I, 355, who argues that Mk intends the ambiguity and plays upon it.

in the first stage (in the tradition) to repeated denials in the second, to outright cursing and total dissociation in the third.

The story comes to a climax when, following Peter's cursing, the cock crows (14:72). This cockcrow performs two functions. First, it clearly links the denial story to the structure of the Passion Narrative. R. H. Lightfoot[20] called attention to the fact that Mk organizes the Passion Narrative according to three hour intervals (14:72; 15:1, 25, 33–34, 42) and according to the divisions of the night watch. In reckoning the times when the Son of Man might unexpectedly return Mk lists the night watches (13:35) and then proceeds to arrange the events of 14:17–15:1 according to those night watches, thereby suggesting a thematic relationship: evening (14:17), midnight (14:41?), cockcrow (14:72), morning (15:1). Thus it is clear that when Mk announces cockcrow in 14:72 he understands it not as the sound of a bird but as a time designation, the end of the third night watch.[21] The second function of the cockcrow is to heighten the drama by causing Peter to remember Jesus' prediction of his denials, a prediction now ironically come to fruition, despite Peter's strong protestation (14:31).

In terms of tradition and redaction, Peter's remembering (14:72b) has the marks of the tradition. In the Gospels *anamimnēskein* occurs only twice, both in Mk (in 11:21 Peter remembers Jesus' curse of the fig tree); but in 14:72 the verb is aorist, a feature characteristic of the traditional material Mk has been using (14:53, 54, 68, 72). Also in this verse we find *hrēma*, whereas Mk by far prefers *logos*,[22] an un-Mkan use of *hōs*,[23] and another aorist, *eipen*. Thus Peter's remembering appears to be from Mk's source.

As for Peter's weeping (14:72) matters are complicated by the exact

---

20. R. H. Lightfoot, *The Gospel Message of St. Mark* (Oxford: Oxford University Press, 1950), 53–54.

21. C. H. Mayo, "St. Peter's Token of the Cock Crow," *JTS* 22 (1921), 367–70. Mk's two cockcrows may refer to the bugle sounded at the end and beginning of each night watch or may be a literal rendering of *dis* in the denial saying (14:30, 72). In Rabbinic literature (b. Yoma 21a; Gen Rab 36.1; Lev Rab 5) demons rule the night until cockcrow, when their power wanes. This motif continues in later folklore where causing a cock to crow or imitating its sound will scare the devil away. On the range of connotations attached to the cock, see H. D. Betz, *Lukian von Samosata und das Neue Testament*, Texte und Untersuchungen 76 (Berlin: Akademie-Verlag, 1961), 30–32.

22. *hrēma* occurs only twice (see 9:32), *logos* twenty-three times.

23. G. D. Kilpatrick, "Some Notes on Marcan Usage," *BT* 7 (1956), 51–52; normally Mk would use *hote* or *hotan*.

agreement of Mt (26:75) and Lk (22:62) against Mk: "And he went out and wept bitterly." In Mt and Lk the aorist tense and the redundant *exelthōn exō* appear more characteristic of the traditional material isolated in Mk (14:54, 68b). The verse (14:72) can at least be claimed on literary grounds as Mkan. One reason that Mk might change the tradition here, if indeed he knows it, is that he has already had Peter exit in 14:68; moreover, *pikrōs* gives a repentant force which Mk would perhaps downplay in Peter's case.

The denial saying itself (14:72; see 14:30) is problematic. It cannot be assumed that the saying followed Peter's remembering of it in the tradition, or that, if it did, it does not appear in redacted form here (or that it is even the saying originally referred to in the story; note that the traditional story has no cockcrow motif, although the denial saying would demand this element in the story).

The saying appears twice in each of the Synoptics, once in a prediction setting and once in a story setting; in Jn it is found only in the prediction setting. Mt (26:34, 75) is clearly dependent upon Mk's version of the saying. However, Lk, while he adopts Mk's version in the denial story (Lk 22:61/Mk 14:72), has a different version in the prediction setting (22:34): *ou phōnēsei sēmeron alektōr heōs tris me aparnēse mē eidenai.* And this corresponds closely to the saying in Jn (13:38): *amēn legō soi ou mē alektōr phōnēsē heōs hou arnēsē mē tris.*[24] This close agreement suggests the existence of a non-Mkan version of the saying. Kelber[25] has argued the existence of a pre-Mkan prophetic sayings tradition present both in Q (Mt 23:39/Lk 13:35; Mt 5:26/Lk 12:59) and in the Synoptic tradition (Mk 9:1; [9:41]; 10:15; 13:30; 14:25; Mt 5:18; 10:23). These sayings have a history of their own prior to their inclusion in the Gospels and they function as

24. This is just one of a number of parallels between Lk and Jn in the denial complex. In the prediction block: (1) Lk 22:33/Jn 13:37 Peter insists he will (Lk: go to prison and) die for Jesus, then Jesus predicts his denial; in Mk-Mt these are reversed; (2) the disciples are part of the scene in Mk-Mt but only Peter in Lk-Jn; (3) the prediction in Lk-Jn takes place in the upper room, but not in Mk-Mt; (4) Peter rejects the prophecy of denial in Mk-Mt but not in Lk-Jn; (5) yet, Jn, Lk, and Mk-Mt each have different versions of the "I will die for you" saying. In the story block: (1) in Lk 22:55 they "kindled a fire" and in Jn 18:18 they "made a charcoal fire"; Mk-Mt lack this detail; (2) there is no cursing by Peter as in Mk-Mt.

25. W. H. Kelber, "Kingdom and Parousia in the Gospel of Mark" (Ph.D. dissertation, University of Chicago, 1970), 89–92; this material was not included in his recently published book.

prophetic promises hinging upon the imminent irruption of the eschaton. Their literary form is set and complex: (*amēn*) (*legō*) . . . *ou mē* (followed by the subjunctive aorist) . . . *heōs* [*an*] (followed by the subjunctive aorist).

Jn 13:38 is a clear example of this eschatological sayings form, and that form gives the denial saying a much more cosmic and potent tinge than the modified versions found in the other Gospels.[26]   Lk (22:34) has defused it by dropping *mē* (from the emphatic *ou mē*), changing *phōnēsē* to *phōnēsei* (aorist subjunctive to future indicative) and adding *mē eidenai* to deflect and soften further the saying.   Mk, too, has altered the saying and reshaped it according to the needs of his narrative by giving it a much more temporal character, casting it as a prophecy and conforming it to the night watch scheme (specifically by adding *sēmeron tautē tē nykti prin ē* [14:30], and a tense change to the simple future). *Tris* and *dis* can be explained as Mkan additions, *dis* being peculiar to Mk[27] and *tris* reflecting the story's three stages which we now recognize to be a Mkan arrangement (it is conceivable that *tris* was an original part of the saying, originally symbolic, later coming to be taken literally —by Mk).

Thus the traditional denial story concludes with Peter's remembering the word of Jesus and perhaps his weeping. It is not certain that the denial saying was originally attached to the story, although a denial saying is clearly alluded to in the story.

Our analysis reveals a coherent core of tradition and a much simpler narrative embedded within active Mkan redaction. Jesus is led to the High Priest (14:53a), Peter follows (14:54) and is confronted by a servant (14:66b) who accuses him of having been with Jesus (14:67b); this he denies, saying that he neither knows nor understands what she is saying. He flees from the courtyard (14:68) and then, remembering Jesus' prediction, weeps (14:72b, d and par.).

Our analysis also argues for a direct knowledge of Mk by Jn, since Jn adapts at least four elements of Mk's redaction: (1) both Jn and Mk intercalate the hearing story within the denial story; (2) both frame the hearing with references to Peter's warming himself; (3) only Jn and Mk

26. Of twenty-five amen sayings in Jn only 8:51 and 13:38 fit the pattern; others come close: 3:3; 3:5; 5:19; 6:53; 12:24.
27. See notes 15 and 21; *dis* is also found in the Fayyum Fragment, but this does not necessarily evidence pre-Mkan tradition.

use the term *thermainomenos*; (4) only Jn and Mk have a stage in the story where Peter has no direct discourse. These observations also argue against the existence of multiple versions of the denial story in the tradition and support the more probable view that later versions of the story are a combination of a knowledge of pre-Mkan tradition, of Mk (in the case of Jn, a knowledge of the Synoptics), plus the creativity of later redactors: Mt, Lk, and Jn.[28]

2. TRADITION: STORY AND SAYING

We should now assess the two components of Mk's tradition: story and saying.

Mk 14:53a, 54 seem to indicate that the traditional denial story still was part of a larger narrative (as it seems to begin *in medias res*), perhaps a pre-Mkan passion story or a block of Peter material. Yet no judgments can be made regarding the historicity of such a narrative or any of its parts, nor whether it existed in oral or written form, nor what Mk might have omitted from his source.[29] Nor can we determine if this story ever circulated as an independent unit, even though we might suspect such since the story does have a distinct beginning and end (Peter's entering the courtyard and leaving it).

Peter's denial (14:68) has an evasive strategy. Peter appears to

28. For example, Goguel, "Peter," 9, 12, argued that Mk was the only source for both Lk and Jn. However, we must allow for the possibility that the one-stage, traditional story remains concurrent with Mk whose redaction does not also thereby eliminate it. There are affinities between Jn and Mk at precisely those points where Mk seems to be using the tradition: (1) Jn 18:17: *legei tō Petrō hē paidiskē* (Mk 14:67a); (2) Jn 18:26: *eis ek tōn doulōn tou archiereōs* (Mk 14:66b); (3) Jn 18:17 (18:25, 26): *sy ek tōn mathētōn ei tou anthrōpou toutou* (Mk 14:67b); (4) Jn 18:18 and Mk 14:54 use *hypēretēs*, Lk does not; (5) Jn 18:15 and Mk 14:54 use *aulē*, Lk uses *oikia* (22:54); (6) Jn uses the singular of High Priest (18:13, 14) as does Mk's tradition (14:53, 54, 66).

Jn also shows a knowledge of Mt. Only they mention the High Priest Caiaphas by name (Mt 26:57/Jn 18:13, 28) and only they have two different servants who question Peter (Mt 26:69, 71/Jn 18:17, 26).

On Jn's knowledge of Lk, see note 24.

These correspondences suggest that theories of Gospel sources and dependence must allow for greater flexibility. Inter-Gospel contacts appear much more fluid, and it is at least possible that Jn knew the Synoptics and perhaps even post-Synoptic traditions. We might opt for more recent views of oral and folk traditions and for greater creativity and selectivity on the part of the Evangelists rather than for strict and rigid limitations of dependence (see note 29).

29. See, for example, E. L. Abel, "The Psychology of Memory and Rumor Transmission and Their Bearing on Theories of Oral Transmission in Early Christianity," *JR* 51 (1971), 270–81; P. B. Mullen, "Modern Legend and Rumor Theory," *JFI* 9 (1972), 95–109.

deny Jesus directly while hiding behind the claim that he does not
understand; Mk carries this element forward and amplifies it in explicit
terms (14:70, 71).

Thus, what emerges is that Mk's is not a totally new creation, but an
extension of an earlier story, building upon its outline, heightening its
tenor. The negative character of the story exists even prior to Mk.
Recognizing this, Klein[30] has theorized that the denial legend (three
stages) finds its setting amid anti-Petrine traditions and polemics (e.g.,
Mk 8:33; Mt 14:28–31; GosThom 12) produced by persons vying for
power in the Church and specifically opposed to Peter. Perhaps the
story originated as a maliciously spread rumor about Peter.[31]

As for the denial saying, one is inclined to agree with Wilcox[32] that
the basic element of the tradition is the saying and not the story. If our
analysis is correct, we are dealing with a saying which predates Mk and
has survived intact (Jn 13:38). That it is, in fact, an isolated logion is
also indicated by its secondary context in both Jn and Lk. In Jn the
saying has been worked into a setting reflecting Johannine theological
themes.[33] And the Lkan setting (22:31–34) is far from homogeneous; Lk has juxtaposed two independent traditions, one implying
that Peter does not fail (22:31–32a), the other that he does (22:33–
34).[34] In Mk, too, the saying's context (14:27–31) is artificial.[35]

While the saying may have had a proverbial background,[36] which did
refer to the crow of a cock, it seems to have been absorbed into the
context of early Christian prophetic curse traditions.[37] Käsemann has

30. Klein, "Verleugnung," 312–28.

31. Others do not fully appreciate the anti-Petrine flavor of the story. Wilcox, "Denial-
Sequence," 436, claims that the story is not really about Peter at all, but about a time of
trial and testing; LINNEMANN, 93, says that it is symbolic, being a literary concretizing
of a general denial by all of the disciples.

32. Wilcox, "Denial-Sequence," 432, 434; also Goguel, "Peter," 6, 27.

33. R. E. Brown, *The Gospel According to John*, Anchor Bible 29A (Garden City,
N.Y.: Doubleday, 1970), 608–16.

34. Klein, "Verleugnung," 298–302. Lk links the traditions with *epistrepsas*
(22:32b), but they are still discordant: Peter is addressed as Simon in 22:31–32, but
as Peter in 22:34; the plural *hymas* (22:31) is at odds with the singular *soi* (22:34).
See BULTMANN, 267, 435–36.

35. BULTMANN, 278–79; Wilcox, "Denial-Sequence," 435; Goguel, "Peter," 6; against
LINNEMANN, 82–85.

36. Mayo, "Cock Crow," 370; M. Dibelius, *From Tradition to Gospel*, trans. B. L.
Woolf, rev. 2d ed. (New York: Scribner's, n.d.), 216; Betz, see note 21.

37. See E. Käsemann, "Sentences of Holy Law in the New Testament," *New Testament
Questions of Today*, trans. W. J. Montague (Philadelphia: Fortress Press, 1969), 66–
81; W. Wiefel, "Fluch und Sakralrecht," *Numen* 16 (1969), 211–32.

described the strategy and setting of the laws of retaliation and anathematic dicta within these traditions. Their thrust is that eschatological judgment (which is tantamount to membership in the community) is a present event. The behavior of each disciple now is the criterion for future divine action and dictates how each will be dealt with in the final judgment. The possibilities of curse or blessing, exclusion from or inclusion with the community, future condemnation or salvation are opened in the present to each person by the prophet speaking on behalf of Jesus. A decision must be made that will result either in unity with the community or delivery over to Satan (e.g., 1 Tim 1:20; 1 Cor 5:5). One's fate hinges upon confession or denial, to be ratified in kind at the eschaton. This prophetic-communal context seems the appropriate setting for the cockcrow denial saying, as it too has an anathematic function.[38]

Strategically, the saying holds out the inevitability of denial to the hearer, for surely the cock will crow and also will denial be made. There is a cosmic aura to the scene implied by the saying. The orderly working of the cosmos, of which cockcrow is a part, would have to be restrained to forestall denial. The burden of the cosmos is thus placed on the wavering disciple who is then on notice as to the conclusion toward which present behavior is leading. Revealing the course of that behavior may be intended to shock the disciple into a confession (as in fact it does in Mk 14:31). Geared toward preventing the disintegration of the community, the saying holds out denial as its own deterrent.

The use of this saying against Peter would be coherent with Klein's description of the denial story setting if it were an attempt to effect (reflect?) the exclusion (posthumous?) of Peter or to devalue his power or reputation.

Finally, the fact that the traditional denial story has no cockcrow

---

38. By further developing Käsemann's work, we can see more clearly how the denial saying fits into this category. For purposes of description we might regroup his examples (plus others that we add) into three categories: (1) *retaliatory:* Rom 2:12 (cf. Gal 3:10); 1 Cor 3:17; 14:38; 2 Cor 9:6; Lk 12:8–9/Mt 10:32–33; Mk 4:24; 8:38; Mt 5:19; 6:14–15 (cf. Mk 11:25[–26?]); 16:27; Lk 12:10; 2 Tim 2:12b; 1 Jn 4:15; Rev 3:5; 13:10; 18:6–7. Here the action of the disciple is rewarded or punished in kind by God. (2) *anathematic:* 1 Cor 16:22; Gal 1:9; 3:10; Lk 12:59/Mt 5:26; Mk 9:42–48; 10:15; Mt 7:23; 25:12, 41; Rev 22:18–19. These are exclusionary, using the threat of a curse to maintain the community. (3) *regulatory:* Rom 10:11, 13; 1 Cor 14:13, 27–28, 30, 35, 37. These emphasize how members should function if they are to remain in the community, but do not bear the harsh imperative or threat of excommunication as in the above. The denial saying (Mk 14:30, 72) fits most closely the second category.

motif leads one to wonder whether that story might have had an earlier relation to another denial saying, such as Lk 12:8–9/Mt 10:32–33, which could have provoked the creation of the story or be the word which Peter remembers ،(note that traditional story and both denial sayings use *arneisthai*, not the Mkan *aparneisthai*). But there is no way to determine this.

3. MARKAN CONCERNS

Mk tells a story, a story which, within the context of his total work, reveals a set of facts about his literary concerns and perhaps about the realities for which the story was thought pertinent and which may be reflected in the story. Why then has Mk told this story?

Mk reintroduces Peter into the narrative to climax the theme of Petrine opposition to Jesus and to serve as a negative model.

Mk's redaction has expanded Peter's denials from one to three, has intensified the negative tenor of the story, and has placed it over against Jesus' Sanhedrin hearing so that Peter curses Jesus at the same time and in the same place that Jesus makes his confession (14:61–62). Mk has turned a small story into a major narrative and a major incident within the plot of the Gospel. In one of the few times that the Gospel digresses from its main character, Peter who once followed Jesus "at a distance" now becomes the center of attention.[39] One further indication that Mk's concerns are expressed symbolically *within* the story is that the story abruptly ends with no report of any further outcome or any subsequent movements of Peter; Peter drops out of the Gospel.

Whereas in the tradition Peter's confrontation with the maid is a private one, Mk amplifies it to public proportions; in the former Peter is evasive, in the latter he is pushed to an outright cursing of Jesus. A weak Peter is transformed into a hostile Peter, an opponent.

Mk does not intend Peter merely to deny Jesus; if so no redaction of the traditional story would have been necessary. For Mk it is no longer that Peter denies but what he denies and the manner in which he does

---

39. John the Baptist and Herod also get special attention (1:4–8; 6:14–28) as does possibly the young man (16:5–7; 14:51–52). Note that Judas does not get the same kind of attention: being the last listed of the twelve (3:19), he is forgotten until needed to identify Jesus (14:44–45) and then just as quickly is forgotten again (Mk must remind us that he is "one of the twelve," 14:10, 20, 43).

it. The facts of the story, not unnarrated thoughts or feelings or motives, speak for themselves and for Mk. Peter separates himself from Jesus in a progression from a noncommittal "I don't understand" to a public cursing. Within this context are Mk's thematic concerns: (1) Peter curses Jesus—and at the same time that Jesus is condemned to death; (2) in doing so Peter fulfills Jesus' prediction and becomes subject to the general curse that the Son of Man will be ashamed of those who were ashamed of Jesus (8:38); (3) Peter denies Jesus as Nazarene; (4) Peter denies his own Galilean identity (an identity which he shares with Jesus). Jesus' curses (8:38; 14:30, 72) and Peter's curse (14:71) converge in the denial story and bring into sharp relief the opposition which exists between these two characters.

As for Nazarene and Galilean, these are positive identifications of Jesus in the Gospel. The Gospel's orientation toward Galilee and the eschatological overtones of that place have long been noticed.[40] Galilee is the place of Jesus' work and the place to which he shall return (14:28; 16:7) in power as Son of Man (13:26; 14:62). It is also as Nazarene that he has worked and goes to Galilee (16:6). Thus, there is also an eschatological undercurrent to Peter's denials (reinforced when it is recalled that the eschatological night watches clock Jesus' last meal, betrayal, flight, denial, and handing over to Pilate).[41] In sum, Peter rejects identities which have come to represent the thrust of Jesus' entire ministry: past, present, and future. Here also Peter abandons his own Galilean identity and so further dissociates himself from Jesus.

The double function of the denial story can now be seen: on the one hand it discredits Peter and those who would attach themselves to this cursed disciple while, on the other hand, it rescues and promotes the eschatological interests which he denies.

As a complement to the denial story, the Sanhedrin hearing (14:55–65) further focuses Mk's intentions. The synchronized contrast between a Jesus who confesses and Peter who denies is patent, as is the fact that Jesus is condemned while presumably Peter extracts himself from that same fate. Peter, too, functions as a false witness, failing to

40. Recently, see MARXSEN, 54–116; PERRIN, 37–45; KELBER, 129–47.
41. Again expectations are reversed: during the night watches Jesus is pictured not as a master in the end time (13:32–37), but as passive, obedient, and powerless. See notes 12, 13.

confess. Thus, the Peter-Jesus opposition is further emphasized here. Moreover, Mk's anti-Temple and anti-Jerusalem themes, which Jesus enacts (Mk 11–13) culminate here.[42] In substitute for Temple and city Jesus promises a new Temple, one not made with hands, which will house the future eschatological community (13:27). Implicit in the promise of this "house of prayer for all nations" is Mk's concern for the importance of the Gentile mission as well as for the hope of an imminent parousia and the coming of the Son of Man, symbolized by Galilee.[43] If Peter is in opposition to Jesus, then, it is inferred, he will be found on the side of Temple and city with the connotations of isolation and static orientation toward the present. If so, Peter, more than the betrayer, is the chief antagonist.[44] By rejecting his own Galilean identity he negates the hope for Jesus' return and the establishment of an end-time community. Again, Peter's ultimate exclusion from that community is suggested.

In 14:26–31 the denial theme is linked to the overriding theme of the falling away (scandal) of the disciples. Jesus prophesies that they will all be scandalized and, when Peter protests, he predicts precisely how Peter will fulfill the prophecy (i.e., by denial). The movement of this story is toward the prophecy of the denial.[45]

The scandal theme originates in the programmatic parable chapter, where, when seed is thrown on rocky ground, it springs up, but having no root (*hriza*) withers (*xērainein*), 4:5–6. These seeds are those who hear the word but, having no root, are scandalized (*skandalizein*) when persecution and tribulation come (4:16–17; see 13:19, 24)—Mk addresses his readers very directly here. For Mk, that which scandalizes should be excised whatever the cost (9:42–50); Peter whose denial is a scandal to himself and to the community may well come under this ordinance (as may current members of Mk's community). In 11:20–21, Peter is again linked to the Temple when he sees the fig tree (symbolically the Temple) withered (*xērainein*) to its roots (*hriza*) and remembers Jesus' curse on it—an ironic foreshadowing of their

42. DONAHUE, 103–38; KELBER, 87–138.
43. PERRIN, 37–45; KELBER, 45–65, 129–47.
44. J. B. Tyson, "The Blindness of the Disciples in Mark," *JBL* 80 (1961), 266–68; W. H. Kelber, "Mark 14:32–42: Gethsemane," *ZNW* 63 (1972), 181–87.
45. So Dibelius, *Tradition*, 161.

fates. Then, echoing the preceding, the theme again emerges in 14:26–31.

Reflecting the sequence established in 14:26–31, all of the disciples are scandalized and do "scatter" in 14:50 (even Peter, who later follows "at a distance"), and Peter does deny Jesus, rather than die with him (14:31; here Peter appears to accept the possibility of Jesus' death, cf. 8:31–33).

However, of the three predictions made by Jesus in this complex (14:27, 28, 30), one, that Jesus will go ahead of his disciples into Galilee after he is raised (14:28), is completely ignored by Peter and the disciples. They respond to the predictions of flight and denial but not to that of resurrection and parousia. This is no surprise since the disciples have opposed, ignored, or misunderstood Jesus' earlier predictions of death and resurrection as well (8:32; 9:10; 9:32; 10:33–45). Prediction of eschatological return falls on deaf ears, and, within the dynamic of the scene, it is again Peter who has deflected attention away from Jesus' future and toward his own fate in the present.

Finally, within the theme of Petrine opposition we should consider the Caesarea Philippi incident (8:27–33). It resembles the hearing-denial unit in that here again Jesus makes a confession, again in terms of the Son of Man (8:31, see 14:62), while Peter is placed in the role of opponent. The hostility and opposition between Jesus and Peter are exposed in Peter's faulty confession of Jesus as the Christ and his rebuke of Jesus following a prediction of passion and resurrection. In the context of Mk, the scene has much more the character of a demonic battle with each side rebuking the other (8:30, 32, 33; as for *epitiman*, cf. 1:25; 3:12; 4:39; 9:25), and ending with the astounding but thematically coherent identification of Peter as Satan (versus Jesus who is on the side of God).

Thus it is clear that by his opposition to and denial of Jesus Peter must come under the jurisdiction of 8:35–38: having been ashamed of Jesus, Peter is and will be excluded from the present and future communities; in saving his life he loses it. Peter fails in the proper role of discipleship, self-denial (8:34). He has indeed cursed himself and become one with Satan. Those who attach themselves to Peter or to his view will suffer the same fate.

Models: Jesus and Peter. In excising Peter and the disciples, Mk's *coup de plume* not only has made Peter a negative model but also has relativized his own readers' foundations. In overturning their apostolic base Mk has opened his readers to an uncertainty having no present resolution, but pinned instead to future hope symbolized in Galilee and the Son of Man. To understand the total function of the denial story in the Gospel, then, we might look at the two opposing character models: Jesus and Peter.

At least since W. Wrede, who used the rubric, "Messianic Secret," the ambiguity of Jesus' identity in Mk has been recognized.[46] Jesus is a paradoxical figure: a miracle worker who sometimes can do no miracles (6:5), subject to marvel and faith or scandal and laughter (5:40; 6:3), with a family and yet without (3:31–35), who speaks in riddle, who has supernatural knowledge and yet not (5:30–33), accused of blasphemy (2:7; 14:64) but is himself blasphemed (15:29), then forsaken by God (15:34), who saves others but not himself (15:31), who promises to return after death but has not. Mk presents not two conflicting views of Jesus (miracle worker *versus* suffering Son of Man) but one paradoxical view.

This incongruity (illustrated by the phantasmagoria of christological titles) is underscored by the misunderstanding of the disciples, as well as by repeated questioning about Jesus' identity (1:27; 2:12; 4:41; 6:2; 6:14–16; 8:27–30; 14:61; 15:2). All of the characters are caught up in this ambiguity and their response to it seems to be either flight or opposition. The disciples flee, Judas betrays, Peter denies, the women at the tomb flee and are silent. Jesus himself, reversing the expected, rises from the dead, leaving an empty tomb. At the Gospel's end, all have disappeared except for the young man at the tomb.[47] Apparently none of the other characters can cope with this Jesus, including opposing Jewish groups whose plot to kill Jesus succeeds only temporarily.

Jesus' ambiguity (which he seems to encourage, 1:34; 1:43; 3:12; 5:43; 7:36) and these defective responses may reflect the uncertainty of Mk's readers. Knowing or not knowing Jesus is a divisive task with

---

46. See, for example, WREDE, 19–20, 53–81, 93–114, 124–28, 146–47.   See also notes 12, 13, 41.

47. The *anonymous* young man (14:51–52; 16:5–7) may be a symbolic (of Jesus) escape figure, who escapes (leaving behind his *sindōn*) later to point the way of Jesus' own escape (Jesus is wrapped in a *sindōn*, 15:46) in Jesus' own words (16:7; cf. 14:28).

serious consequences. Precisely: the community cannot seem to identify Jesus (13:6, 21–23). The possibilities of betrayal and denial, of
inadvertently turning against Jesus, of being led astray exist (8:38;
13:9–12; 14:21). In confusion, hope may disintegrate. But, unable to
resolve the ambiguity, their only choice is to affirm it, for their own
identity is centered in it.

This is precisely where Peter, in tribulation, fails and gives up his own
identity. For Mk's readers he becomes not only a negative model but
also a cause of this uncertainty, since he, as a leader, fails. His role
becomes dysfunctional, one of opposition to Jesus: from his geographical misplacement, to his eschatological misalignment, to his failure as a
disciple and his satanic antagonism. Therein lies the ironic tragedy of
the Peter who curses Jesus.

4. TOWARD A PETRINE TRAJECTORY

Finally, we want to look briefly at the subsequent history of the denial
story. We are just beginning to develop the possibility of describing a
Petrine trajectory: the roles into which Peter is cast in early Christian
literature, the character and images of Peter, how they functioned or
were made to function, how "Peter" has been employed in various and
changing texts and contexts. The denial is just one strand, but an
enduring one.

After Mk, there is a rather consistent effort to amend the harshly
negative image given Peter, and yet the denial is so solidly entrenched
already that it cannot be simply ignored. In Mt Peter is the rock upon
which the church is built, is given the keys of heaven (16:17–19), and
while his faith wavers, he does walk on water (14:28–31); by the end
of the Gospel denial is forgotten (28:16–20). Mt tends to work
around Mk's negative Peter stories by juxtaposing more positive material (but see 16:23). Lk deals directly with the denial saying by
appending another saying foretelling Peter's restoration (22:31–32); in
the story he removes Peter's cursing. Lk restores Peter (24:34) so
much so that in Acts this miracle worker and inspired leader accuses
*other*s of having *denied* Jesus (3:13)! In Jn even in competition with
the other disciples Peter is given a very positive role (20:3–6: 21:7–
23); the denial is made less dramatic and more matter of fact. With

Acts of Peter, the denial is so much under control that it is Peter himself who recalls his denial and uses it for his own enhancement: "Satan overthrew me whom the Lord held in such great honor, if he subdued me, what do you expect who are new to the faith?"[48]

The denial is burlesqued in a folktale in which two soldiers who are refused admission to heaven remind Peter of his denial and are then admitted.[49]   In another tale, which exemplifies the folly of Peter's opposition to Jesus, Peter and Jesus are sleeping in the same bed in an inn, when the host returns home drunk and beats Peter. Peter changes places with Jesus; but because of this, when the host returns to beat the other lodger, Peter is beaten again![50]

Thus the negativity which shadows Peter, while it may be downplayed, countered with positive material, or offset with humor, is a seed which was planted prior to Mk and continued to exist. The denial has been a prominent factor, so that we might ask how much later material was designed not only to idealize Peter but also consciously or unconsciously to offset the denial strand (or other negative strands) of the trajectory. To what extent does the trajectory become proprioceptive, feeding upon and reacting to itself (as opposed to a historical person)? Does in fact "Peter" become a creation of the trajectory, a literary product, a multivalent symbol which can be plugged into numerous and contrasting roles, images, and types? We will want to distinguish "Peter's" literary roles and Gospel themes from the implications that they convey (although both contribute to the trajectory). Describing this trajectory will not be a task of merely blocking out typologies (e.g., martyr, shepherd, fisherman, rock, chief apostle, impetuous and weak disciple, etc.) but of going below them to an underlying flexibility that makes accommodation of various roles, images, and types possible and to the undercurrents that have buffeted the character "Peter" along.[51]

48. E. Hennecke and W. Schneemelcher, *New Testament Apocrypha*, trans. R. McL. Wilson (Philadelphia: Westminster Press, 1965), II, 288–89.

49. Stith Thompson, *Motif Index of Folk Literature* (Bloomington: Indiana University Press, 1934), III, J1616.

50. Antti Aarne and Stith Thompson, *The Types of the Folktale*, Folklore Fellows Communication 184, 2d rev. (Helsinki, 1961), type 791 (cf. Thompson, *Motif Index*, K1132); the parody of Peter continues in a number of folktales: 750, 751, 774A-P.

51. See for example: O. Cullmann, *Peter: Disciple, Apostle, Martyr*, 2d ed. (Philadelphia: Westminster Press, 1962); R. E. Brown et al., eds., *Peter in the New Testament* (Minneapolis, Minn.: Augsburg Publishing House, 1973); P. Perkins, "Peter in Gnostic Revelation," *1974 Seminar Papers* (Cambridge, Mass.: SBL, 1974), 1–13.

VII.

The Cross as Power in Weakness

(Mark 15:20b–41)

Theodore J. Weeden, Sr.

In the crucifixion scene (15:20b–41) not only the Passion Narrative but the whole Mkan drama reaches its climax. That the death scene is the climactic event toward which the entire Gospel points is an inescapable conclusion thrust upon the reader by the unfolding drama. The Evangelist prepares us for Jesus' death early (3:6). And soon in mounting intensity he interjects, either through direct reference or by allusion, death "notices" (8:31, 34; 9:11, 31; 10:34, 38, 45; 11:18; 12:6–8; 14:1, 8, 10, 17–24, 27, 31, 34, 36, 41, 64; 15:13–15). Even in the burial and Empty Tomb stories, the Gospel's denouement, Mk draws our attention back to the death scene (15:43–45; 16:6). Why is the crucifixion story so central to the Mkan drama? What clues does it offer for understanding the Evangelist's literary and theological purpose in creating his Gospel?

In search of answers to these questions I will not begin with the customary redaction critical starting point, that is, separating tradition from redaction via analysis of vocabulary, grammar, style, and composition techniques. Rather, I will begin with a literary critical investigation of motifs and thematic configurations. Insights derived from this investigation will then be used along with help from various redaction critical analytical procedures to arrive at both an understanding of the literary processes which led to the creation of the cross narrative and an explanation of Mk's literary/theological purpose.[1]

1. Methodologically, this approach seeks to avoid some of the reductionistic pitfalls of redaction criticism to which D. O. Via calls attention. Via (*Kerygma and Comedy*

1. CRUCIFIXION THEMES

The Mkan crucifixion drama (15:20b–41) contains the following motifs: (a) the crucifixion act itself (15:20b, 24, 25); (b) Simon's bearing of Jesus' cross (15:21); (c) the offering of a drink (15:23, 36); (d) the dividing of Jesus' garments and casting lots for them (15:24); (e) demarcation of the temporal process in three-hour intervals (15:25, 33, 34); (f) two thieves crucified with Jesus (15:27, 32); (g) ridicule and blaspheming (15:29, 31, 32); (h) the Temple (15:29, 38); (i) salvation (15:30, 31); (j) christological identification (15:32, 39, [26]); (k) seeing (15:32, 36, 39) and believing (15:32, 39); (l) darkness (15:33); (m) crying in a loud voice (15:34, 37); (n) divine abandonment (15:34); (o) Elijah (15:35, 36); (p) expiration (15:37, 39); (q) witness of women followers (15:40–41). Among these motifs, the motif of christological identification is, as we shall see, not only the one in relationship to which most of the other motifs play supportive roles; but it stands out as possessing crucial significance for the Evangelist. The primal importance Christology has for the Evangelist is manifested both by the fact that the centurion's christological confession serves as the climactic point of the crucifixion scene and by the major role Christology plays in the crucifixion story and in the Gospel as a whole.

2. THE CHRISTOLOGICAL MOTIF

I have detailed elsewhere my interpretation of the critical importance given to the issue of Christology by Mk.[2] Briefly, two different christological orientations stand in conflict with each other in the Gospel. One of them, the suffering Son of Man Christology, first introduced in 8:31, the Mkan Jesus acclaims as the authentic Christology. The other

---

in the New Testament [Philadelphia: Fortress Press, 1975], 3, 71–73) contends that redaction critics, primarily motivated by historical questions, are more interested in dismantling a composition to reconstruct the historical trajectory that led to it rather than respecting the literary integrity of the composition and understanding it on its own terms. While not dismissing historical questions, the approach here will be directed first to understanding the message of the crucifixion narrative as a whole before raising the questions about the historical trajectories and the component parts of material prior to the creation of the narrative.

2. See WEEDEN, 52–100, 159–68.

Christology, a divine man (*theios anēr*) Christology, a power-oriented Christology that is demonstrated by, among other things, extraordinary miracle working activity, is the christological role into which Jesus is primarily cast prior to 8:31.

I have argued that Mk is an advocate of the suffering Son of Man Christology. Against him are those in his community who avow a divine man Christology. Mk polemicizes against the divine man Christology by presenting at the outset a portrait of Jesus as a great miracle worker, a divine man. Then he has Jesus, at a high dramatic moment, when the question of christological identification is most sharply focused (Caesarea Philippi), repudiate the divine man christological orientation by proclaiming himself to be the suffering Son of Man (8:31; 9:31; 10:33–34, 45). My contention is that, as in earlier sections of the Gospel, the central issue in the crucifixion story is the conflict between a divine man Christology and a suffering Son of Man Christology. Only in the crucifixion story the conflict is even more sharply dramatized, a dramatization which now finally leads to a resolution of the conflict, at least as Mk perceives it.

In 15:20b–41 the Evangelist has woven motifs into a configuration which consists of these two christological viewpoints. With regard to the presentation of the suffering Son of Man Christology in the scene, Mk has drawn upon motifs from certain Old Testament passages portraying the figure of the innocent Righteous One who suffers, yet is finally vindicated in his suffering. Motifs which coalesce to produce this image of the Righteous One are the motifs of crucifying (Ps 22; Isa 53); the offering of a drink (Prov 31:6; [Ps 69:21?]); the dividing of Jesus' garments and casting lots for them (Ps 22:18); execution of two thieves with Jesus (Isa 53:12); ridicule and blaspheming (Ps 22:6–7); divine abandonment (Ps 22:1).[3] All of these motifs function to fulfill the rubrics for the suffering Son of Man Christology: suffering many things, being rejected, mocked and killed (8:31; 9:31; 10:33). While an Old Testament text has no bearing on it, the depiction of Simon carrying Jesus' cross also supports the suffering Son of Man configuration imaged by these Old Testament allusions. It has not gone unno-

3. On these Old Testament motifs in Mk's portrait of the suffering Innocent One, see now J. H. Reumann, "Psalm 22 at the Cross: Lament and Thanksgiving for Jesus Christ," *Interpr* 28 (1974), 39–58.

ticed that the depiction of Simon's carrying the cross of Jesus parallels quite closely Jesus' appeal for a cross-bearing life in 8:34.[4]

With regard to the presentation of the divine man christological gestalt, two sections of the crucifixion story, 15:29b–32 and 15:34–36, are noteworthy. First, as to 15:29b–32, it is now commonly recognized that the antagonists in this passage are challenging Jesus to demonstrate his Messiahship by an extraordinary miracle, descent from the cross. Christological belief for them is predicated on seeing an exhibition of miraculous power (15:32). Another motif reinforcing the divine man christological imagery of our passage is the soteriological motif of saving one's self and saving others (15:30–31). The most puzzling aspect of this motif is the taunt, "he saved others; he cannot save himself" (15:31b). Where in the Gospel has Jesus saved others in the theological sense?

The reference is likely a flashback to Jesus' ministry of healing. The word *sōzein* (save) is used by Mk not only in the technical soteriological sense familiar to us (8:35; 10:26; 13:13, 20). It is used also to describe the restoration of health which Jesus effects as a consequence of his healing ministry (3:4; 5:23, 28, 34; 6:56; 10:52). When *sōzein*, i.e., make well, is used in the context of Jesus' miracle working, there is good reason to believe that it denotes not only restoration to physical health but also an implicit soteriological aspect associated with the divine man theological orientation. The fact that *sōzein* on occasions is found in conjunction with cognates of the word *pistis* (faith or belief: 5:34, 36; 10:52; 15:32) and the fact that faith is often associated with efficacious miracle working (2:5; 4:40; 5:36; 9:23–24) strongly underscore this soteriological significance of the use of *sōzein* in healing miracles.[5] Consequently, it is my opinion that *sōzein* in 15:30, 31 bears intentionally a divine man soteriological orientation. Jesus is challenged to resort to divine man soteriology.[6] Of course, for the

---

4. E.g., E. Schweizer, *The Good News According to Mark*, trans. D. H. Madvig (Atlanta, Ga.: John Knox Press, 1970), 345; SCHENK, 29.

5. SCHENK, 52–53; K. Kertelge, *Die Wunder Jesu im Markusevangelium*, StANT XXIII (Munich: Kösel, 1970), 29, 39, 115, 124–25, 175–78, 197–99; H. J. Held, "Matthew as Interpreter of the Miracle Stories," *Tradition and Interpretation in Matthew*, trans. P. Scott (Philadelphia: Westminster Press, 1963), 180, 189–90, 239, 275–84.

6. According to divine man piety, at least as depicted in the Mkan miracle tradition, belief in the divine man's soteriological power is normally the requisite for the effecting

Mkan Jesus, salvation comes not by miraculously extricating oneself out of life-threatening situations (15:30–31) but by self-losing (8:34–35; 10:42–45).

One final comment on the divine man christological character of 15:29b–32: the challenge to Jesus to justify faith in him as "the Christ, the King of Israel" by miracle working proof suggests that the christological title "Christ" is to be understood in this context in terms of a divine man christological perspective. I have argued previously that the same divine man interpretation of the title "Christ" lies behind the Petrine confession (8:29).[7] What both these passages indicate (8:29; 15:32), is that in Mk's mind, and likely in the understanding of his community, the title "Christ" was associated with a divine man christological position in much the same way that the Son of God title was. The probability of this fact is strengthened by the conjunction of the two titles in 14:61, a key Mkan passage in which the divine man Christology is corrected by the Son of Man Christology.[8]

The focus on miraculous deliverance encountered in 15:29b–32 is found also in 15:34–36. In this case the bystanders are cast in the incredible posture of misunderstanding Jesus' voicing of the words from Ps 22:1 as a cry to Elijah for intervention (mistaking "Eloi" for "Elijah") and miraculous rescue. In this incident we have one of the rare cases in the New Testament where Elijah functions as a divine man rather than in the more common role of eschatological prophet. That the divine man tonality of this passage is being emphasized is suggested by (1) the repeated note that Jesus is asking for Elijah's miraculous aid (15:35, 36), (2) the high relief given this divine man perspective in the

---

of that power (e.g., 2:5, 11–12; 5:25–34; 6:2–6; 9:20–27; 10:46–52; cf. Kertelge, *Die Wunder Jesu*, and Held, "Matthew as Interpreter"). The reversal of this divine man format in 15:32 (seeing then believing) serves as a caricature of divine man piety and soteriology.

7. WEEDEN, 52–69.

8. The two titles also occur conjointly in the conclusion of the divine man Signs Source (Jn 20:30–31). See R. Fortna, *The Gospel of Signs* (Cambridge: Cambridge University Press, 1970), 198, 223–34. On "Christ" as divine man title in the New Testament, see H. Koester, "One Jesus and Four Primitive Gospels," *Trajectories through Early Christianity* (Philadelphia: Fortress Press, 1971), 188. With regard to Mk, see N. Perrin, *A Modern Pilgrimage in New Testament Christology* (Philadelphia: Fortress Press, 1974), 108–21. DONAHUE, 198–200, is convincing in interpreting the title "King of Israel" (15:32) eschatologically (King of an eschatological, true Israel) rather than politically.

mistaking of "Eloi" for "Elijah," and (3) the stark contrast between the psalm-guided meaning of Jesus' evocation and the radically different, divine man interpretation given to that evocation by the bystanders.[9]

Not only are the Son of Man Christology and divine man Christology pitted against one another throughout the crucifixion story in a theme/countertheme pattern, but the end result of this theme/countertheme pattern is the discrediting of divine man Christology and the vindication of Son of Man Christology. The divine man Christology is discredited, first of all, because its only advocates in the drama are the enemies of Jesus. Even that advocacy is pressed sarcastically. Second, the manner in which the advocacy is pressed ironically heightens the image of Jesus as the suffering Son of Man. The Son of Man Christology is vindicated in the course of the narrative, first, by the fact that what happens to Jesus in his suffering and death transpires exactly as he predicted would take place. Second, the Son of Man Christology is vindicated because it alone in the drama conforms to the rubrics of Old Testament prophecy.

The final and complete repudiation of the divine man Christology and the vindication of the Son of Man Christology occurs in the climax of the crucifixion story, in the confession of the centurion (15:39). The centurion in contrast to others in the drama proclaims Jesus to be the Son of God—not because Jesus produced a miraculous feat, as Jesus' adversaries require for belief, but because he *saw how* Jesus died.[10] The only person with real power at the cross paradoxically verifies Jesus' christological status not because Jesus awed him with his power but because Jesus died a suffering, "powerless" death. By his confession, particularly via the divine man title "Son of God," the centurion eviscerates by conceptual reversal divine man Christology. As a closing touch to the whole servanthood theme in the Passion Narrative, Mk notes the servant-follower profile of the women watching "from the wings" (15:40–41).

Up to this point our discussion has focused on the thematic point and counterpoint in the crucifixion story. I shall next deal with three motifs

9. See WEEDEN, 58, 166; LINNEMANN, 148–51.

10. "Seeing" in 15:39 echoes with intended irony the divine man association of "seeing" with miracle working (thus also SCHENK, 57–58). Cf. 2:5, 12; 5:14, 16; 6:48–50; 9:20, 25, 38; 15:32, 36. DONAHUE's claim, 204, that the centurion's "seeing" symbolically points to the parousia is untenable.

which are seemingly unrelated to the two christological viewpoints. These motifs are first and foremost the Temple motif, and furthermore the themes of the three-hour intervals and darkness. I shall establish their connection with the christological point and counterpoint, and in the process inquire into the possible pre-Mkan setting of these Christologies.

3. THE TEMPLE MOTIF

There are a number of mystifying features about the Temple motif that make it difficult to fathom Mk's interest in it. The first problem is the ambiguity 14:57–59 causes with respect to the proper interpretation of 15:29, 38 and also with regard to the proper interpretation of Jesus' specific posture toward the Temple in the Gospel. One might argue that the rending of the Temple veil in 15:38 is Jesus' "delivering" on the sarcastic challenge hurled at him in 15:29. The splitting of the veil might suggest that at least part of the boast was "made good."[11] But this hypothesis fails because the Evangelist has made it indisputably clear in 14:57–59 that the boast of 15:29 was falsely ascribed to Jesus. Did Jesus boast he could destroy the Temple and build it in three days or not? If he did not, what is the import of 15:38?[12]

Similarly, in Mk 11–13 Jesus' attitude toward the Temple and Temple cult is clearly negative. He opposes the cult and predicts the destruction of the Temple.[13] Yet, when one compares this well-attested attitude with the force of 14:56, 57–59, one is confused. The repeated emphasis on the falseness of the anti-Temple charge leads one to wonder whether the Evangelist is trying to disassociate Jesus from an anti-Temple position. Was Jesus opposed to the Temple or not? Did he intend to build a new one himself in three days or not? Moreover, why does 14:58 designate Jesus as the destroyer of the old and builder of the new Temple, whereas 13:2, 14 and 15:38 make no reference to Jesus as

11. The rending of the veil is a symbolic reference to the destruction of the whole Temple (see DONAHUE, 201–203).

12. The focus of these questions is not on the historical Jesus but on the Jesus of the Mkan narrative. The question of historical authenticity (see LINNEMANN, 116–19) is quite a different matter.

13. See DONAHUE, 113–38; KELBER, 97–128; cf. L. Gaston, *No Stone on Another*, NTSup 23 (Leiden: E. J. Brill, 1970), 472–81.

the agent of destruction?[14]   Why are there no explicit references to the building of a new Temple aside from 14:58 and 15:29?[15]

The second curious feature of the Temple motif, both in the crucifixion story and the rest of the Gospel, is the close contextual association it has with the christological motif.   In 15:29–32 the taunt about destroying the Temple is followed by christological mocking.   In 15:38–39 the splitting of the Temple veil is followed by a christological confession.   In the trial narrative the false accusation against Jesus as destroyer of the Temple is followed by an inquiry about his christological identity (14:61–62).   In Mk 13 the disciples' question about the destruction of the Temple is followed immediately by Jesus' warning about Messianic impostors (13:1–6).   We should also note that the christological adoration of the crowd upon Jesus' entry into Jerusalem is followed by Jesus' entrance into the Temple (11:9–11).   Noteworthy, too, is that the christological discussion in 12:35–37 is explicitly set in the Temple.[16]

The third striking characteristic of the Temple motif is related to the second.   At practically every point at which the motif of the destruction of the Temple is introduced it is eclipsed by the christological motif.   In 15:29–32, although Jesus is taunted about a boast to destroy the Temple and rebuild it, the challenge hurled at Jesus is not to demonstrate his ability to destroy and rebuild the Temple, but to verify his Messiahship by extricating himself from his plight.   In 15:37–39, if the rending of the veil is meant to have any significance with respect to Jesus' death, it is almost completely overshadowed by the centurion's christological response to the death.   Similarly, in the trial narrative the Temple motif is dismissed quickly as the narrative moves to the christological question which is the issue the High Priest is primarily concerned about, the only issue to which Jesus responds, and the issue which finally brings about Jesus' condemnation.

Likewise, in Mk 13 the christological motif eclipses the Temple motif. The chapter begins with Jesus' prediction of the destruction of the

14. There is a key difference between Jesus proclaiming the end of the Temple and claiming that *he* is the agent of destruction.

15. Against DONAHUE, 122–27, and with Gaston (*Stone*, 213–17, 476) and LINNEMANN, 123–24, Mk 12:1–12 does not present Jesus as the creator of a new community (Temple)—unless one reads 14:58 back into the parable.   The point of the parable is christological not ecclesiological.

16. See KELBER, 93–97, on 11:9–11 and 12:35–37.

Temple (13:1–2). Yet when the disciples ask Jesus for the clue to
that event, Jesus responds not with information about the Temple but
with information about Christology (13:3–6). From that point on,
the Temple is referred to only once and then only obliquely (13:14).
The dominant theme throughout the chapter is Christology (13:6, 9,
13, 21–27).[17] If it were not for the initial statement about the destruction of the Temple in 13:1–2, and the oblique reference in 13:14,
the Temple would play no part at all in the discussion of Mk 13.

We need to make one further observation on the relationship between
Christology and Temple motifs in Mk. Isolated from their context, the
Temple sayings in 14:58 and 15:29 are the only instances in the Gospel
in which the Temple motif is not suppressed by the christological motif.
Only in these verses do the two motifs stand in an almost mutually
supportive interrelationship. In each case the Temple image has been
preserved in terms of the "new Temple" so as to communicate the
christological (and ecclesiological) message. This same equivalence of
Temple theme and Christology occurs in Jn 2:19–21.[18]

The fourth curious feature about the Temple motif is that in all cases
but three in Mk the word used to refer to the Temple is either *hieron* or
oikos. In the three cases, namely, 14:58, 15:29, and 15:38, the word
for Temple is *naos*.

What sense can be made out of these mystifying, sometimes contradictory, features of the Temple motif? One thing is clear. If we de-
leted 14:57–59 and 15:29, 38, the problematic features we have noted
would no longer exist. Without these passages the Mkan presentation
of Jesus' stance toward the Temple would be free of ambiguity. In the
excised version Jesus would emerge as one who opposed the Temple cult
and its leaders, anticipated and predicted the destruction of the Temple
(along with the city). Yet Jesus would not be linked directly with the
Temple destruction per se, nor would he be cast as the builder of a new
Temple in either a christological or ecclesiological sense. Such an excised version would exhibit no positive or mutually supportive correlation between the Temple motif and Christology.

Deletion of 14:57–59 would remove the Evangelist's strange re-

---

17. WEEDEN, 70–100.
18. See B. Lindars (*New Testament Apologetic* [Philadelphia: Westminster Press,
1961], 105–106) who discusses the body-Temple equivalence in Jn 2:19–22 and the
process leading up to the formation of Jn 2:19.

course to redundancy to prove to the reader that the old/new Temple charge against Jesus was contrived, ungrounded in fact. The deletion of 14:57–59 and 15:29, 38 would remove in the process the uncharacteristically Mkan use of the word *naos* to designate the Temple.

Recently J. Donahue has renewed the argument that Mk is responsible for the insertion of 14:57–59 and 15:29 into the Mkan drama. Donahue contends that Mk affirms the position ascribed "falsely" to Jesus in both passages. Jesus *will* bring an end to the old Temple and *will* establish a new Temple, the eschatological Christian community.[19] Donahue makes this claim on the basis of his understanding of the function of the sayings and the entire Mkan anti-Temple theology in the Mkan *Sitz im Leben*. According to Donahue, the Mkan community finds itself in the immediate aftermath of the destruction of the Temple and the related events of the Roman-Jewish War (A.D. 66–70). Estranged from Judaism and suffering persecution from Jews, the community needed a theological rationale for its plight and for the relationship of the Temple destruction to that plight. Some Christians (13:6, 21–22), drawing upon an anti-Temple tradition attributed to Jesus, have falsely identified the end of the Temple as *the* eschatological signal for the imminent dawning of the parousia. For Mk this eschatological position is in error.

Mk, according to Donahue, does subscribe to Jesus' opposition to the Temple and the prediction of its destruction. But the eschatological value of the Temple destruction for the Mkan community, so the Evangelist tells us, must be delimited to an attestation of God's judgment on Judaism. There is no intrinsic relationship between the destruction of the Temple and the return of Jesus (13:1–27). The reader must forget the Temple and focus attention upon patient waiting for the irruption of the parousia event (13:28–37). Then Jesus will create a new Temple, an eschatological community whose cornerstone is Jesus (12:10), a community promised by Jesus (14:58b) and fully manifested at the parousia.[20]

Donahue argues that Mk, in opposition to the false eschatology which

---

19. DONAHUE, 77, 134–36, 175–77. See also J. Donahue's essay in the present volume, "Temple, Trial, and Royal Christology."

20. DONAHUE, 114, 131, is dependent on KELBER, 87–137, in his reconstruction of the Mkan *Sitz im Leben* with respect to a false eschatology associated with the Temple.

links Temple destruction with parousia, takes a traditional saying of Jesus about the destruction of the Temple (see 13:2) and adds a second saying to the first to establish the validity of his own eschatological interpretation.   Thus: Mk takes the Temple motif of the original Temple-destruction logion (14:58a) and turns it into a positive eschatological metaphor for the new community (14:58b).   Mk then puts this expanded saying into the trial account to remind and assure the reader of Jesus' promise of a new community.   He introduces the saying again in 15:29 to play a double function: (1) to relate "the final decision to execute Jesus for his opposition to the temple to its carrying out in the crucifixion," and (2) to put "an incorrect eschatology [linking Temple destruction with the parousia] on the lips of the mockers and an incorrect understanding of Jesus' Passion[circumvention of the cross] . . . as a foil for an eschatology and Christology which he rejects throughout his Gospel."[21]

I support Donahue in his basic thesis that behind the Mkan use of the anti-Temple motif lies an attempt by the Evangelist to discredit an eschatological position which associated the destruction of the Temple with the imminence of the parousia.   As should now be obvious, I also concur that Mk is unmasking and attacking a false Christology in his Gospel and that that Christology is being discredited through its sarcastic advocacy in 15:29–32.   I furthermore agree with Donahue that the use of the Temple saying in 15:29 is, in its placement on the lips of the revilers of Jesus, an attempt to expose the "heresy" of an eschatology linking the destruction of the Temple with the parousia.

I dissent from Donahue, however, when he argues that the Temple saying is introduced in 15:29 to relate the issue upon which Jesus was condemned to crucifixion.   I find no evidence in the Mkan trial account to argue that the Sanhedrin judgment against Jesus was provoked by his opposition to the Temple.   Nor is Jesus' opposition to the Temple identified as a charge in the hearing before Pilate (15:1–5).   I cannot share the view that the reader, on the one hand, should recognize that the Temple saying as it occurs in 15:29 functions as a foil for a false eschatology yet, on the other hand, should also know that the saying as it appears in 14:58 represents authentic eschatology.   Contextual and

21. DONAHUE, 197–98; see also 103–37, 205–24.

intrinsic factors related to the Temple boast of 14:58 persuade me that
it is being discredited as false eschatology for the benefit of the reader
just as the same boast is discredited as false eschatology in 15:29.

Contextually, I find this to be so despite the common view that the
Evangelist in 14:58 is asseverating that Jesus did claim he would destroy the Temple and build, without hands, another one in three days.
If this were in fact Mk's intent, then he has a strange way of proclaiming
the truth by convincing the reader of its falseness (14:56, 57, 59).
The narrative logic of 14:55–59 leaves the unmistakable impression
that it is a malevolent misrepresentation of the Mkan Jesus to attribute
to him the old/new Temple claim of 14:58.

Furthermore, two distinctive and intrinsic facets of the Temple logion
found in 14:58 (and also 15:29) cast Jesus in the role of Temple
destroyer/rebuilder, a role glaringly incompatible with the Mkan Jesus'
position elsewhere in the Gospel. The logion 14:58 evinces an inherent
instrumental and eschatological continuity. The instrumental continuity is manifest in the fact that Jesus himself is the agent of destruction
and rebuilding. The eschatological continuity is evident in the fact that
destruction of the old Temple and building of another are conceived as
tandem acts accomplished within the imminent eschatological time-
frame of three days.

Aside from 14:58 and 15:29, support for such an instrumental and
eschatological continuity fails in Mk. As far as the instrumental continuity is concerned, there is no indication in the rest of the Gospel that
Jesus is himself the destroyer of the old Temple, although he clearly
predicts its end (13:2). In fact Mk 13 informs us that, in the history
between Easter and the parousia, the period in which the Temple is
destroyed, Jesus is absent from the world and the Church. This particular epoch is a negative time, an era of "heresy," both christological and
eschatological. It is a period when false claims are made for Jesus'
presence (13:6, 21–23). Jesus, in this schema, only returns when the
epoch comes to its destructive end (13:24–26).[22] If, then, he is
absent in the epoch in which the Temple is destroyed, he cannot be its
destroyer.

Nor does Mk 13 support the specific instrumental continuity of 14:58

22. WEEDEN, 85–89.

and 15:29 by citing Jesus as the builder of another Temple. It is true that after the end of the old epoch Jesus, according to 13:27, 33–37, will be reunited with his followers in a new community. Yet, if the instrumental imagery of 14:58b is intended here, it is surprising that the Temple motif does not explicitly evidence itself in the depiction of the founding of the community.

With regard to eschatological continuity, Donahue and Kelber[23] have persuasively argued that Mk opposes any direct eschatological link between the destruction of the Temple and the parousia. Mk 13 indisputably supports this position by locating the destruction of the Temple as one event, albeit important, among many events in the negative period of world history, a period quite separate and distinct from the time of the parousia, a period in which false claims are made with regard to the eschatological import of the Temple destruction.

Expanding the discussion, I share, as noted above, Donahue's position that both a false eschatology and a false Christology has been placed under attack in 15:29–32. Against Donahue I am persuaded that the very same false eschatology and false Christology is being discredited and/or corrected in the trial narrative.

Earlier in this essay the argument was made that the christological polemic in the trial and crucifixion is against a divine man Christology. Now, on the basis of what we have seen to be Mk's consistent aversion to the old/new Temple logion, there is reason to conclude that what Mk attacks as eschatologically objectionable in 15:29 is also being attacked by Mk as eschatologically objectionable in 14:58. Thus, the contention that the Evangelist polemicizes against the same Christology and eschatology in the trial and crucifixion scenes is logically warranted.

Moreover, the fact that these attacks on Christology and eschatology are contextually interrelated, particularly in the crucifixion, prompts a further deduction. In Mk's mind there is an integral link between the "heretical" advocacy of a divine man Christology and the advocacy of a false old/new Temple eschatology. Support for such a thesis is found when one compares the Mkan treatment of divine man Christology and Temple eschatology in Mk 13 with his treatment of both in the trial and crucifixion accounts. In all three of these key sections of the Gospel

23. KELBER, 111–28.

there is a material link between the subjects of Temple and Christology. In each there is a uniform pattern of response to divine man Christology and Temple eschatology. Divine man Christology is repudiated as false and replaced by a Son of Man Christology.[24] In each case an eschatology which associates the destruction of the Temple as a penultimate act of Jesus, leading to his ultimate parousia act of full establishment of a new community (Temple), is exposed as fraudulent. All of these factors bring me to this conclusion: *Mk is combating a divine man Christology conjoined with a realized eschatology which depicts Jesus as the destroyer of the old Temple and builder of the new.*

Using this conclusion as a working hypothesis, I think it can be argued (1) that Mk used a trial tradition which originally consisted of, among other elements, 14:58 (without reference to the falsity of the charge) and 14:61–62a (without mention of Son of Man Christology); and (2) that this trial narrative belonged to a divine man tradition. Unfortunately, space limitations do not permit me to marshal a full defense for such an argument.[25] We can only touch on some reasons for assuming a divine man origin of the trial. As already noted, the christological interchange in the trial (14:61–62a) before the affixing of the Son of Man Christology (14:62b) evinces a divine man orientation. With regard to the old/new Temple logion, it appears likewise at home in the divine man context. I shall elaborate.

First, aside from Mt's incorporation of Mk 14:58 and 15:29, the closest parallel to the old/new Temple saying is found in Jn 2:19 where it is affirmatively cited in the story of the cleansing of the Temple, a story the Fourth Evangelist borrowed from his divine man Signs Source.[26] Notable in the Signs Source cleansing story is the fact that Jesus' saying is provoked by a challenge to support his Temple-cleansing authority by a sign (miracle).[27] Both the challenge and Jesus'

---

24. See our discussion above; WEEDEN, 70–100.

25. Narrative logic, theme, and character continuity support an argument for a pre-Mkan trial containing (1) two principals, Jesus and the High Priest (14:53, 60, 61, 63); (2) anti-Temple charge (14:58); (3) the High Priest's demand for response to the charge (14:60, now a logically motivated query); (4) the High Priest's christological question (14:61b) provoked by an implicit christological claim in the charge; (5) Jesus' affirmative christological response (14:62a); (6) the High Priest's pronouncement of judgment (14:63–4).

26. Fortna, *Signs*, 145–47.

27. Thus R. Bultmann, *The Gospel of John*, trans. G. R. Beasley-Murray et al. (Philadelphia: Westminster Press, 1971), 124–25.

counterchallenge exemplify the type of divine man power confrontation which Mk disdains and which he discredits by his sarcastic use of the old/new Temple saying in 15:29.

Second, one of the closest parallels to the first half of our saying lies in the charge levied against Stephen at his trial (Acts 6:14). Whether one argues that Lk derived the charge from the Mkan trial of Jesus or from a divine man Stephen tradition,[28] it is clear that in the Acts context the view that Jesus is the Temple destroyer is linked to a divine man Christology. Third, the close conceptual and linguistic (*katalyein, oikodomē, acheiropoiētos*) correspondence between 2 Cor 5:1 and Mk 14:58 has been noted.[29] Is it mere coincidence that these terms and the particular conceptualization characteristic of 14:58 occur only here in Paul, in the context of a letter responding to a divine man challenge (so D. Georgi) in Corinth? It is my opinion that the pre-Mkan trial account belonged to Mk's divine man opponents. In his use of the trial, Mk edits it to convince the reader (1) that Temple eschatology is fraudulent, and (2) that Jesus acknowledges christological status only when it is interpreted by Son of Man Christology.

If this is Mk's way of dealing with the aberrant Temple eschatology of his opponents, why does he permit the reference to the rending of the Temple veil? Does not this notice tend to play into the hands of the opponents' position by its association with the death cry of Jesus, or at least introduce ambiguity into Mkan Temple theology which seems homogeneous up to this point? The answer to this question returns us to a consideration of two important motifs in the crucifixion we have until now delayed: the motifs of three-hour intervals and darkness.

4. MARKAN SETTING AND PRE-MARKAN TRADITION

There is a growing consensus that the hour and darkness motifs along with the motif of the veil rending and, perhaps, the loud cry motif convey a pronounced apocalyptic orientation. Recently J. Schreiber, E. Linnemann, and W. Schenk have formulated the position that Mk possessed a crucifixion tradition in which these particular motifs play

28. See J. Schreiber, *Theologie des Vertrauens* (Hamburg: Furche-Verlag, 1967), 66–82; Gaston, *Stone*, 154–61.
29. See Gaston, *Stone*, 185–86.

important parts.[30]   Schreiber and Schenk have argued, Linnemann to the contrary, that this particular tradition was cast in the apocalyptic format.   Schreiber and Schenk contend that in addition to this tradition Mk possessed another crucifixion account, an account shaped from both the "memory" of Simon of Cyrene and Old Testament allusions.   This account belonged to a group tracing its origin to Stephen.   Schreiber claims that the apocalyptic tradition also came from the Stephen group, a group with a decidedly divine man orientation.[31]

I am not so confident as Schreiber, Schenk, and Linnemann are in the ability of redaction criticism to reconstruct the precise content and contextual parameters of the pre-Mkan tradition or traditions.   Although I do not believe it is possible to identify more than the general thematic contours of this tradition, even identifying these contours significantly advances our understanding and interpretation of Mk's use of the tradition.   It may be that Mk possessed a tradition in which Simon of Cyrene played a significant part in aiding God's innocent sufferer.   If such a tradition did exist, Mk obviously aligned himself with the theological viewpoint of that tradition.   The same cannot be said for an "apocalyptic" crucifixion tradition which Mk likely did possess.

The narrative logic of the "apocalyptic" tradition sketches, as Schenk and Schreiber helped me to see, a drama unfolding according to the predetermined plan of God (exact three-hour intervals; 15:25, 33, 34a) in which forces of chaos reassert themselves and sweep over good (defeat of God's anointed; 15:25) and capture and control God's creation (darkness; 15:33).   This conquest of evil is finally halted and abruptly brought to an end by a *coup de main*, a triumphant loud cry of Jesus (15:34a [37]).   In the triumphant cry of Jesus, good, reversing its plunge toward apparent defeat, emerges victorious from the cosmic battle, and seals the final judgment and ultimate destruction of evil (rending of the Temple veil; 15:38).[32]   Schenk hypothesizes that the

---

30. The tradition is variously assessed.   See Schreiber (*Theologie*, 22–40, 66–82): 15:25, 26, 29a, 32c, 33, 34a, 37, 38; LINNEMANN (137–70): 15:22a, 24a, 25a, 33, 34a, 37, 38; SCHENK (13–24, 37–52): 15:25, 26, 29ac, 30, 33, 34a, 37, 38, 39 (in part).

31. On the Simon tradition: Schreiber (*Theologie*, 22–33, 62–66): 15:20b–22a, 24, 27; SCHENK (13–36): 15:20b–22a, 23a?, 24, 27, 29b?; on Mkan redaction: Schreiber (24–32, 41–49): 15:22b, 23, 29b–32b, 34b–36, 39–41; SCHENK (13–24, 52–64): 15:22b, 23b, 31, 32, 34b–36, 39 (in part), 40–41.

32. Cf. Schreiber, *Theologie*, 33–40, 66–69; SCHENK, 37–52.   O. Betz (*"phōnē,"*

apocalyptic crucifixion tradition belonged to Christians who avouched a realized eschatology and who viewed Jesus' death as the final end time moment in which the old, evil age was destroyed and the new age of God irrupted in full realization.

What I find most striking about Schenk's reconstruction of this tradition is the correspondence between some of its constitutive elements and key features of the theological posture of Mk's divine man opponents derived from the investigation of the Temple logion in 14:58 and 15:29. As in the case of the opponents' logion, the apocalyptic tradition avers a realized eschatology manifested by the destruction of the Temple. As in the christological imagery of the logion, the pre-Mkan crucifixion account casts Jesus as the agent of Temple destruction (rending of the veil by the cry).[33] Furthermore, the christological portrait of Jesus, as Schreiber has seen, comports well with the divine man pattern of martyrdom which in the Christian context culminates in the reversal of fate, with a triumphalist Christ emerging victorious over his enemies.

The similarity between Mk's treatment of the apocalyptic crucifixion tradition, both with regard to its constitutive elements and theological gestalt, and his treatment of his opponents' traditions elsewhere, enhances the probability that the crucifixion tradition belonged to his opponents. First of all Mk completely eviscerates the theological thrust of the tradition by the way in which he interweaves it with other material to create his crucifixion story.[34] By historicizing the tradition, i.e., setting the death of Jesus in the context of world history (15:1–20, 43–45), and even viewing Jesus' death in historical retrospect (15:44–45), Mk divests the elements in the tradition of their original apocalyptic function.

The time notices no longer serve the reinforcement of apocalyptic determinism. They only mark the temporal span of the crucifixion

---

TDNT IX, 294) suggests that Joel 3:15 (LXX), where God's voice effects judgment and destruction of the earth, may lie behind Mk 15:37. Cf. Schreiber and Schenk for apocalyptic passages (e.g., in New Testament: 1 Thess 4:16–17; Rev, *passim*) where a loud cry connotes triumphant power and judgment.

33. The image of Temple rebuilding does not surface in the Mkan text, although some have mistakenly read it in under the influence of 14:58 and 15:29 (cf. Schreiber, *Theologie*, 43, 242; SCHENK, 62).

34. Thus SCHENK, 52–64.

event. Historicizing the death into the past has deeschatologized the tradition's realized-eschatological character of both the death of Jesus and the "proleptic" Temple destruction. By historicizing the triumphant apocalyptic death cry and transforming it into the anguished prayer of a servant of God victimized by his enemies (Ps 22:1), Mk has robbed the cry of its triumphalist character. He has turned what was once a climactic moment of apocalyptic reversal into an expiring cry of dereliction. By this same historicizing process, the central role the veil rending played as a symbol of the final apocalyptic vanquishing of the forces of evil has now been obscured by the transformed character of the cry, the "upstaging" of the centurion's confession and the attention given to the faithful followers watching from afar (15:40–41).

But it is not just in the eviscerating of the theological thrust of the tradition that Mk's treatment of the apocalyptic crucifixion story corresponds closely to the way in which he reacts to divine man traditions elsewhere. Mk has in this case, as elsewhere, taken his opponents' material and effectively turned it into the service of his own suffering Son of Man apologetic. This is particularly evident in the way the cry of the apocalyptic tradition and the veil rending, in conjunction with the centurion's confession, the watching women, and other elements, have been fashioned into a new narrative imagery, an imagery in which the cry and the veil rending have undergone transvaluation. To help understand the consequence of this transvaluation of imagery we need to turn to some conceptual insights of the structuralist hermeneutic.

From what structuralists would call the deep structure of the composition[35] there pulsates through the Mkan narrative a dialectic characterized by the clash of two opposing ways to attain and sustain personal well-being. One way seeks well-being by conquest, leading to dominance or destruction of others. Its instrument is coercive, brute power. The other way seeks personal well-being by self-effacement and self-giving love—suffering servanthood—which leads ultimately to self-realization through self-actualization of others. Whereas authority of the former lies in coercive power, the authority of the latter lies in compassionate, persuasive love. The first way's weakness is in its power. The second way's power is in its weakness. One method by

35. See Via, *Kerygma and Comedy*, 1–33.

coercive force transforms life into death. The other by the paradoxical mystery of self-giving love transforms death into life.

These two contrasting forces clash with each other most prominently in the Gospel after 8:27. It is in the second half of Mk that one finds such diverse figures as the Jewish authorities, the disciples, Barabbas, and the Roman soldiers in pursuit of personal well-being by dominance or destruction of others (9:33–34; 12:12; 14:10; 15:7, 16–20). They gain life by taking life. Set over against these are children, women, Simon of Cyrene, and, of course, Jesus—those who gain life by life-giving (8:34–35; 9:35–37; 10:42–45; 14:3–9; 15:40–41).

This same dynamic dialectic permeates the Mkan crucifixion narrative. Obviously in the crucifixion scene the champions of coercive power are the Jewish leaders, the soldiers, robbers, and the centurion. By contrast one finds persuasive, self-giving power represented by Simon of Cyrene, the watching women, and Jesus. The most profound meaning of the clash between these two forces, however, lies at an even deeper dimension both in terms of the narrative as narrative and the probable historical/theological trajectory which the materials transversed prior to being woven into the present narrative mosaic.

In terms of the historical/theological trajectory, it is apparent, as I reconstruct the Mkan *Sitz*, that Mk's opponents advocate in their theology (Christology, eschatology) self-actualization through the demonstrative use of awesome power. Mk, by contrast, aligns himself with the persuasive love of suffering servanthood.

An interesting result ensues when Mk brings these opposing theological traditions together. The coercive forces in the final composition ironically become instruments for dramatizing and actualizing the potential of the persuasive force of love. Thus by coercion Simon is compelled to carry Jesus' cross, but in so doing he becomes a model of cross-bearing and life-giving discipleship (8:34–35). The coercive forces directed against Jesus (crucifixion, dividing his garments, derision, etc.) serve to actualize his suffering servanthood.

But it is in the transvaluation of coercive images, some drawn from the tradition of Mk's opponents, that the crucifixion story finally on the narrative level discredits the argument for self-actualization via coercive power, and authenticates life actualized by self-giving. The cry of triumph which originally effected the "proleptic" destruction of the Temple by divine force now has been transformed into a cry of dereliction. In its transformed state the cry (15:34, 37), as we have seen, plays a key role in the suffering-servant portrayal of Jesus' death. In that role the cry is instrumental in causing the surrogate of supreme coercive power (the Roman centurion) to avow paradoxically the power of suffering servanthood. Similarly, through an ironic twist the centurion makes his confession with a christological title, Son of God, which originally certified omnipotence but now through transvaluation attests to total weakness. Likewise, the Temple, symbol of dehumanizing power, caricatured as a den of thieves (11:17), is ironically reduced to impotency not by the destructive force of the Roman army or even the mistakenly expected, militant agency of Jesus (14:58), but by the powerlessness of his death.

And thus it is that the crucifixion story, both on the level of narrative and in the history of the struggle of theological traditions in the Mkan community, dramatizes the mysterious paradox of authentic Christian existence: "Power [life] is made perfect in weakness" (2 Cor 12:9).

VIII.

Empty Tomb and Absent Lord

(Mark 16:1–8)

John Dominic Crossan

The thesis of this essay is that Mk created the tradition of the Empty Tomb (ET) as the precise and complete redactional conclusion for his Gospel (16:1–8). The argumentation for this must be tripodal so that the failure of any one section will destroy support for the whole. Three interlocked and mutually supportive arguments confirm this thesis. First, there are no versions of ET *before* Mk. Second, those *after* Mk all derive from him. Third, the ET *in* Mk is completely consistent with and required by Mkan redactional theology.[1]

There are three major presuppositions that need to be explained immediately. First, the primary question addressed to Mk 16:1–8 should *not* be: what actually happened that morning insofar as this can now be

---

1. For a full discussion of the Easter traditions see: (1) bibliographies: (a) 1940–57, C. M. Martini, *Il Problema Storico della Risurrezione negli Studi Recenti*, AnGreg 104 (Gregorian University Press, 1959), 158–71; (b) 1957–68, G. Ghiberti, "Bibliografia sull' Esegesi dei Raconti Pasquali e sul Problema della Risurrezione di Gesú," *ScuolC* 97 (1969), 68*–84*. (2) surveys: F. H. Drinkwater, "Resurrection Chronicle," *Clergy Review* 52 (1967), 960–64; 53 (1968), 258–63; 54 (1969), 251–59, 332–36, 412–19, 621–27; J. J. Smith, "Resurrection Faith Today," *TS* 30 (1969), 393–419; G. Ghiberti, "Discussione sul sepulcro vuoto," *RivB* 17 (1969), 392–419. (3) recent books: L. Schenke, *Auferstehungsverkündigung und leeres Grab*, Stuttgarter Bibelstudien 33 (Stuttgart: Katholisches Bibelwerk, 1968); E. L. Bode, *The First Easter Morning*, AnBib 45 (Rome: Pontifical Biblical Institute, 1970); C. F. Evans, *Resurrection and the New Testament*, SBT, 2d Ser. 12 (Naperville, Ill.: Allenson, 1970); R. H. Fuller, *The Formation of the Resurrection Narratives* (New York: Macmillan, 1971); R. E. Brown, *The Virginal Conception and Bodily Resurrection of Jesus* (New York: Paulist Press, 1973), 69–129.

historically reconstructed from the varying accounts? *But rather*: what type of language and what sort of story is being told to us in 16:1–8? Not, what is its historical core, but, what is its linguistic function? One has the clear impression that much recent work intends to find that historical core which is therefore presumed as an incontrovertible datum at the start.[2] This article neither presumes nor denies such historicity but it relegates it to a second stage of the investigation, after, and only after, the study of the linguistic intentionality of the text. The second presupposition applies Occam's razor to traditions: these should be multiplied only when necessary, not just possible. One should not postulate divergent and independent traditions as methodological discipline, if textual differences can be *as easily* explained by redactional creativity on one and the same tradition. A third presupposition is that a *presumption* is not the same as a *tradition*. It is possible that those who believed Jesus was with God might have presumed there was, therefore and somewhere, an empty grave. But this is not yet a tradition of where it is, how it was found, when, by whom, etc. No doubt Mk presumed Jesus had an infancy but there is no tradition of an infancy in Mk as there is in Matthew and Luke. Presumption of fact is not tradition of event.

1. THE TRADITION BEFORE MARK

Recent attempts to separate Mkan redaction from pre-Mkan tradition in 16:1–8 have been far from successful. The rather wan minimum of pre-Mkan tradition that five scholars agreed on was 16:2 and 8a.[3] Such a wide disagreement makes one wonder if there was any such pre-Mkan tradition at all. Is there any clear evidence of its presence *before* the writing of Mk himself?

1. The Burial. If Jesus was buried by his friends, someone would surely have visited the grave, for example, Joseph of Arimathea. Re-

---

2. On the basic historicity of the events in 16:1–8 there is a spectrum from totally unhistorical, in I. Broer, "Zur heutigen Diskussion der Grabesgeschichte," *BiLe* 10 (1969), 40–52; to totally historical (without angels), in W. Nauck, "Die Bedeutung des leeren Grabes für den Glauben an den Auferstanden," *ZNW* 47 (1956), 243–67; to historical (with angels), in P. Gaechter, "Die Engelerscheinungen in den Auferstehungsberichten," *ZKT* 89 (1967), 191–202.

3. See the analyses of L. Schenke, M. Goguel, W. Grundmann, E. Gutwenger, and E. Hirsch given in Bode, *Easter Morning*, 25, note 1.

cent study has shown, however, that the burial tradition bears strong evidence of apologetical change so that an incomplete burial by enemies is being gradually changed into a very complete entombment by friends.[4] The earliest stage of the tradition may still be visible behind Jn 19:31–32 (burial by the Romans?) and the latest is underlined in Jn 19:38–41 (burial by disciples). Removal of the body (Jn 19:31, *arthōsin*) may therefore be closer to what actually happened on Easter morning than any presupposed burial of Jesus by his friends and disciples.

2. The Lord's Day. Did the tomb's finding result in Sunday becoming "the Lord's day"? It is just as likely that the phrase "on the third day," as in 1 Cor 15:4 for example, was historicized both prophetically on the lips of Jesus and posthumously as the day of resurrection, therefore Sunday as the Lord's day. And it was because of all this that Mk had to put ET "on the third day."

3. 1 Cor 15:4. It has often been argued that Paul's understanding of bodily resurrection demanded ET between the burial and resurrection in 15:4 and that his "on the third day" referred to its discovery. First, even if one concedes a presumption, there is no evidence he had any tradition concerning it. Second, "on the third day" was not intended as historical chronology but as prophetic and/or eschatological symbolism.[5]

4. Lk 24:22–24. Is this pre-Mkan tradition? It is much more likely to be Lkan redaction to smooth the Emmaus incident into the preceding 24:1–12. First, the narrative moves easily from 24:21a into 24:25.[6] Second, the women of 24:1–11 and Peter in 24:12 reappear

4. Fuller, *Resurrection Narratives*, 54–55. See also I. Broer, *Die Urgemeinde und das Grab Jesu*, StANT 31 (Munich: Kösel, 1972).

5. On the presumption, see E. Gutwenger, "Zur Geschichtlichkeit der Auferstehueng Jesu," *ZKT* 88 (1966), 257–82, and J. Mánek, "The Apostle Paul and the Empty Tomb," *NovTest* 2 (1958), 276–80, but disputed by M. Brändle, "Musste das Grab Jesu leer sein?" *Orientierung* 31 (1967), 108–12. On "the third day" (and Hos 6:2), see J. Dupont, "Ressuscité 'Le Troisième Jour,'" *Bib* 40 (1959), 742–61; B. Lindars, *New Testament Apologetic* (Philadelphia: Westminster Press, 1961), 59–72; J. Wijngaards, "Death and Resurrection in Covenantal Context (Hos. VI 2)," *VT* 17 (1967), 226–39; H. K. McArthur, "'On the Third Day,'" *NTS* 18 (1972), 81–86. On the third day as "the day of divine salvation, deliverance and manifestation," see Bode, *Easter Morning*, 125.

6. So Fuller, *Resurrection Narratives*, 105. But P. Schubert ("The Structure and Significance of Luke 24," *Neutestamentliche Studien für Rudolf Bultmann*, ed. W. Eltester [Berlin: A. Töpelmann, 1954], 165–86) holds that all of 24:17–27 is Lkan redaction. See also F. Schneider and W. Stenger, "Beobachtungen zur Struktur der Emmausperikope (Lk 24, 13–35)," *BZ* 16 (1972), 94–114.

in 24:22–23 and 24:24 respectively. Third, four redactional phrases from 24:1, 3, 5, 7 reappear in 24:21b–23 (early, find the body, living, third day). Fourth, "a vision of angels" in 24:23 uses a word for vision found only in Lk 1:22, Acts 26:19, and 2 Cor 12:1. Most likely then 24:22–24 (and possibly all of 24:17–27) is Lkan redaction not pre-Mkan, independent tradition.

The general conclusion is that there is no strong or even convincing evidence of pre-Mkan traditions concerning the tomb. Presumptions maybe, but such are not traditions.

2. THE TRADITION AFTER MARK

The next question is whether ET in Mt 28:1–15, Lk 24:1–12, and Jn 20:1–18 indicate independent traditions or whether these are all redactional adaptations of one original creation.[7]

There are four major elements in ET and these can be quite easily separated from one another as already indicated by their presence and/or absence across the texts. In summary format:

AT THE TOMB	Mark	Matthew	Luke	John
Guards (GT)		28:4, 11–15		
Women (WT)	16:1–8	28:1–3, 5–8	24:1–11	20:1, 11–13
Apostles (AT)			24:12	20:2–10
Jesus (JT)		28:9–10		20:14–18

The argument is that WT originated in Mk and went thence into all the other Gospels. These both adapted WT in their own versions and also added either GT in Mt, AT in Lk and Jn, or JT in Mt and Jn. One discerns in all this a steady desire to replace the Women of Mk with Apostles, and the Messenger of Mk with Jesus himself.

A. GUARDS AT THE TOMB (GT)

Mt 27:62–66 and 28:4, 11–15 alone has GT. I accept Fuller's arguments and conclusion: "Bultmann has designated Matthew 27:62–

---

7. It is not adequate to note the resemblances and argue from these to a common origin without also asking if one of the versions is that common origin. See A. Descamps, "La structure des récits évangeliques de la resurrection," *Bib* 40 (1959), 726–29.

66 an 'apologetic legend.' We cannot but agree."[8]   The GT element indicates that there was already Jewish polemic against the Mkan story within the Matthean environment and that GT represents a triangular relationship among Mt, his Mkan source, and his Jewish surroundings.[9] GT is neither prior to nor independent of Mk.

B. WOMEN AT THE TOMB (WT)

1. Matthew.   WT in Mt 28:1–8 can be satisfactorily explained as his redactional handling of Mk 16:1–8.   I accept the argument and conclusion of F. Neirynck: *"Matt. xxviii. 1–10 ne suppose aucune tradition évangélique autre que Marc xvi. 1–8."*[10]

2. *The Gospel of Signs* (GS).   Two important units of recent research must now enter the discussion.   First, R. T. Fortna[11] has offered a reconstruction of the narrative source underlying the Fourth Gospel and has termed it the Gospel of Signs (GS).   Second, F. L. Cribbs[12] has studied the textual contacts between Lk and Jn and concluded: "Fortna's reconstruction of the supposed narrative source underlying the fourth gospel . . . is quite similar . . . to . . . our own delineation of those Johannine passages with which Luke is in agreement against both Mark and Matthew."[13]   In other words Lk knew "some early form of the developing Johannine tradition,"[14] and the best example of this early form presently available is the GS proposed by Fortna or some modification thereof.

---

8. Fuller, *Resurrection Narratives*, 73.

9. See, however, B. A. Johnson, "Empty Tomb Tradition in the Gospel of Peter," *HTR* 59 (1966), 447–48.

10. F. Neirynck, "Les Femmes au Tombeau: Étude de la Rédaction Matthéenne (Matt. XXVIII:1–10)," *NTS* 15 (1969), 168–90, especially directed against P. Benoit, "Marie-Madeleine et les Disciples au Tombeau selon John 20: 1–18," *Judentum, Urchristentum, Kirche. Festschrift für Joachim Jeremias*, ed. W. Eltester, BZAW 26 (Berlin: A. Töpelmann, 1960), 14–52.   P. Benoit had argued for the originality of JT in Jn over Mt and of AT in Lk–Jn over Mk 16:1–8.

11. R. T. Fortna, *The Gospel of Signs* (Cambridge: Cambridge University Press, 1970).   See also B. Lindars, "The Composition of John XX," *NTS* 7 (1961), 142–47, as well as G. Hartmann, "Die Vorlage der Osterberichte in Joh 20," *ZNW* 55 (1964), 197–220.

12. F. L. Cribbs, "A Study of the Contacts That Exist Between St. Luke and St. John," *1973 Seminar Papers* (Cambridge, Mass.: SBL, 1973), II, 1–93.   See also J. A. Bailey, *The Traditions Common to the Gospels of Luke and John*, NTSup 7 (Leiden: E. J. Brill, 1963), and P. Parker, "Luke and the Fourth Evangelist," *NTS* 9 (1963), 317–36.

13. Cribbs, "Contacts," 91 n. 12.

14. Ibid., 92.

The immediate problem, then, is whether WT (only Mary Magdalene?) as reconstructed by Fortna and as hypothetically known to Lk is totally independent of Mk. Fortna's GS includes, basically, Jn 20:1, 11–12, but not 20:13, that is, the dialogue between Mary and the angels.[15] He considers that 20:13 is a Johannine paraphrase of the source's 20:2. The question is whether WT in this source could have come from Mk, however such derivation is to be explained, be it direct or indirect, be it oral or written.

Four arguments make an affirmative answer at least possible. Obviously, a fuller understanding of the relationship between GS and Mk will support or destroy the hypothesis. First, another unit of recent research must be introduced. P. Achtemeier[16] has written a very persuasive analysis of Mk 4–8 which included as a most important item the claim that it was Mk who *first* united the feeding miracle in 6:30–44 with the walking on the waters in 6:45–52: "Such evidence renders it increasingly difficult to maintain that the connection of the story of the feeding of the 5,000 and the walking upon the sea antedates Mark, despite the evidence of their connection in John."[17] Indeed, we have to go even further, for Fortna's GS had the feeding in Jn 6:1–15 and the walking immediately following it in 6:16–21. If both these scholars are correct, then either GS/Jn 6:1–21 is due to Mk 6:30–52 or we have a pure coincidental connection of these two incidents in both Gospels. In other words, the relationship of GS and Mk can no longer be presumed to be one of total and mutual independence: GS may have known Mk.

Secondly, it must be noted that WT in GS/Jn is in a state of severe dismemberment. GS is not at all interested in WT but rather in AT and this new element destroys completely the internal coherence of WT. Mary is not even allowed to look into the tomb before she returns a report of its emptiness to the disciples, and it is difficult to imagine what sort of anticlimactic dialogue she might have had with the angels *after* Peter had visited the empty tomb and we had read GS/Jn 20:9. Even

15. Fortna, *Signs*, 139.
16. P. Achtemeier, "Toward the Isolation of Pre-Markan Miracle Catenae," *JBL* 89 (1970), 265–91, and "The Origin and Function of the Pre-Marcan Miracle Catenae," *JBL* 91 (1972), 198–221.
17. Achtemeier, "Isolation," 282.

when Jn wished to replace this dialogue with his redactional 20:13 he could only create a banal and ungracious repetition of 20:2.

Third, there is nothing positively present in GS/Jn 20:1, 11–12 which indicates an independent tradition. There are, of course, special features which derive from GS/Jn 11, the raising of Lazarus, such as the weeping, the face-cloth, etc.[18] But an independent tradition for WT can be postulated only on the general preliminary hypothesis of total Johannine independence from the Synoptics and this is now severely in question once again.

Fourth, there is one element in the GS version which makes very little sense there save as residual debris of a Mkan source where, as we shall see later, it makes eminent redactional sense. In GS/Jn 20:12 there are "two angels in white, *sitting where the body of Jesus had lain*, one at the head and one at the feet." This quite anomalous seated position derives from the "young man *sitting* on the right side, dressed in a white robe" of Mk 16:5. He is not, of course, sitting where Jesus had been laid but instead he points out to the women, "See the place *where they laid him*" (16:6).

The conclusion, even allowing for the general uncertainty of GS and Mk relationships, is that the WT in Mk is most likely the source for the residual WT in GS.

3. *Luke*. There is no independent WT tradition in Lk 24:1–11. This depends on his own redactional combination of Mk 16:1–8 and GS.[19]

4. *John*. Again there is no independent tradition for WT but a very thorough redactional amplification of his GS source.

C. Apostles at the Tomb (AT)

This element appears only in Lk 24:12 and in Jn 20:2–10.

1. *The Gospel of Signs* (GS). Fortna[20] has reconstructed GS as omitting any reference to the Other Disciple and as noting Peter's bewilderment (from Lk 24:12) rather than this Other's faith in 20:8. As seen above, AT is clearly intended to bring Peter and not Mary to the forefront of the story even at the expense of narrative consistency.

---

18. See Fortna, *Signs*, 238–40.
19. See Cribbs, "Contacts," 82–85.
20. Fortna, *Signs*, 135–38, 245.

Mary is reduced to misunderstanding and the force of the original GS/Jn 20:9 would have meant that Peter did not understand *up until that point*: "for as yet they did not know the scripture, that he must rise from the dead." It must be stressed that, for writer and reader alike, the message is given clearly and unambiguously by this sentence in 20:9. What counts for GS is that Peter, scripture, and resurrection are mentioned together when first they are mentioned at all. All of which destroys quite firmly the story in Mk 16:1–8.

2. Luke. AT is present in Lk 24:12 and this verse is here taken as critically authentic as it will be in the twenty-sixth edition of the Nestle/Aland New Testament.[21] Once again, Cribbs[22] has explained this by Lk's knowledge of something like GS/Jn 20:2–10 as reconstructed above: Lk 24:12 comes from GS.

3. John. AT in Jn 20:2–10 is a redactional exaltation of the Other Disciple over Peter. The former arrives first (20:4), looks in and sees first (20:5), and believes first, or only (20:8), while poor Peter is left to enter first and no more (20:6–7).[23] All of which is Johannine redaction of his GS source.

D. JESUS AT THE TOMB (JT)

This element is found in Mt 28:9–10 and in Jn 20:14–18.

1. Matthew. Once again I presume the argument and conclusion of F. Neirynck that *"la christophanie des femmes* (vv. 9–10) *s'explique au mieux à partir du message angélique de Marc xvi. 6–7."*[24] In fact, Mt 28:9–10 (JT) is an almost complete copy of Mt 28:1–8 (WT) and is a totally redactional creation of Mt to offset the negative conclusion of Mk 16:8 and to prepare, transitionally, for his own Mt 28:16–20 as a new conclusion.

2. *The Gospel of Signs* (GS). Fortna finds his GS in Jn 20:14–18 but omitting all of 20:15 (gardener) and those parts of 20:17 concerning the ascension. The message of Jesus can no longer be reconstructed.

---

21. K. Aland, "Neue Neutestamentliche Papyri II," *NTS* 12 (1966), 193–210; K. Snodgrass, "Western Non-Interpolations," *JBL* 91 (1972), 369–79; Bode, *Easter Morning*, 68–69.

22. Cribbs, "Contacts," 84.

23. See G. F. Snyder, "John 13:16 and the Anti-Petrinism of the Johannine Tradition," *BR* 16 (1971), 5–15.

24. Neirynck, "Les Femmes," 190.

The source ends with Mary's delivery of the message in 20:18 and, Fortna hypothesizes, with a statement of their disbelief.

At this point a serious problem arises with regard to the integrated presence of WT + AT + JT as postulated by Fortna in his GS. It has two facets and, together, they make it very difficult to feel certain that JT was ever present in GS. First, if the function of AT was to downplay Mary as the recipient of resurrectional message (GS/Jn 20:1) and to elevate Peter to association with, if not reception of, that crucial faith (GS/Jn 20:9), why would any JT be present after all this: what would be the content of its message and the function of its presence? GS would seem to have reduced Mary's role to a vision of angels, and it was most likely this alone that she announced back to the disciples in GS/Jn 20:18. Second, and much more important, is the total absence of any JT in Lk. If Cribbs is right that Lk, in effect, knew GS, he would have had to omit JT if such were present in that source. This is not unthinkable and one might be able to give reasons for it, but it is a difficulty. And it is compounded by the Lkan redactional summary of 24:1–12 on the road to Emmaus in 24:22–24. Lk's sense of literary style gives this as an undetailed summary, since it is for a stranger, and hence the vague "some women of our company" in 24:22 and "some of those who were with us" in 24:24. But it should be noted that he seems to recall the GS source rather than his own previous redaction of it in 24:1–12. He says the women "amazed us . . . saying that they had seen a vision of angels" which is GS/Jn 20:12 rather than Lk 24:4. The question is whether Lk would have omitted JT had he known it from GS, and then written his own 24:22–24 as a summary of the morning's events. Tentatively, then, I shall presume that GS contained only WT + AT and that this latter element represented its solution to the problem posed by the WT in Mk 16:1–8, just as WT + JT represented the solution of Mt.

3. John. JT is present in Jn 20:14–18 as a Johannine composition. Once GS had reduced WT by its creation of AT any message from the angels to Mary would have to be quite redundant. But Jn, as distinct from GS, uses the angels to allow a second statement of her misunderstanding (20:2 = 13) and then creates JT not as a message of resurrection but as one of ascension. Resurrection faith is already clearly established by his reformulation of 20:7–8, so Mary's message does not

take precedence over the faith of the Other Disciple but is an interim report pending the arrival of Jesus to the disciples in 20:19–23. There is no danger that Mary's vision of the Lord in 20:15–18 will become overly important since the Thomas incident in 20:24–29 puts any such vision in definite second place to the faith of the Other Disciple in 20:8. It is also clear that, as with Mt, Jn has modeled his creation of JT in 20:14–18 on the preceding WT in 20:11–13.

4. Matthew and John. How does one explain JT in both Mt 28:9–10 and Jn 20:14–18 and with both formally modeled on their preceding WT elements in 28:1–8 and 20:11–13? Once again, I would refer to the wider and preliminary problem of Synoptic and Johannine relationship and specifically to the statement of F. Neirynck: *"Notons surtout qu'il y a, dans le récit de l'ensevelissement, des contacts spécifiques avec Matthieu."*[25] These contacts between Jn and Mt make it *"une hypothèse raisonnable"* that, with regard to the burial and the ET at least, Jn not only depends on a tradition like that in the Synoptics but *"comme certaines resemblances précises semblent le suggérer, une tradition qui s'est formée en partie à partir de nos évangiles synoptiques."*[26]

E. History of the Tradition

Mk, for reasons yet to be seen, created ET containing only one element, WT (stage 1). What followed was a combination of acute inability ever to eliminate his WT and equally acute embarrassment with his having ended his Gospel in this fashion. One solution is that of Mt who created JT in 28:9–10 in order to mediate a new conclusion in 28:16–20 (stage 2a). An alternative solution is that of *The Gospel of Signs*, known to both Lk and Jn, which created AT (just Peter actually) in Jn 20:2–10 and Lk 24:12 (stage 2b). These are the obvious two alternatives. Mk created Women and Messenger (WT): Mt replaced Messenger by Jesus (JT) and GS replaced Women by Peter (AT). Nobody, however, succeeded in fully eliminating Mk's WT, nobody gave us Jesus and the Apostles at the tomb together. Jn combined both these two alternatives (AT + JT) but his Thomas incident denotes an antiapparition attitude close to Mk's (stage 3). Next, the textual tradition of Mk tried to add in new endings, shorter or longer, in 16:9–20 (stage

25. Ibid., 189.
26. Ibid.

4). Finally, modern scholarship climaxes this historic dissatisfaction with Mk's work by attempting to compose a hypothetical reconstruction for an equally hypothetical lost ending of Mk (stage 5).[27] This can be schematically outlined as follows:

$$\text{Mark: WT}\begin{cases}\text{Matthew: } GT + WT + JT \\[2mm] \textit{The Gospel of Signs: } WT + AT\end{cases}\begin{cases}\text{Luke: } WT + AT \\[2mm] \text{John: } WT + AT + JT\end{cases}$$

To accept this hypothesis, at least as here formulated, one must also accept the possibility of Mkan influence on GS (for WT) and of Matthean influence on Jn (for JT). One must also accept the possibility, which has long embarrassed the tradition and which still continues to do so, that Mk knew exactly what he was doing and did exactly what he wanted in ending his Gospel with and at 16:1–8.

3. THE TRADITION IN MARK

It was noted above that redaction critics have been quite unsuccessful in obtaining any consensus on the pre-Mkan tradition in 16:1–8. My thesis has been that there was no such source and that this renders its reconstruction quite problematic. The final stage of the argument is the analysis of 16:1–8 as the complete creation of Mk himself. As an artificial but necessary disjunction content will be examined first, and then form. Function will be determined in the process of studying both these aspects.

A. THE CONTENT AND FUNCTION OF 16:1–8

This section presumes the basic validity of certain recent redactional research on Mk. It is precisely these studies which make it clear why

---

27. For recent discussion, see E. Linnemann, "Der (wiedergefundene) Markusschluss," *ZTK* 66 (1969), 255–87; K. Aland, "Bemerkungen zum Schluss des Markusevangeliums," *Neotestamentica et Semitica: Studies in Honour of Matthew Black*, ed. E. E. Ellis and M. Wilcox (Edinburgh: Clark, 1969), 157–80; and "Der wiedergefundene Markusschluss? Eine methodologische Bemerkung zur textkritischen Arbeit," *ZTK* 67 (1970), 3–13; H.-W. Bartsch, "Der Schluss des Markus-Evangeliums. Ein überlieferungsgeschichtliches Problem," *TZ* 27 (1971), 241–54; J. K. Elliott, "The Text and Language of the Ending to Mark's Gospel," *TZ* 27 (1971), 255–62; G. W. Trompf, "The First Resurrection Appearance and the Ending of Mark's Gospel," *NTS* 18 (1972), 308–30.

Mk created and indeed had to create the new ET tradition to conclude his Gospel.

I accept the general hypothesis that Mk created the genre Gospel, and thereby created Gospel as we know it, as an intra-Christian polemic against theological opponents characterized by (1) interest in miracles and apparitions rather than in suffering and service; (2) very little sympathy with the Gentile mission especially insofar as this questioned the validity of the Law; (3) an appeal to the authority of the Jerusalem mother Church, based both on the family of Jesus and on the original disciples of Jesus: the twelve, the inner three, and Peter in particular.[28]

If these scholars are basically correct, Mk had a very serious problem in *ending* his Gospel. If we accept a skeletal sequence such as 1 Cor 15:3–5a (death, burial, resurrection, and apparition/revelation to Peter) as a creedal summary on which a *story* might be constructed and the Gospel concluded, Mk would have been forced to end in a way that would negate the polemical thrust of the entire preceding Gospel. He would have had to conclude with an apparition and mandate for Peter/ James and the twelve/Apostles. My thesis is that it was precisely to avoid and to oppose any such apparition to Peter or the Apostles that he created most deliberately a totally new tradition (*traditio tradenda* not *traditio tradita*), that of ET. This can now be detailed verse by verse.

1. 16:1. The names of the women are already known from other tradition in 15:40. Their purpose is explained by postulating an inadequate burial in 15:42–46, although there was no indication of such inadequacy there: note the *agorasas* of 15:46 which Mt 27:59 and Lk 23:53 wisely suppress.

2. 16:2. The phrase *lian prōi* of this new "Galilean" (see 16:7) dawn and mission recalls the inaugural one in 1:35 with its *prōi ennycha*

---

28. A. Kuby, "Zur Konzeption des Markus-Evangeliums," *ZNW* 49 (1958), 52–64; J. B. Tyson, "The Blindness of the Disciples in Mark," *JBL* 80 (1961), 261–68; J. Schreiber, "Die Christologie des Markusevangeliums," *ZTK* 58 (1961), 154–83; É. Trocmé, *La Formation de l'Évangile selon Marc*, ÉtHistPhilRel 57 (Paris: Presses Universitaires de France, 1963), 100–109; U. Luz, "Das Geheimnismotiv und die Markinische Christologie," *ZNW* 56 (1965), 9–30; E. Schweizer, "Zur Frage des Messiasgeheimnisses bei Markus," *ZNW* 56 (1965), 1–8; L. E. Keck, "Mark 3, 7–12 and Mark's Christology," *JBL* 84 (1965), 341–58; K. Tagawa, *Miracles et Évangile*, ÉtHistPhilRel 62 (Paris: Presses Universitaires de France, 1966), 174–85; N. Perrin, "The Son of Man in the Synoptic Tradition," *BR* 13 (1968), 3–25 (see 21), and "The Creative Use of the Son of Man Traditions by Mark," *USQR* 23 (1968), 357–65 (see 357); J. D. Crossan, "Mark and the Relatives of Jesus," *NT* 15 (1973), 81–113. And see most especially WEEDEN, and KELBER.

lian anastas. Mk alone uses *lian* of time in the New Testament. And just as "Simon and those who were with him" (1:36) wanted to keep him there that first morning, so also they will fail his message now (16:7–8). Note how Lk 4:42 restates Mk 1:36 so that it is the crowds that wish to detain him and not the disciples. But in 1:35–38 and in 16:1–8 the call of Jesus is: "Let us go" and in both places it encounters resistance.

The phrase *tē mia tōn sabbatōn* is also important. By means of his three indications of time in 15:42 (*prosabbaton*: not in Mt 27:57, 62 and Lk 23:50), 16:1a (*diagenomenou tou sabbatou*) and 16:2 (*tē mia tōn sabbatōn*), Mk has given a harmonized chronology with the "three days" of the prophecies in Mk 8:31, 9:31 and 10:33–34. Three days: before the sabbath, the sabbath, the first day after the sabbath.

3. 16:3–4. The dialogic style recalls such places as, for example, 4:41. Since the tradition had securely closed the tomb with 15:46, Mk, having used 15:47 as preparation, now reopens it in almost verbatim language in 16:3–4.[29]

4. 16:5. There are three significant points: the messenger, his position, and his dress. (a) Messenger. This is the crux of the discussion and it presumes two important recent studies. A. Vanhoye[30] linked together the *neaniskos* of 14:51–52 and 16:5 as symbolic representations of Jesus himself who leaves in his enemies' hands the burial *sindōn* (twice in 14:51–52; elsewhere in the New Testament only from Mk 15:46) and reappears robed in victorious white (16:5). But R. Scroggs and K. I. Groff[31] have argued that one must go even further than this since in the two cases the *neaniskos* both represents Jesus and is clearly distinguished from him: in the garden by Jesus' concomitant presence and in the tomb by the reference to Jesus' absent body. The authors conclude: "The *neaniskos* is a representation of the exalted Christ *because he symbolizes the believer who, now baptized, partici-*

---

29. É. Dhanis, "L'ensevelissement de Jésus et la visite au tombeau dans l'évangile de saint Marc (Mc. XV, 40–XVI, 8)," *Greg* 39 (1958), 367–410.

30. A. Vanhoye, "La fuite du jeune homme nu (Mc 14, 51–52)," *Bib* 52 (1971), 401–406. See also J. Knox, "A Note on Mark 14, 51–52," *The Joy of Study*, ed. S. E. Johnson (New York: Macmillan, 1951), 28; H. C. Waetjen, "The Ending of Mark and the Gospel's Shift in Eschatology," *ASTI* 4 (1965), 114–31.

31. R. Scroggs and K. I. Groff, "Baptism in Mark: Dying and Rising with Christ," *JBL* 92 (1973), 531–48.

pates in the resurrection of Christ."[32] To this I would add only one
qualification. The *neaniskos*-messenger is not just the Christian initiate
in general. It is the neophyte in the Mkan community and therefore it
is that community itself, including Mk. It is not the risen Lord and
neither is it some accidental angel who delivers the message: it is the
Mkan community of those reborn in the resurrected Christ. (b) Position. This is now immediately clear. Christ was seated at the right
hand of God in Mk 12:36 and 14:62, and this is proleptically promised
to the Mkan community by the position of the messenger (see also Col
3:1–13; Eph 2:4–6). (c) Dress. The white robe (*stolē leukē*) is
that worn in heaven (Rev 6:11; 7:9, 13, 14) and the *peribeblēmenos* of
16:5 is likewise a heavenly description (Rev 7:9, 13). It should also
be noted that Mk 9:3, as against Mt 17:2 and Lk 9:29, stresses the
whiteness of Jesus' dress at the transfiguration; and Mk also omitted any
mention of Jesus' face, as also against both Mt and Lk, thereby keeping
transfiguration and tomb closer together.

5. 16:6. The verbs *exethambēthēsan* (16:5) and *ekthambeisthe*
(16:6) are exclusively Mkan in the New Testament and are always
omitted or changed by the other Synoptics. The names Jesus receives
are also significant. *Nazarēnos* is almost exclusively Mkan in the New
Testament. It recalls the opening 1:9 and, looking forward to the
mention of Galilee in 16:7, underlines Jesus as the Galilean, the non-
Jerusalemite. The term *ton estaurōmenon* is almost titular and is found
elsewhere only in Paul: 1 Cor 1:23; 2:2; Gal 3:1. For Mk, Jesus is the
Crucified One and Jesus is the Galilean, and both titles beckon also to
the followers of Jesus.

The basic resurrection faith is given in the *ēgerthē*. The codicil, "he
is not here; see the place where they laid him," is another connective
between the burial tradition in 15:46, the redactional comment in
15:47, and the new unit of the ET. It also underlines the negativity of
presence intended by Mk's formulation: "he is not here."

6. 16:7. The preceding verse announced Jesus as the Crucified and
Risen One. But this announcement is followed by a command and this
is a second crucial point in the Mkan creation of 16:1–8. It must be
stressed that the message is *not* about the resurrection. Mt 28:6 noted

32. Ibid., 543.

this long ago and changed Mk 16:7 so that it included the message of the resurrection. Two separate points. (a) Recipients. These are given as "tell his disciples and Peter" which is almost unique in the New Testament where Peter, if present, is almost always in first place (Peter and . . .). The reason is because this formulaic precedence does not highlight Peter enough for Mk's present intent. Not just: tell Peter and the disciples; but: tell the disciples, and especially Peter. In other words, Peter is singled out not only as being in authoritative first place but as especially designated to receive *this* message. (b) Message. Once again I presume recent studies on "Galilee" in Mkan theology.[33] Galilee is both place and symbol and the latter because first the former. Galilee is the *past* of Jesus' own dual mission on both sides (Jews/Gentiles) of the lake. It is the *present* of Jesus' call through the Mkan community to the Jerusalem community to inaugurate a mission to both Jews and Gentiles, and it is all that has happened since their failure to heed that call. And it is the *future* of Jesus' eschatological return to those who have participated in the preceding call. The *proagei* of 16:7 had already been promised the disciples in 14:28. But the verb also recalls, the more ominously, the *proagōn* of Jesus in 10:32 where he led them (and they failed to follow) up to suffering and death at Jerusalem.

7. 16:8. The reaction of the disciples to Jesus' leadership toward Jerusalem in 10:32 was *ethambounto* and *ephobounto*. So also now with the women. This is no temporary response of numinous awe as the other Synoptics were easily able to recognize, and so they changed their Mkan source quite drastically in Mt 28:8 and Lk 24:8. Flight, fear, and silence end the Mkan story. The women, the relatives of Jesus (cf. 3:34–35; 6:3), fail to communicate the message. In plain words, the Jerusalem community led by the disciples and especially Peter, has never accepted the call of the exalted Lord communicated to it from the Mkan community. The Gospel ends in a juxtaposition of Mkan faith in 16:6–7 and of Jerusalem failure in 16:7–8.

---

33. On Galilee and the Gentile mission, see G. H. Boobyer, "Galilee and Galileans in St. Mark's Gospel," *BJRL* 35 (1953), 334–48; C. F. Evans, " 'I will go before you into Galilee,' " *JTS* 5 (1954), 3–18. On Galilee and the parousia, see R. H. Lightfoot, *Locality and Doctrine in the Gospels* (New York: Harper and Brothers, 1938); MARXSEN, 54–116; N. Q. Hamilton, "Resurrection Tradition and the Composition of Mark," *JBL* 84 (1965), 415–21. But most especially, see KELBER.

B. THE FORM AND FUNCTION OF 16:1–8

It has been argued that the content of 16:1–8 served functionally as an anti-tradition to the creedal statement that the Risen Lord had appeared to Peter and/or James and to the twelve and/or the Apostles. One images some such aphorisms as those now contained in 1 Cor 15:5–7.[34] But while this explains the content of 16:1–8, it does little to explain the form of Mk's creation. Why did he compose it in this format and not in some other possible one?

The answer to this question involves a wider interpretation of the tradition of risen appearances which can only be indicated but not argued in detail. First, the historical sequence and development of the appearances tradition was from creedal *statement* (as in 1 Cor 15:5–7) to creedal *story* as stages in the articulation of Easter faith. Second, one example of such creedal stories is the walking on the waters in Mk 6:45–51. This is especially important because we are certain that Mk knew at least this one no matter what he knew about any other such stories. Third, the form of Mk 16:1–8 is derived directly and deliberately from that of 6:45–51. Both form and content of 16:1–8 coalesce as an anti-tradition to any concluding story of an apparition to the apostles or to any one of their leaders. One important point must be stressed in all this. Before Mk wrote his Gospel there was no "before" and "after" Easter. Hence a community confessed the revelatory and salvific presence of its exalted Lord either in brief statement or longer story but nobody asked questions such as: did this story happen in the "earthly" or the "risen" life? Only after Mk would all such stories have to be located either before or after Easter (or both: Lk 5 and Jn 21). Hence Mk 6:45–51 is not an accidentally "misplaced" resurrection apparition but a deliberately "placed" one, placed by Mk (and Jn!) safely in the earthly life of Jesus he had created.

The proof for this thesis can be clarified by recalling the form critical study of C. H. Dodd[35] on the appearances of the Risen Christ. Apart from internal weaknesses due to the lack of redactional sophistication,

---

34. See WEEDEN, 47–50, 102–11; Hamilton, "Resurrection Tradition."

35. C. H. Dodd, "The Appearances of the Risen Christ: An Essay in Form-Criticism of the Gospels," *Studies in the Gospels: Essays in Memory of R. H. Lightfoot*, ed. D. E. Nineham (Oxford: Blackwell, 1955), 9–35.

the article has one serious external problem. Dodd had noted that the form postulated for the risen appearance stories reappears in the walking on the waters in Mk 6:45–51 and Jn 6:16–21 and that "so striking a similarity" has to be explained either by its being a "transplanted" risen appearance or by its being "influenced" by these later stories.[36] But what has been missed completely is the fact that there is an *even* closer formal similarity between Mk 16:1–8 and Mk 6:45–51 than between either of these and the risen appearances. This can be indicated schematically using the five basic formal elements of Dodd but adding a final sixth one, the Result. Here is the outline:

Formal Elements (Dodd)	Walking on Sea: Mark	Tradition of Empty Tomb		
		WT: Mark	JT: Matt	JT: John
Situation	6:45–48a	16:1–4	28:8	20:14a
Apparition	6:48b	16:5abc	28:9a	20:14b
Greeting (Address)	6:50b	16:6	28:9b	20:15–16a
Recognition (Response)	6:49–50a	16:5d	28:9c	20:16b
Command	(6:51b?)	16:7	28:10	20:17
Result	6:51c	16:8	–	20:18

Two notes. First, the formal sequence is followed, as Dodd outlined it, by the two JT columns but there is a reversal of his elements of Greeting and Recognition in both the walking on the sea and the ET units in Mk. This means that these two Mkan pericopes are in very close formal parallel and are much closer to one another than either is to the other stories cited by Dodd. Second, one cannot note formal similarities such as these without asking functional questions, which Dodd does not, such as: why is Mk 16:1–8 so formally similar to 6:45–51 and why are other traditions of risen appearances also somewhat similar to

36. Ibid., 24.

these two stories? Is it possible, for instance, that the walking on the waters (Mk and Jn!) is the formal basis for the risen appearances tradition Dodd has investigated?

4. THEOLOGICAL CONCLUSIONS

It is most probable that Jesus was buried by the same inimical forces that had crucified him and that on Easter Sunday morning those who knew the site did not care and those who cared did not know the site. The major reason for this conclusion is that the tradition has protested too much: an indifferent burial by Roman soldiers becomes eventually a regal entombment by his faithful followers (cf. Jn 19:31–32 and 38–41).

Easter faith, the belief that Jesus is with God and that the crucifixion was not divine rejection but divine acceptance, arose in a manner no more and no less inexplicable than all faith before or after it. At an earlier stage it appeared in creedal *statements* in such places as 1 Cor 15:3–7. In a different manner, and presumably at a later stage, it appeared in creedal *stories* in narratives such as Mk 6:45–51. This confesses, in story, that Jesus has conquered the waters of death and comes, at dawn, to save his followers from danger and despair. It is from or around such stories that the Apparition tradition developed. But it is clear that such apparitions, or apparition-stories, are the effects of Easter faith and not its cause or even its occasion. The cause was God, the occasion, the crucifixion of Jesus.

Mk's theology was very different. Jesus does not return in apparition to save his own from danger before the parousia. Instead of the present Jesus of the Apparition tradition, he offers us an absent Jesus in his newly created anti-tradition of the ET. On earth there are no apparitions but only the harsh negative of the ET and the Lord who "is not here." And there is the stern challenge of the Mkan community in Galilee that calls in vain to the Jerusalem community to obey its Lord by preparing for his return in suffering, in service, and in mission to the world.

IX.

Conclusion:
From Passion Narrative to Gospel

Werner H. Kelber

The purpose of this final chapter is to summarize the major conclusions of the preceding essays, to develop their implications for interpreting the Mkan Passion Narrative and the Gospel as a whole, to consider some points of relevance for systematic theology, and to indicate future directions for Mkan research.

1. THE ISSUE OF A PRE-MARKAN PASSION NARRATIVE

It is a chief feature of these essays on the Mkan Passion Narrative that each author links his interpretation of a passion unit with motifs and material from the pre-passion section of the Gospel. In each case the author takes hermeneutical clues for an understanding of a passion pericope from Mk 1–13. We shall briefly review the seven exegetical essays from this perspective.

Robbins views the Last Supper (14:12–25) as Mk's answer to an intra-Christian dispute over meal Christology which was highlighted in the two Feeding Stories (6:30–44; 8:1–10). The dating of the "first day of Unleavened Bread" (14:12) is polemically directed against the "leaven" of misunderstanding perpetuated by the disciples, Herod, and the Pharisees (8:14–21). The motif of bread which had played a key role in the meal controversies (Mk 6–8) is interpreted by Jesus' body (14:22), and the cup motif which had earlier figured in Jesus' prediction of the disciples' martyrdom (10:35–40) is likewise used in reference to the death of Jesus (14:24). The last verse of the Supper scene (14:25) continues the Mkan Kingdom theme (1:14–15), while the Mkan leitmotif Gospel (1:1, 14) is taken up in the Anointing story (cf. 14:9) and again interpreted through Jesus' burial and death.

Kelber views the Gethsemane story (14:32–42) as a culmination of passion Christology and discipleship failure. Mk's Son of Man Christology (8:31; 9:31; 10:33–34) progresses systematically to a peak in 14:41, the Gospel's last suffering Son of Man saying. The "coming" of Judas for the purpose of "delivering up" Jesus literally recalls the "coming" of the Kingdom of God (1:15). The motif of "the hour" of passion (14:35, 41) brings to mind "the (eschatological) hour" of Jesus' parousia (13:32), and Jesus' prayer for the removal of "this cup" (14:36) revives the earlier controversy over the drinking of "the cup" (10:38–39; cf. 14:22). The singling out of the three confidants (14:33) presupposes their initial appointment by name-giving (3:16–17) and continues a characteristic Mkan feature of making the three privileged witnesses of crucial events (5:35–43; 9:2–8). The disciples' inclination to sleep (14:37, 40, 41) bids defiance to Jesus' earlier warning not to sleep (13:35–36), and Peter's resistance to a suffering Son of Man (14:37) is in keeping with his deficient Christ confession at Caesarea Philippi (8:29–31).

Donahue explains Jesus' trial before the Sanhedrin (14:53–65) as a complex weaving together of the Mkan death theme, Temple theology, and royal Christology. The condemnation (14:64) concludes a series of references to the death plot (3:6; 11:18; 12:12; 14:1). Mk's dramatization of Jesus' conflict with Jerusalem (3:22; 7:1) and opposition to the Temple (11:1–14:1) reaches a new height in the first half of the Temple saying (14:58), and the Evangelist's concern for the eschatological community (1:16–20; 3:13–19; cf. 14:28; 16:7) finds expression in the second half of the Temple saying (14:58). The High Priest's identification of Jesus (14:61) employs characteristically Mkan titles: Christ (1:1; 8:29) and Son of the Blessed, i.e., Son of God (1:1; 3:11; 5:7; cf. 15:39). Mk uses this latter title, Son of God, not in a Hellenistic *theios anēr* sense, but in a Jewish, Messianic sense and hence in agreement with the Gospel's paradigmatic Kingdom theme (1:14–15). While the High Priest ironically affirms the Kingship of Jesus (14:61), Jesus' own confession (14:62) also confirms his royal identity by pointing to future enthronement and coming. Mk 14:61–62, therefore, constitutes Jesus' formal identification as royal King of the end time as outlined in 1:14–15.

Perrin traces the three christological titles which coalesce in 14:61–62 and defines Jesus' confession as a Mkan christological summary. The Christ title, headlined in the superscription (1:1) but misused by Peter (8:29) and the mockers (15:32), receives Jesus' confirmation in 14:61–62. Son of the Blessed, i.e., Son of God, continues a long-standing Mkan interest in this title (1:1, 11, 24; 3:11; 5:7; 9:7; 14:61) which reaches its final resolution only in the centurion's confession (15:39). The combination of these two titles in 14:61 deliberately echoes their coexistence in the superscription (1:1). Jesus' own confession through the Son of Man title concludes Mk's three-stage Son of Man Christology. After Jesus' pronouncement of his earthly authority (2:10, 28), of his suffering identity (8:31; 9:31; 10:31, 45; 14:21, 41) and his apocalyptic future (8:38; 13:26), the moment has arrived to complete his identification as Son of Man in the trial scene. The Messianic claim formula *egō eimi* characterizes the confession before the High Priest as the breaking of the Messianic Secret (1:34; 3:11–12; 8:30; 9:9, 30–31). If retrospectively the confession summarizes Mkan Christology, it functions prospectively by anticipating what is yet to come in the Gospel's story: Jesus' crucifixion-enthronement and parousia.

Dewey observes a thematic reenactment of the Caesarea Philippi incident (8:27–33) in the combined scene of Peter's denial and Jesus' trial (14:53–72). By virtue of the intercalation of the trial (14:55–65) into the denial story (14:53–54, 66–72) Mk invites comparison between Peter's rejection of Jesus and Jesus' Son of Man confession which incurs the death sentence. At Caesarea Philippi likewise Jesus makes a suffering Son of Man confession (8:31) which exposes the inadequacy of Peter's preceding "confession" (8:29). Peter's specific denial of Jesus as Nazarene (14:67), furthermore, links up with Jesus' Nazarene-Galilean identification which provides a frame for the Gospel (1:9, 21–28; 16:6–7). By denying Jesus as Nazarene-Galilean, Peter negates his own Galilean identity (14:70–71) and thus deprives himself and his followers of the promised Galilean future (14:28; 16:7). Hence Peter becomes subject to Jesus' curse as he did at Caesarea Philippi (8:33), not paying attention to Jesus' explicit warning (8:38). Peter's denial in conjunction with Jesus' confession in the trial is thus a variation of the Peter-Jesus confrontation of Caesarea Philippi.

Weeden finds the Mkan theme of Jesus the miracle worker polemically reintroduced into the crucifixion story (15:20b–41). Both the contemptuous challenge of the passers-by (15:29–33) and the mocking by the bystanders (15:34–36) revive the image of Jesus the miracle worker (throughout 1:21–8:26) by playing out the miracles against the cross. The use of Christ by the passers-by reflects the christological misconception foreshadowed in Peter's Christ "confession" (8:29). Moreover, Weeden uncovers in two Temple sayings (14:58; 15:29) an eschatological viewpoint—correlation of Temple destruction with Jesus' parousia—which the Evangelist opposes in Mk 13. In sum, Weeden detects a polemical strand in the Passion Narrative which appears to be in continuation of Mk's pre-passion argument against a specific type of Christology and eschatology.

Crossan argues the thoroughgoing redactional nature of the Empty Tomb narrative (16:1–8) both on the basis of the history of tradition and in view of a thematic coherence with the minutiae and fundamentals of Mkan theology. As for the details, for example, Jesus' journey to Galilee defined by the term *proagei* (16:7) is in continuation of his earlier journey to Jerusalem (10:32: *proagōn autous ho Iēsous*), while the women's reaction to the Galilean invitation (16:8: *ephobounto gar*) equals the followers' previous response to Jesus' leadership role (10:32: *kai hoi akolouthountes ephobounto*). The three time references following Jesus' death (15:42; 16:1, 2) create a time-frame which brings the date of the resurrection into harmony with that announced in the passion predictions (8:31; 9:31; 10:33–34). As for the fundamentals of Mkan theology, 16:1–8 enunciates the Mkan motifs of Jesus' absence from the community (4:13–20, 26–29; 13:1–23; 14:7, 25), the Galilean reorientation (1:14–15; 14:28), and discipleship failure (1:35–38; 4:40–41; 6:52; 8:14–21; 8:32–33; 9:5–6, 32; 10:35–37).

What follows from these studies may be summed up in three theses:[1]

(1) *Virtually all major (and a multiplicity of minor) Mkan themes*

---

1. On the following, see also J. Donahue's introductory essay, "From Passion Traditions to Passion Narrative," to this volume.

converge in Mk 14–16. The major ones are: passion Christology, meal Chrisotlogy, titular Christology, Messianic Secret, Temple theology, Kingdom eschatology, discipleship failure, Petrine opposition, anti-Jerusalem theme, Galilean thesis, the leitmotif Gospel, as well as a christological, eschatological undercurrent.

(2) *Mk 14–16 constitutes a theologically inseparable and homogeneous part of the Gospel whole.* Thematically, Mk 1–13 dovetails into Mk 14–16. The passion section of the Gospel can neither be comprehended nor defined as a *theological* unit set apart from the remainder of the Gospel. The very term Passion Narrative may therefore not adequately reflect the nature of Mk 14–16, if the latter is viewed as the culmination of *all major Mkan theological themes.*

(3) *The understanding of Mk 14–16 as a theologically integral part of the Mkan Gospel calls into question the classic form critical thesis concerning an independent and coherent Passion Narrative prior to Mk.* Thematically it is difficult to identify a major non-Mkan thrust or theme in Mk 14–16, let alone extrapolate a coherent pre-Mkan source.

In addition, the authors observe a very intense redactional activity in Mk 14–16. The Evangelist inserts the Anointing story into a context of hostility toward Jesus; he takes a tradition of Jesus' words about bread and cup and develops it into a Last Meal scene; he adds the largely redactional section dealing with Jesus' prediction of Peter's denial and the return to Galilee; he composes the three-stage Gethsemane narrative out of a lamenting Jesus saying or prayer; he creates Jesus' trial (including Jesus' words of confession) before the Sanhedrin out of a story about Jesus' presentation before Jewish officials; he expands a short story of Peter's denial into a lengthy, three-stage account and intercalates it into the newly created trial narrative; he rewrites a crucifixion tradition; and he composes the Empty Tomb story as a fitting conclusion to his Gospel. Mkan vocabulary, Mkan stylistic features, and Mkan compositional techniques further corroborate the impression of the overall Mkan literary character of Mk 14–16.

We will again sum up our conclusions in three theses:

(1) *From the perspective of the history of tradition there exists no appreciable difference between Mk 14–16 and what is known about the literary genesis and composition of Mk 1–13.* Mk is no more tradition-bound in Mk 14–16 than he is in Mk 1–13. He edits and unifies

individual traditions, composes new material, and creates the total narrative sequence in Mk 14–16 in the same manner in which he edits and unifies individual traditions, composes new material, and creates the total narrative sequence in Mk 1–13.

(2) *No single pre-Mkan tradition exercises an authoritative influence upon Mk.* The Evangelist refashions and composes a narrative in view of his current situation and in the interest of a religious response to it. He is master over his traditions and pays no deference to an alleged time or tradition-honored Passion Narrative.

(3) *Mk's literary achievement is to compose what he calls the Gospel out of a multiplicity of disparate tradition units.* His literary activity is ill-defined in terms of a prefixing of a lengthy introduction to an authoritative passion source, and it is amiss to consider the passion section of the Gospel as a *literary* unit set apart from the remainder of the Gospel. The issue is not why Jesus' passion demanded an early pre-Mkan connected narrative form, because it did not, but the issue is why Mk created the Gospel whole in its present form.

The theological and literary conclusions derived from these studies on Mk 14–16 show that the Mkan Passion Narrative does *not* constitute the exception to the form critical canons which govern the formation of the Synoptic tradition. While it may not be possible at this point in the discussion to win a firmly grounded agreement, the thesis of a Mkan creation of the Gospel whole out of a multiplicity of individual tradition units is more probable than that of Mk the writer of an introduction to a given Passion Narrative.[2]

The issue of a pre-Mkan Passion Narrative hinges in part on an assessment of the relationship between the Gospels of Jn and Mk, for a striking resemblance between the Johannine and Mkan Passion Narratives has been used as corroboratory evidence for the existence of a pre-Mkan passion source. The three authors who touch on this issue discount a Johannine-Mkan dependence on a pre-Mkan source and suggest instead a relationship of some sort between Jn and Mk.[3]

---

2. The thesis of an independent, pre-Mkan Passion Narrative has recently been questioned by LINNEMANN; E. Güttgemanns, *Offene Fragen zur Formgeschichte des Evangeliums* (Munich: C. Kaiser, 1970), 227–29; H. C. Kee, *Jesus in History* (New York: Harcourt, Brace & World, 1970), 274; P. J. Achtemeier, *Mark*, Proclamation Commentaries (Philadelphia: Fortress Press, 1975), 82–91.

3. On the following, see also J. Donahue's introductory essay, "Passion Traditions," to this volume.

Dewey observes that Jn in his treatment of the denial story specifically appropriates material from Mk, as well as from Mt and Lk. Most spectacularly, Jn intercalates the denial story into Jesus' trial in the manner of Mk. Kelber argues that the caesura between the Mkan Gethsemane and arrest stories, a break traditionally taken as an indication for the commencement of a pre-Mkan passion source, is of Mkan making and not source-conditioned. He also indicates that the fragmentation of the Gethsemane tradition in Jn is the result of Jn's *theologia gloriae*, while the extant fragments are for the most part taken from the Mkan account. Crossan is convinced that in the case of the Empty Tomb story the *Signs Source* may have played an intermediary role between Mk and Jn, but he also recognizes contacts between Jn and Mt.

The evidence in favor of a Mk-Jn relationship consists of close verbal agreements, resemblance in story traditions, and parallel sequence structures.[4] This evidence may be evaluated in terms of Johannine knowledge of Mk, but it must not be pressed toward Johannine dependence on Mk. According to Dewey's observation, Jn works selectively with elements taken from a broad spectrum of the Synoptic tradition, and not in sole reliance upon one single source. Similarities and correspondences between Jn and Mk must therefore not be taken as an argument for a single underlying source, but rather as evidence for floating traditions and creative Synoptic interchange.

4. The following authors argue for a Jn-Mk relationship in varying degrees: B. F. Westcott, *The Gospel According to John* (London: John Murray, 1908), CLXVI–CLXVIII; F. W. Worsley, *The Fourth Gospel and the Synoptists* (Edinburgh: T. & T. Clark, 1909), 23; B. W. Bacon, *The Fourth Gospel in Research and Debate* (New York: Moffat, Yard and Co., 1910); B. H. Streeter, *The Four Gospels* (London: Macmillan, 1924), 393–401, *passim*; H. Windisch, *Johannes und die Synoptiker*, UNT 12 (Leipzig: J. C. Hinrichs, 1926); W. F. Howard, *The Fourth Gospel in Recent Criticism and Interpretation* (London: Epworth, 1931); M. Goguel, "Did Peter Deny His Lord? A Conjecture," *HTR* 25 (1932), 1–27, esp. 9, 12; R. M. Grant, "The Fourth Gospel and the Church," *HTR* 35 (1942), 95–116, esp. 95; C. K. Barrett, *The Gospel According to John* (London: SPCK, 1955), and "John and the Synoptic Gospels," *ExpT* 85 (1974), 228–33; R. H. Lightfoot, *St. John's Gospel*, ed. C. F. Evans (Oxford: Oxford University Press, 1956), 26–42; E. K. Lee, "St. Mark and the Fourth Gospel," *NTS* 3 (1957), 50–58; S. Ivor Buse, "John V.8 and Johannine-Marcan Relationships," *NTS* 1 (1954), 134–36, and "St. John and the Marcan Passion Narrative," *NTS* 4 (1958), 215–19, and "St. John and the First Synoptic Pericope," *NovTest* 3 (1959), 57–61, and "The Gospel Accounts of the Feeding of the Multitudes," *ExpT* 74 (1963), 167–70; A. Schlatter, *Der Evangelist Johannes*, 3d ed. (Stuttgart: Calwer Verlag, 1960), 144, 165, 263, 265, *passim*; E. Stauffer, "Historische Elemente im vierten Evangelium," *Bekenntnis zur Kirche: Festschrift für E. Sommerlath* (Berlin: Evangelische Verlagsanstalt, 1960), reprinted in *Homiletica en Biblica* 22 (1963), 1–7; P. Guichou, *Evangile de St. Jean* (Paris, 1962) 10; H. M. Teeple, "Methodology in Source Analysis of the Fourth Gospel," *JBL* 81 (1962), 279–86; C. W. F. Smith, "Tabernacles in the Fourth Gospel and Mark," *NTS* 9 (1963), 130–46, esp. 135–42; H. Balmforth, "The Structure of the Fourth Gospel," *SE* II (Berlin: Akademie-Verlag, 1964), 25–33, esp. 33; J. Blinzler, *Johannes und die Synoptiker*, Stuttgarter Bibelstudien 5 (Stuttgart: Katholisches Bibelwerk, 1965); N. Perrin, *The New Testament: An Introduction* (New York: Harcourt Brace Jovanovich, 1974), 226–29, and *A Modern Pilgrimage in New Testament Christology* (Philadelphia: Fortress Press, 1974), 122–28; W. G. Kümmel, *Introduction to the New Testament*, trans. H. C. Kee, 17th ed. rev. and enlarged (Nashville, Tenn.: Abingdon, 1975), 202–204, 211.

2. CHRISTOLOGY

The Gospel's three principal christological titles, Christ, Son of God, and Son of Man, continue into Mk 14–16 and receive conclusive definition in the passion drama. The three titles converge in Jesus' confession before the High Priest (14:61–62), and the Son of God title is resumed by the centurion's confession (15:39). In addition one new title, i.e, King, is introduced in Mk 15 and placed in control over the events leading up to and including the crucifixion (15:2, 9, 12, 18, 26 [32]). From the perspective of titular Christology, therefore, the central title, King, is framed by Jesus' Son of Man confession and the centurion's Son of God confession.

The High Priest's question (14:61) links up Christ with Son of the Blessed, i.e., Son of God. Both titles had up to this point been in suspense or under suspicion (Donahue, Perrin). Peter's Christ confession is rejected by Jesus apparently on grounds that it lacks the dimension of suffering (8:29–31). The title Son of God is the address to Jesus not only by God (1:11; 9:7) but also by the demons (1:24; 3:11; 5:7). Furthermore, this title is issued in private (1:11), is not to be disclosed until a future appointed time (9:9), and is stamped with the seal of secrecy (3:12). It is not until his confession before the High Priest (14:62) that Jesus gives personal affirmation to his status as Christ and Son of God. He confirms these two titles by means of the third one, Son of Man, which is defined by its eschatological quality. This Son of Man saying, the last of its kind in the Gospel, concludes the Mkan Son of Man Christology which encompasses the epiphany of Jesus' earthly *exousia* (2:10, 28), his passion identity (8:31; 9:31; 10:33; 14:21, 41) and its soteriological significance (10:45), as well as his eschatological future (8:38; 13:26).

These three titles in conjunction summarize Mk's titular Christology, and the Messianic claim formula, *ego eimi*, characterizes this first and last confession of Jesus as the break or disclosure of the Messianic Secret (Donahue, Perrin). On the face of it no new christological truth is revealed by 14:61–62. What had been communicated in private, kept in secret, or misunderstood patently was always meant to be understood by the readers of the Gospel. On the discourse level, secret and private testimonies are fully disclosed, and the readers are meant to profit from the misconceptions surrounding the identity of Jesus in the Gospel. On the story level, however, it is significant that Jesus' full identity remains unconfirmed until this specific moment in the Gospel's story. By making his one and only full confession at his trial Jesus incriminates himself before his accusers. His confession provokes and indeed causes the death sentence (14:63–64). The latter does not follow from political or judicial reasoning, but out of the logic of Mkan Christology. The death sentence must result from Jesus' confession, just as his confession must be confirmed by the death sentence, because the full identity of Jesus as Christ, Son of God, and Son of Man is established "during and in the light of the passion" (Perrin).

As the three titles were assembled in 14:61–62 under the prompting of Mkan Christology, so does also the emergence of the title King in Mk 15 result from the Evangelist's christological reflection (Perrin, Kelber). This royal title which according to 1:14–15 (cf. 4:11, 26–29, 30–32; 10:23–27; 11:9–10) could be expected to be the authentic designation of Jesus is withheld until the crucifixion events because for Mk Jesus is King through suffering and cross. The ambiguity surrounding the title (Kelber) is rooted in the paradoxical nature of Mk's royal Christology: Jesus is the crucified King. The crucifixion of the two robbers "one on his right and one on his left" (15:27) enhances the imagery of enthronement. The cross becomes a means of accession to royal power.

Mk offers neither description nor mention of Jesus' physical suffering, and yet the crucifixion is anything but the dramatization of docetic Christology. Jesus does suffer, but his suffering is of a quality which exceeds that of physical pain. The cross marks his defeat by the forces of evil and his abandonment by God. Global darkness (15:33) symbolizes the triumph of darkness and the demonic seizure of power.[5] At the cross demonic forces reach the height of their power, and Jesus is crushed by those very powers which he himself had come to exorcise. The cries of dereliction (15:34) and expiration (15:37) likewise depict Jesus as being overpowered by the forces of evil. Both are "loud cries" (*phōnē megalē*) which are uttered in the state of demonic possession

5. J. Schreiber, *Theologie des Vertrauens* (Hamburg: Furche-Verlag, 1967), 38–39, 95, 118, *passim*; F. W. Danker, "The Demonic Secret in Mark: A Reexamination of the Cry of Dereliction (15, 34)," *ZNW* 61 (1970), 50–51.

(cf. 1:26; 5:7).[6]   As Jesus' own authority formerly caused demons to convulse, so does the demonic presence make him suffer at the cross. Engulfed by demonic darkness and overcome by the powers of evil, Jesus suffers the absence of God, for the cry of dereliction is not shouted in triumph but out of absolute powerlessness (Weeden). With it Mk's passion Christology is raised to a new and piercing level. Jesus is "delivered up" (14:10, 11, 18, 21, 41, 42, 44; 15:1, 10, 15) not merely into the hands of the Jewish-Roman power structure, but beyond that into demonic darkness and God-forsakenness. God's noninterference at the cross, his abandonment of Jesus in the hour of greatest need constitutes the ultimate depth of Jesus' suffering. Rejected by his followers, taunted by his enemies, derided even by those who suffer the cross next to him, delivered into the hands of Satan, and abandoned by God, Jesus paradoxically fulfills his royal mission. His Messianic identity is cited by the *titulus* over the cross (15:26) because it is consummated in total abandonment on the cross.

Death coincides with (or effects) the rending of the Temple curtain (15:38) and causes the centurion's confession (15:39). The moment of absolute powerlessness generates a "transvaluation" of the symbols of power and weakness, and life and death (Weeden). The Temple, established representation of life, comes to an end, and Jesus' true identity is confirmed in view of his death. As yet no human being has testified to Jesus as Son of God until this moment of God-forsakenness. The centurion "sees" that "the man was Son of God" in the circumstances surrounding the crucifixion and by the manner of Jesus' dying. Defeat by the demons and abandonment by God reveals his Sonship of God.

As Son of Man Jesus incurs the death sentence, as King he is crucified, and as Son of God he dies in powerlessness.

The cross, therefore, becomes the ground of Easter hope, for it is not by resurrection but in abandonment by God that Jesus is appointed Son of God, King, and Son of Man. It is not Easter that vindicates the cross, but the cross is the *conditio sine qua non* of Easter.

If the cross is the moment of epiphany and the primal datum of faith for Mk, what is the role of resurrection? Mk 16:1–8 opposes the view that the resurrection could either be ground for faith or proof of Jesus' presence in the

6. Danker, "Demonic Secret," 51–54. *Phōnē megalē* occurs four times in Mk, twice in exorcism stories (1:26; 5:7), and twice in the crucifixion story (15:34, 37).

community (Crossan). This is contrary to the classic concept of resurrection Christology which in recent times has been forcefully argued by W. Pannenberg.[7] In his systematic assessment of Mk 16:1–8 Pannenberg makes five fundamental affirmations:

(1) Mk 16:1–8 is an Easter tradition in the sense that it testifies to the historicity of the Empty Tomb and provides the presupposition for the resurrection kerygma.

By rejoinder we would suggest that Mk 16:1–8 is not an Easter tradition which promotes Easter faith and the resurrected Lord in the community. To the contrary, these verses form an anti-apparition tradition or an "anti-tradition of the Empty Tomb" (Crossan). Not the presence of the resurrected Lord is emphasized, but the "negativity of the presence" then and thereafter (Crossan). The angel identifies Jesus as Nazarene, the Crucified One, and points to his resurrection as the ground for his absence (16:6d: *ēgerthē, ouk estin hōde*). Mt (28:6) and Lk (24:6) reverse the Mkan logic: Jesus' absence in the tomb becomes the ground for his resurrection. The Empty Tomb tradition, as conceived by Pannenberg, is thus the Matthean and Lkan theological corrective of the Mkan anti-apparition tradition.

(2) In Pannenberg's view, the disciples could never have proclaimed the resurrected Lord on grounds of the Empty Tomb unless they had indeed witnessed the tomb empty.

In contrast to 1 Cor 15:3–5, Mt 28:1–10, 16–28, and Lk 24:1–11, 13–35, 36–49, the disciples in Mk do not witness the Empty Tomb, do not even learn of its existence, do not experience the resurrected Lord, and proclaim nothing regarding Jesus or the tomb in the closing scenes of the Gospel. Mk 16:1–8 purposely deprives Peter and the disciples of a resurrection appearance of the risen Lord (Crossan).

(3) Pannenberg argues that Mk 16:1–8 was part of a pre-Mkan Passion Narrative.

According to Crossan, however, 16:1–8 is Mkan redaction deliberately designed to communicate Mk's anti-apparition Christology. Even if one wishes to postulate the existence of a pre-Mkan Passion Narrative, Mk 16:1–8 was not part of it.

(4) Pannenberg states that 16:1–8 can be traced back to Jerusalem since the pre-Mkan Passion Narrative originated as a local Jerusalem tradition.

While the existence of a pre-Mkan Passion Narrative is doubtful, as argued above, its Jerusalem origin is wholly unproven. In its present form 16:1–8 is not a Jerusalem tradition, but rather an anti-Jerusalem tradition. What might at best be argued is that Mk by withholding the resurrection appearance from

---

7. W. Pannenberg, *Jesus—God and Man*, trans. L. L. Wilkins and D. A. Priebe (Philadelphia: Westminster Press, 1968), 88–106. Pannenberg has admirably utilized current New Testament scholarship in his systematic theological enterprise. The above observations are meant to indicate the impact of Mkan redaction critical studies on a theology of the stature of Pannenberg's.

the disciples may be reversing what used to be a Jerusalem-type pre-Mkan Empty Tomb tradition. But Crossan argues that there never existed pre-Mkan traditions regarding the Empty Tomb, only apparition stories such as Mk 6:45–51.

(5) Pannenberg believes that the inconclusive ending of the Mkan Gospel points to a missing Easter account, i.e., an apparition of Jesus in Galilee.

Nothing is lacking after 16:1–8, however, according to the Gospel's dramatic logic. The disciples cannot experience the resurrected Lord because they did not follow the Crucified One. The Gospel is complete in itself by deliberately *not* recording an apparition event.

In Mk the resurrection is strictly subordinated to the crucifixion. The Evangelist makes his Gospel culminate in a passion account, not in a narrative of Jesus' resurrection appearance! The resurrection ensues from death in godforsakenness and marks the beginning of Jesus' absence from the community. Rooted in the cross the resurrection does not *in itself* carry soteriological significance.

A Christology which peaks in the lowness of the cross, subordinates resurrection to crucifixion, and refrains from displaying the Resurrected One (while stressing his absence) is too harshly focused on the paradox of negation to be of enduring attraction. Mt, Lk, and Jn (if we may assume a Mk-Jn relationship), each in his own way, digress from Mkan Christology. On one point all three are agreed: a Christology devoid of apparition scenes is intolerable.

In what sense does Mk's Christology of the cross communicate to the readers of the Gospel? The anti-apparition thrust of 16:1–8 is noticeable elsewhere in the Gospel. The eucharistic tradition (14:22–25) centers on Jesus' death and culminates in the announcement of his absence until some future point in time (Robbins). Mk 13 defines the Mkan time-frame between Easter and parousia as a period of wars, Temple destruction, flight, heresy, and the absence of Jesus (Weeden). The parables in Mk 4 portray the Mkan present as a twilight zone afflicted by persecution and the onslaughts of Satan. The absence of Jesus is thus a presiding feature in the Mkan Gospel. If, as most contributors to this volume agree, the Gospel was composed in the aftermath of A.D. 70, Mk's emphasis on Jesus' absence might be related to the time and circumstances of the Gospel's composition. The anti-apparition thrust may derive from the fact that Jesus did not intervene in the eschatological struggle against Rome as he was expected to and as was propagated by early Christian prophets at the time (13:6, 21).[8] After the disconfirmation of the parousia expectations of A.D. 70 the absence of Jesus became an intensely Mkan experience. But if the absence of Jesus from the community is a Mkan experience, then the absence of God suffered by Jesus on the cross appears in a new light. In his godforsakenness Jesus suffers the plight of the Mkan Christians. Both divine silence (15:34) and the destruction of the Temple (15:38), the very traumas suffered by the people, are anticipated in and transcended by Jesus' suffering on the cross. His non-miraculous death becomes transitional for himself and for those on behalf of whom he dies (10:45; 14:24). In his very godforsakenness Jesus anticipates in exemplary fashion the traumatic experiences of the Gospel's readers.

3. RIVAL CHRISTOLOGY

In Mk 14–16 the Mkan passion Christology is accompanied by the shadow of its own negation. The Christology of the suffering Son of Man, King, and Son of God is developed in contradiction to an opposite concept of Messiahship, one of miraculous demonstration of power. At crucial points in Mk 14–16 theme alternates with countertheme, claim meets counterclaim, and confession is pitted against anti-confession.

The crucifixion scene itself (15:22–32) is patterned after theme and countertheme. The title "King of the Jews" placed over the cross (15:26) conveys both dramatically and conceptually the cardinal point of Mk's passion Christology: Jesus' Messiahship is consummated by crucifixion. On the other hand, a whole chorus of mockers surrounds the cross and challenges the concept of a suffering King (15:29–32). The passers-by, chief priests, scribes, and robbers provoke Jesus to perform a miracle on behalf of himself so as to prove his identity and to implement his Messianic authority. The mockers wish to see a life-saving miracle, for their faith is predicated on seeing (15:32: *hina idōmen kai pisteusōmen*). "Christ" is the title indigenous to this Christology of miracle-saving power (Weeden), and the mockers' "King of Israel" (15:32) is set in opposition to the *titulus* "King of the Jews"

---

8. R. Pesch, *Naherwartungen: Tradition und Redaktion in Mk 13* (Düsseldorf: Patmos Verlag, 1968), 218–23, *passim*; KELBER, 109–28, *passim*.

(15:26). The latter supports Mk's suffering Kingship, while "King of Israel" represents a "Christ" who performs in power and by self-serving miracles (Weeden). This same concept of "Christ" exhibited by the mockers (15:32: *ho Christos*) seems also to lie behind Peter's anti-confession (8:29: *ho Christos*) which runs into Jesus' confession of suffering Son of Man (Weeden). Peter's anti-confession and denial and the disciples' ineptitude to grasp a suffering Messiahship makes the twelve under the leadership of Peter together with the chorus of mockers the proponents of a rival Christology which thrives on miracle-working power minus suffering and death.

Jesus' confession before the High Priest (14:61–62) functions as an antidote to an opposite viewpoint on at least three different levels. Within the narrow scope of 14:61–62 Jesus' future-directed Son of Man statement may be designed to correct Christ and Son of God, titles which for the High Priest are likely to imply the present realization of power (Weeden). Within the larger framework of 14:53–72 Jesus' confession forms part of a trial scene which is set in intercalated position within the story of Peter's denial (Dewey, Donahue). The net effect of this construct is such that confession and anti-confession occur "at the same time and in the same place" (Dewey). On a still larger scale Jesus' confession is directed against the false Messianic claimants of 13:6, 21–22. Their concept of a realized Messianic presence summoned by the *egō eimi* formula (13:6) is opposed by Jesus' *egō eimi* confession which projects his full manifestation into the future.

A further instance of the confession/anti-confession pattern is provided by the cry of dereliction (15:34) and its subsequent misinterpretation (15:35–36). While the cry displays Jesus' utter helplessness and powerlessness, the bystanders take it to be a call for help and miraculous rescue from suffering (Weeden). Once again, the seeing of a miracle is fundamental to the anti-confession position (15:36: *aphete idōmen*). The centurion's climactic confession (15:39), by contrast, turns the bystanders' concept of seeing right side up. He "sees" (*kai idōn*) the Son of God revealed in the void of godforsakenness and death, and thus becomes the Gospel's first and only true believer.

Consistent with this theme/countertheme pattern are two types of meal Christologies (Robbins). The Feeding Stories (6:30–44; 8:1–10) function within a context of thoroughgoing misunderstanding which reflects Mkan controversy over the christological significance of ceremonial meals. As conceived by the disciples and requested by the Pharisees, the feedings ought to celebrate the presence of the risen Lord. But in his own last meal celebration (14:22–25) Jesus rights the wrong meal Christology by focusing upon his death and absence from the community. Again, a Christology of Messianic presence receives correction from a Christology which is rooted in the cross and devoid of apparitions (Robbins).

The full dimension of Mkan Christology involves its polemical underside, for Jesus is vindicated by reversing the opposite model. Christology and rival Christology condition each other, indeed feed on each other in unexpected, paradoxical ways. Jesus' first suffering Son of Man confession is provoked by Peter's anti-confession. The High Priest facilitates disclosure of the Messianic Secret which in turn brings about death out of which comes life. The centurion, symbol of power and instrumental in the cross, stands in awe of power made manifest in weakness (Weeden). The Mkan Jesus thrives on turning around the opposite model of Messiahship until in the end he triumphs in suffering death, not in celebration of resurrection life. Mkan Christology thus unfolds by a process of reversal.

A number of authors of this volume are of the opinion that the Gospel's christological dialectic derives from an intra-Christian conflict in the Mkan environment. Among the general features of the opponents' profile they would list the following: interest in miracles and apparitions, stress on present realization of eschatological hope, a minimal appreciation of the religious validity of Jesus' suffering and death, and a possible appeal to the twelve under the leadership of Peter. Weeden has argued that the Christology of the opponents was drawn from a Hellenistic *theios anēr* milieu in which Jesus was identified as a superhuman worker of miracles. Kelber attempted to trace the opponents' Christology (and eschatology) to Jewish apocalypticism which evoked a Jesus returned or imminently expected to return at the parousia. Weeden, Kelber, and Crossan recognize a direct or indirect association of the opponents with Jerusalem. Weeden sees behind them the Hellenistic-Jewish Stephen party,[9] Crossan and Kelber the Jewish Christian core of the Jerusalem Church. Two observations may be

9. T. J. Weeden, "The Conflict between Mark and His Opponents over Kingdom Theology," *SBL Seminar Papers*, ed. G. MacRae (Cambridge, Mass.: SBL, 1973), II, 226–28.

added at the present stage of the discussion: (a) The actual agreement (among some authors) on the opponents as a religious phenomenon is obscured by the disparate *religionsgeschichtliche* designations of *theios anēr* versus apocalypticism. This raises the question whether (b) both terms may not be inappropriate in reference to the specific type of Christian faith against which Mk appears to polemicize.

While the authors recognize the existence of the theme/countertheme pattern in Mk, not all would attribute it to the force of a Mkan opposition. Donahue, for example, questions Weeden's thoroughgoing reconstruction of a *theios anēr* Christology and his interpretation of Mk by way of a dialogue with such an opposition. For Donahue, Mk is not repudiating a Hellenistic notion of Son of God, but rather reinterpreting a Jewish, Messianic concept of Son of God. Hence, Mk 14–16 is not viewed as the reversal of a divine man Christology, but as the culmination of Mk's pervasive royal Christology refashioned through the medium of the cross. Irony and paradox in Mk 14–16 may therefore not necessarily reflect a *theios anēr* challenge, but could be the natural component of a Christology of the crucified King, and the theme/countertheme pattern would not inevitably indicate the existence of a distinct group of opponents with whom Mk is debating.

4. THE ISSUE OF THE TEMPLE

One of the interpretive puzzles of Mk 14–16 has been an anti-Temple theme which seems out of accord with the theological issues raised by trial and crucifixion. Specifically, the discussion has revolved around 14:58, a saying attributed to Jesus and dealing with his threat to destroy the Temple and his promise to build another one. There are three problems involved in the emergence of the anti-Temple theme in the trial (14:58) and in the crucifixion (15:29). (1) Is the saying 14:58 intended by Mk to be true or false on the lips of Jesus? If it is meant to be a true statement of Jesus, why is it attributed to false witnesses? (2) In 14:58 does the other Temple not made with hands (which will replace the one made with hands) refer to the Temple of the end time, to the eschatological community, or to the risen Jesus? (3) In what sense, if at all, is 14:58 related to other anti-Temple sayings or scenes in the Gospel such as the mocking of the passers-by (15:29), Jesus' prediction of the destruction of the Temple (13:2), his so-called cleansing of the Temple (11:12–20), and the rending of the Temple curtain (15:38)?

Donahue interprets the first half of 14:58 as an integral part of Mk's pervasive anti-Temple theology (11:11–14:1). Jesus enters Jerusalem with the intention to disqualify the Temple, and it is his anti-Temple activity which causes arrest, trial, and crucifixion. Mk establishes the connection between Jesus' anti-Temple mission and death by reporting three times a plot on the life of Jesus, and each time in reaction to his anti-Temple words or actions. Initially the plot is provoked (11:18) by Jesus' eschatological "cleansing" of the Temple. The plan to kill Jesus is reiterated (12:12) after Jesus announces the replacement of the Temple by the Christian community.[10] Jesus' outright prediction of the destruction of the Temple (13:2; cf. 13:14) prompts a third plot on his life (14:1) which in turn is transformed into action through the arrest, trial, and crucifixion. Since, therefore, the trial arises directly out of Jesus' anti-Temple activity, the latter has to become an issue in the trial, and 14:58, according to Donahue, functions as a true statement.

The matter of the false witnesses Donahue explains in terms of an Old Testament tradition of the suffering Just One. To be surrounded by false accusers belongs to the traditional image of the Just One whose fate it is to suffer innocently. The motif of false witnesses (14:56, 57, 59), therefore, enhances the image of Jesus as the suffering Just One, while it does not affect the truth or falseness of the charge of 14:58. The Mkan Jesus, Donahue argues, is tried and killed because of his opposition to the Temple, but he is tried and killed as the Righteous One.

The second part of 14:58 is in Donahue's view also intelligible as a continuation of a Mkan theme, i.e., that of Jesus the preparer of the eschatological community (1:16–20; 3:13–19; 11:17; 14:28; 16:7). For Donahue, the other Temple not made with hands symbolizes the new Christian community in Galilee.[11]

---

10. DONAHUE, 122–27. The setting for the parable of the Vineyard and the Tenants (12:1–11) is established by 11:27. The parable is spoken in the Temple and against the Temple authorities.

11. Donahue is less confident about the compatibility of 15:29 with Mkan Temple theology. Within a thoroughgoing context of contempt (15:29–32a), 15:29 is placed on the lips of mockers because the verse represents for Mk an incorrect viewpoint. See, DONAHUE, 196–201.

In this double focus on the destruction of the Temple and a new Galilean center, 14:58 speaks effectively to Christians who have experienced the fall of Jerusalem and are faced with the problem of finding a new communal place. For them the trial of Jesus serves as a model for their own trials and tribulations.

Weeden does not consider Mkan Temple theology as much of a linear, homogeneous complex as does Donahue. According to Weeden, the Evangelist places 14:58 and 15:29 on the lips of false witnesses and revilers because he wishes to dissociate himself from the viewpoint expressed in these verses. A study of content indicates to Weeden that the two sayings are out of step with Mkan Christology and eschatology. Both sayings consider Jesus himself the agent of the Temple's destruction (emphatically so 14:58: *egō katalyso*), while the Jesus promoted by Mk remains personally uninvolved in the actual Temple crisis, even though he opposes the Temple, disqualifies it, and predicts its downfall. Furthermore, the two sayings advocate a correlation between Temple destruction and Jesus' parousia, for the other Temple rebuilt in three days points, in Weeden's view, to the risen Jesus and his coming—and not to the eschatological community. By contrast, the structure of Mk 13 reveals the Mkan intent to disconnect the parousia of Jesus from the destruction of the Temple.

For Weeden the Temple eschatology of 14:58 and 15:29—Jesus the agent of Temple destruction, the realization of Jesus' presence, realized eschatology in conjunction with Temple destruction—is part of the same divine ideology which he sees Mk opposing throughout the Gospel. Against this divine man eschatology of 14:58 and 15:29 Mk argues that the destruction of the Temple falls into the period of Jesus' absence from the Church (13:1–23), that Jesus is the suffering Son of Man who dies divested of power and not the triumphal Jesus who makes his appearance in Jerusalem (16:1–8), and that Jesus' full identity is reserved for the future (14:62), i.e., a point in time after the fall of the Temple (13:1–27).

These insights of Donahue and Weeden allow us to draw an outline of what is a multifaceted Mkan Temple theology.

(1) Donahue rightly stresses the Mkan anti-Temple theme. Jesus disqualifies the Temple (11:12–20) and predicts its downfall (13:2), and death plots and arrest do result from his mounting Temple opposi-

tion. Within the broad structure of the Mkan narrative, therefore, Jesus' death is caused by his mission against the Temple.[12] By way of an ironic twist, however, Jesus reverses the expectations of his enemies. If the Jewish officials sought to protect the Temple by putting Jesus to death, they merely hastened the fate of the Temple, because the very death of Jesus constitutes a prolepsis of the end of the Temple (15:37–38).[13]

(2) Jesus the opponent of the Temple is not to be confused with a Jesus who is the agent of its destruction. The latter view is expressed in 14:58 and 15:29. While Weeden's *theios anēr* nomenclature remains an open question, his interpretation of the two verses as false statements is persuasive. Throughout the Gospel Jesus suffers a mistaken identity through enemies and friends, false accusers and false confessors, false Christs and mockers, his own disciples and especially Peter. By putting 14:58 and 15:29 on the lips of false witnesses and revilers Mk has formally relegated these sayings to his theological counterstructure. For Mk, Jesus cannot be the personal destroyer of the Temple for two reasons. One, he is not a militant, triumphal Christ, but one who in the process of his mission against the Temple is destroyed himself. Two, it is in the last analysis the Temple establishment, and not Jesus, which by killing Jesus effects the end of the Temple.

(3) For Mk the fall of the Temple is in no way related to Jesus' resurrection or parousia. Such a connection between the crisis of the Temple (and Jerusalem) and the miraculous appearance of Jesus is assumed by 14:58 and 15:29. The reference to three days in both sayings favors an interpretation of the Temple not made with hands in terms of the risen Jesus. But it is noteworthy that the three-day formulas in both 14:58 (*dia triōn hēmerōn*) and 15:29 (*en trisin hēmeras*) do not conform to the resurrection formula of Jesus' own passion/resurrection predictions (8:31, 9:31, 10:34: *meta treis hēmerais*). This is a further indication that the eschatological Jesus invoked by false wit-

---

12. Both Mkan and Pauline Christology are distinguished by an iconoclastic quality: the Mkan Jesus puts an end to the Temple much like the Pauline Christ puts an end to the Law.

13. Mk is the first Christian theologian known to us who reflects on the relationship between the two principal traumas suffered by first century Christians: the death of Jesus and the destruction of the Temple. He accomplishes meaning by coordinating the two: Jesus' death anticipates the death of the Temple (15:38).

nesses and revilers is at variance with the dying, risen Jesus sponsored by Mk: Jesus rose three days after death, hence not three days after the Temple destruction.

(4) Despite Mk's pervasive anti-Temple scheme Weeden rightly alerts us to the fact that in the trial Jesus is not charged with opposition to the Temple (assuming that 14:58 is false for Mk). The fifth and last reference to the death plot, the condemnation itself (14:63–64), is not caused by an anti-Temple confession or anti-Temple charge. As we noted above, what precipitates the death sentence is Jesus' confession before the High Priest, his disclosure of the Messianic Secret (14:62). For Mk, Jesus dies because he reveals his full identity which includes, but is not limited to, his authority to take action against the Temple. In the last analysis Jesus dies because he confesses to be the Christ and Son of God who as Son of Man claims authority for the future.[14]

(5) The Mkan Temple theology speaks to the Gospel's readers after A.D. 70. Jesus' mission anticipated the end of the Temple, while he himself was not instrumental in bringing about the fall. Jesus rose three days after death and pointed the way toward Galilee. The predicted destruction of Jerusalem and the nonappearance of Jesus in Jerusalem makes any Christian involvement in the city unjustifiable. In the trial Mk repudiates Christian hopes which had been invested in Jerusalem. Jesus died not because he had engaged himself miraculously in the city's crisis, or because he pledged allegiance to Jerusalem, but rather because he confessed his future authority as Son of Man. As enthroned and coming Son of Man Jesus had died for a future which lies beyond the crisis of the city.

5. CHARACTERS[15]

The importance of studying the role of characters as a key to Mk's theological intent has come to be recognized in recent work on the Gospel.[16] On the one hand, characters have an internal function.

---

14. In the trial, therefore, 14:58 is not vindicated but repudiated by Jesus' confession. The witnesses' claim of Jesus' eschatological presence is contradicted by Jesus' revelation of his identity in terms of future enthronement (which implies absence) and future coming.

15. I am grateful to Kim Dewey for having drawn up a first draft of this section.

16. WEEDEN, 20–51; PERRIN, 52–54, and *Pilgrimage*, 107–10.

They *participate* in the inner dynamic of the Gospel, advance the plot, and bring it to the desired resolution. On the other hand, characters serve an external function. They *represent* something to the audience, symbolize realities which link up with the readers' present, and serve as models of meaning and conduct.

The women: The entire passion section in Mk is framed by two stories whose chief characters are women. On one end is the story of an anonymous woman who anoints Jesus for burial (14:3–9) and on the other end stands the report of women who come to the tomb to anoint Jesus' body (16:1–8). Both stories mention anointment and the absence of Jesus (14:7; 16:6). These women demonstrate discipleship which consists in honoring and following Jesus as the Crucified One. With this the similarities end, for while one woman anoints Jesus in anticipation of his death, the other women fail to anoint Jesus because of his absence from the tomb. The anonymous woman is applauded, but the very women who had followed Jesus in Galilee (15:40–41) flee the tomb in fear and trembling. The outsider succeeds, but the insiders fail.

Judas: Not mentioned since his first and unfavorable listing in 3:19, Judas is consistently introduced into the passion section as "one of the twelve" (14:10, 20, 43). Identified as one of the twelve who shares table fellowship with Jesus (14:18–20), the Judas figure shocks the reader into the realization that enmity arises from within (Robbins); as Jesus was "delivered up" by one of his own, so are the Christians likewise "delivered up" by their own (13:12).[17] But the very term used to describe the act of betrayal, *paradidonai* (14:10, 11, 18, 21, 42, 44), integrates the betrayal into a purposeful scheme of passion. Judas, although guilty and cursed by Jesus (14:21), functions to translate Jesus' passion predictions (9:31; 10:33; 14:41, 42) into action. In his own paradoxical fashion he initiates the passion and advances Jesus' enthronement by crucifixion. Hence the framing of the anointment scene (14:3–9) by the themes of death and betrayal (14:1–2, 10–11): Jesus' Messianic anointment is paradoxically instituted by human malice and betrayal.

The twelve, the three, and Peter: In Mk 14–16 the twelve, the three,

---

17. DONAHUE, 170.

and Peter consummate their function as negative models of discipleship. They prepare the passover meal but seem unprepared for Jesus' exposure of the enemy within at his last meal (14:19). Ceremonially, they *all* drink of the cup (14:23), but for all practical purposes they escape drinking the cup when they flee that same night. The three confidants, acting in lieu of the twelve, yield to the temptation to circumvent suffering and passion (14:37–42), and when Jesus' passion begins with his arrest *all* the disciples flee (14:50: *ephygon pantes*), as in the end the three women flee (16:8: *ephygon*). With the arrest the disciples are phased out of Jesus' passion, except for Peter. By juxtaposing his denial with Jesus' confession Mk elevates him into the role of Jesus' chief antagonist (Dewey). As Jesus divulges his Messianic identity, Peter fulfills his role as satanic opponent. With the disciples there is an element of disintegration in the Gospel story, and the readers are alerted to the fact that to follow the twelve, or the three, or Peter, is to court disaster.

The High Priest and Pilate: Both characters function in parallel fashion in Jesus' twin trials (14:55–65; 15:2–15). Both ask Jesus about his Messianic identity (14:61; 15:2), both encounter Jesus' silence (14:61; 15:5), and both receive a qualifying or indirect answer (14:62; 15:2). But while the High Priest seems determined to gain Jesus' conviction, Pilate is a more complex figure. He remains unconvinced of Jesus' guilt (15:14), proposes to release Jesus instead of a man of violence (15:6–9), and "wonders" (15:5) while Jesus is alive, and still "wonders" (15:44) after Jesus is dead. With this characterization of the High Priest and Pilate, Mk reverses the conventional model of friend and enemy. Jesus' own High Priest forces the condemnation, while Pilate, representative of a foreign, hostile power, suspects priestly envy (15:10) and tries to save the life of Jesus.

The young man: The mysterious figure of the naked young man (*neaniskos*) symbolizes Jesus' escape from death. After the flight of the disciples (14:50) he is the only person who still "follows" Jesus (14:51). Then he too is "seized" (14:51) as Jesus was "seized" before (14:44, 46). But he escapes naked by leaving his linen cloth (*sindona*) behind. In similar fashion, Jesus is wrapped in a linen cloth (15:46: *sindona*) from which he escapes by resurrection. The analogy is completed by the reappearance of the young man (*neaniskos*) in

Jesus' tomb (16:5), sitting at the right hand, and dressed in a white robe of eschatological coloring (Crossan). The young man mimics Jesus' escape from death and almost comically exposes the failure of the plot to kill Jesus. He plays the role of transition from the Gospel's disintegrating process toward reintegration.

Barabbas, the soldiers, Simon of Cyrene, the centurion, and Joseph of Arimathea: A number of participants in the passion are representatives of destructive power or indifference who by a reversal of role, however, become instruments in the Gospel's parallel process of reintegration. Barabbas who has destroyed life facilitates life, for his release brings about Jesus' death out of which comes life (15:6–15). The soldiers, determined to make a brutal caricature of Jesus, unwittingly enact the scene of enthronement by humiliation (15:16–20). Simon of Cyrene fulfills the model of cross-bearing discipleship by carrying the cross of Jesus (15:21; cf. Weeden). The centurion in charge of the execution is the only character who faces Jesus on the cross. His ambiguous role is characterized by the phrase *parestēkōs ex enantias autou* (15:39): he stands in opposition to Jesus as his executioner, but he also stands opposite to Jesus so as to face him and recognize his identity.[18] As an opponent facing up to the dying Jesus, he confesses Jesus as the Son of God. Joseph of Arimathea likewise undergoes a dramatic reversal. Mk states that he was a respected member of the council (15:43), and only Mk claims that *all* the members of the council condemned Jesus (14:64). By implication, Joseph also cast his vote against Jesus.[19] After having been instrumental earlier in the death of Jesus, Joseph afterward arranges the burial and thus prepares for the Kingdom (15:43–46). All these characters are drawn into the process of reversal at the center of which stands Jesus' reversal of death into life.

Jesus: The Gospel's chief character is a model hard to define and difficult to follow. He is a character of authority and in possession of

18. By contrast, the women watch "from far away" (15:40: *apo makrothen*), as Peter had earlier followed Jesus into the court "from far away" (14:54: *apo makrothen*; cf. Dewey).

19. J. Schreiber, *Die Markuspassion. Wege zur Erforschung der Leidensgeschichte Jesu* (Hamburg: Furche-Verlag, 1969), 58–59. Mt and Lk sense the Mkan implication and object to it, Mt by transforming Joseph from a council member to a disciple of Jesus (Mt 27:57), Lk by explicitly rejecting the Mkan insinuation (Lk 23:51). In addition, both Mt and Lk disapprove of the Mkan notion that *all* the members had cast their votes against Jesus (Mt. 26:66; Lk omits Mk 14:64c).

detailed foreknowledge of all that is coming to pass. He anticipates the precise location of his Last Meal (14:13–16), the global spread of the Gospel (14:9), his disciples' flight (14:27), Judas' betrayal (14:20), Peter's denial (14:30), his own death (14:8, 21–24, 27, 41), his resurrection (14:28), his absence from the community (14:7, 25), as well as his movement toward Galilee (14:28). There is an "authoritative aura around Jesus" (Robbins) who is in control over the events of the passion. On the other hand, he is beaten and spat upon, sentenced to death, humiliated, and rejected by his followers. The only affection bestowed upon him is anointment unto death and the kiss of death. Abandoned by God he dies engulfed in demonic darkness. As a character model Jesus is a complex and ambiguous symbol. He is the speaker of a Messianic confession who also veils himself in enigmatic silence. He is the King who dies a criminal's death. He is a figure of power who achieves victory through powerlessness. He is a Messiah who dies but rises from death. Even his confession lacks definitive clarity for it points proleptically into an open-ended future. Despite resurrection his final victory is not celebrated because the completion of his role hinges on still future aspects. In the wake of his paradoxical performance the world around him is turned upside down. He changes expectations and identities for better and for worse. He upsets the disciples' conventional concept of Messiah, and reverses the traditional symbols of Jerusalem and Galilee, friend and enemy, insider and outsider, disciple and persecutor, power and weakness, life and death. As one who rose from death he promises life to those who will lose it.

6. MARK 14–16 AND THE GOSPEL

Weeden has argued the significance of Christology and rival Christology as a clue to the theological purpose of the Mkan Gospel. His thesis is well known and widely discussed. Mk, according to Weeden, promotes his Christology of a suffering Son of Man not merely in point/counterpoint fashion, but also by relegating one half of the Gospel to the opponents' viewpoint and the other half to his own. In 1:1–8:29 Mk portrays a Jesus engaged in miracle activity which is capped by Peter's divine man confession (8:29). After the silencing of Peter (8:30) Mk presents Jesus' first public confession as suffering Son of Man (8:31) which is systematically developed from that point on to its logical climax in the passion section. Mediated through the vehicle of the disciples' misunderstanding of the suffering Jesus, Mk conveys the message that their Christ of miracles and manifest power is rejected by the suffering, crucified Jesus. As a result, the passion Christology of the second half of the Gospel renders obsolete the divine man Christology of the first half.

According to Weeden's model Mk 14–16 would be both the Gospel's dramatic culmination and the near-exclusive carrier of Mkan Christology. In this case, the Gospel could appropriately, if "somewhat provocatively," be defined as a Passion Narrative with a lengthy introduction.[20]

An alternative conception of the Mkan Gospel might proceed from the assumption that Mk intends to *combine* the models of Jesus the miracle worker and suffering Son of Man. In this case the miracles would not negatively relate to Mk 14–16 in the sense that the passion disqualifies their validity. Rather the miracles would be the presupposition for fully understanding the Jesus of passion, while the passion would provide the criterion by which the significance of the miracles were to be measured. Jesus' abandonment by God on the cross would have to be grasped in light of his investment with divine power at baptism, and his Galilean triumphs over death and disease would have to be weighed in conjunction with the cries of dereliction and expiration. The full identity of Jesus would therefore comprise the notions of *exousia and* passion, while transcending the particularities of both miracle worker and suffering Just One. This inclusive model would perhaps aptly be articulated by the centurion's confession: "Truly *this man* was *Son of God.*"[21]

---

20. M. Kähler, *The So-Called Historical Jesus and the Historic, Biblical Christ*, trans. and ed. C. E. Braaten (Philadelphia: Fortress Press, 1964; 1st German ed. 1892), 80 n. 11. The following scholars have—without subscribing to Weeden's specific thesis— in recent times adopted Kähler's definition of the Gospel of Mk: BULTMANN, 371, and *The Theology of the New Testament*, trans. K. Grobel (New York: Scribner's, 1951), I, 86; MARXSEN, 30–31, 132; H. Koester, "One Jesus and Four Primitive Gospels," *Trajectories through Early Christianity* (Philadelphia: Fortress Press, 1971), 162; N. R. Petersen, "So-Called Gnostic Type Gospels and the Question of the Genre 'Gospel' " (unpublished paper, 1970), 32–33; N. Perrin, "The Literary Gattung 'Gospel'— Some Observations," *ExpT* 82 (1970), 4–7, and *The New Testament*, 148. A noticeable objection to Kähler's definition has come from H. C. Kee, *Jesus in History*, 119.

21. This seeming contradiction of Jesus' revelation as Son of God in power (baptism, transfiguration) and in humiliation (cross) has been philosophically interpreted in

According to this model, what Mk calls the Gospel would have to be viewed as a thematic and prototypical composite, a combining of the incompatible, a deliberate tension between power and powerlessness in a sense perhaps not tolerated before in the theological history of early Christianity. By synthesizing the diverse models of miracle worker and suffering Just One Mk would have arrived at a new model. It is this new synthesis of a miracle worker who dies in abandonment which would set the pattern for the Gospel form, a form not so much chosen by adoption of an external model but forced upon Mk by the very nature of his theological enterprise.

In the case of this composite model, the Gospel could be defined neither in terms of an aretalogy (understood as a collection of miracle stories) nor as the prefixing of a long but christologically anemic introduction. The same weight would have to be given to the miracle and to the passion sections of the Gospel, and the passion could not be played out against the miracles. Even though Mk 14–16 would form the dramatic and theological culmination of the Gospel, this could not justify an evaluation of the Gospel through the logic of a *reductio ad passionem*. Mk 14–16 would be considered a crucial, but theologically integral part of the Gospel, and not its exclusive determiner.[22]

While the two preceding models are based on the assumption that the Gospel divides conceptually into two separate parts, a third model seeks to pay closer attention to the Gospel's total configuration. If the Gospel constitutes a literary, theological unity, it must be understood by the cohesion of the whole rather than by collision or combination of its parts. Indeed, if Mk 1–13 and 14–16 are interlocked with each other by the convergence of virtually all major Mkan themes in the passion section, then the Gospel's conceptual pattern may not simply be that of thaumaturge versus suffering Just One.

---

terms of a reversal of the noetic and ontic order by J. Moltmann, *The Crucified God*, trans. R. A. Wilson and J. Bowden (New York: Harper & Row, 1973), 91: "What is the last thing for human knowledge is the first with regard to being. Whereas Jesus is not recognizable as the Son of God until his death on the cross and his resurrection, in the order of being he is the Son of God before history takes place."

22. Perhaps it is worth noting from this perspective that the oldest Christian Gospel anticipates in striking fashion a classic christological dispute of later centuries, that of the two natures of Christ, one divine and one human, and of the two states of Christ, one of exaltation and one of humiliation. Inasmuch as the Gospel may have contributed to this christological dispute, it may also suggest an answer.

A major requirement of any Gospel model is that it does justice to the text as an *undivided whole* and to *all the elements* which compose it. While the Mkan Jesus is conspicuous in his role as miracle worker and suffering Son of Man, these features by no means exhaust the Jesus character. He is also the herald of the Kingdom and gifted with extraordinary prophetic powers, a teacher of taboo-shattering quality and a revolutionary who turns against the Temple. If one refrains from reducing the Jesus figure by organizing seemingly contradictory features on two opposite sides, a character emerges who is fraught with ambiguity and steeped in paradox. Jesus announces the Kingdom but opts for the cross; he is King of the Jews but condemned by the Jewish establishment; he asks for followers but speaks in riddles; he is identified as Nazarene but rejected in Nazareth; he makes public pronouncements but also hides behind a screen of secrecy; he saves others but not himself; he promises return but has not returned; he performs miracles but suffers a non-miraculous death; he is a successful exorciser but dies overcome by demonic forces; he is appointed by God in power but dies abandoned by God in powerlessness; he dies but rises from death. His beginning is nebulous and his future status is indefinite, and at the moment of Messianic disclosure he still speaks enigmatically of himself in the third person (14:62; cf. 8:31; 9:31; 10:33–34). If there is one single feature which characterizes the Mkan Jesus it is contradiction or paradox. It might therefore be argued that "Mk presents not two conflicting views of Jesus" but one complex "paradoxical view" (Dewey).

This model of the paradox is not limited to Christology, but affects the total Gospel story. Rival Christology, Temple theology, the characters, Messianic Secret, titular Christology, cryptic teaching, discipleship failure, misunderstanding and unexpected understanding—all these themes and features lend dramatic support to Jesus as a model of contradiction. Jesus transforms the plans and expectations of followers and opponents, overturns an opposite concept of Messiah, and discharges the validity of the Temple. Reversal is his mode of action: clean is declared unclean and unclean becomes clean; the rich are warned and the poor praised; the last will be the first and the first last; the appointed followers are blind and a blind beggar receives sight; Jews are hostile and Gentiles believe; Peter denies and the centurion "sees."

In Mk 14–16 Jesus completes his characteristic role as paradoxical model by the ultimate act of transformation, i.e., that of death into life. Virtually all major themes and a large variety of characters are centripetally organized around the cross and drawn into the process of reversal. Now the world is turned upside down: the disciples stand exposed as negative models; Peter the leader is revealed as the leading opponent; the Temple is turned into a negative symbol; Jerusalem is replaced by Galilee; Son of God is sanctioned by Jesus' suffering and the silence of God; the Kingdom is consummated by crucifixion; death is reversed by life.

According to this model, Mk 14–16 could be defined neither as the *sole* carrier of Mkan Christology, nor as the representative of *one half* of Mk's Christology. Rather, Mk 14–16 would be the *continuation and summation of Mk's paradoxical theology,* a theology informed by and culminating in the paradox of the cross.

Selected Bibliography

Aland, Kurt. "Bemerkungen zum Schluss des Markusevangeliums." *Neo-testamentica et Semitica: Studies in Honour of Matthew Black.* Edited by E. Earle Ellis and Max Wilcox. Edinburgh: Clark, 1969.
————. "Der wiedergefundene Markusschluss? Eine methodologische Bemerkung zur textkritischen Arbeit." *ZTK* 67 (1970), 3–13.
Aytoun, R. A. "'Himself he cannot save' (Ps XXII 29 and Mk XV 31)." *JTS* 21 (1920), 245–48.
Bahr, Gordon J. "The Seder of Passover and the Eucharistic Words." *Nov Test* 12 (1970), 181–202.
Barbour, Robin S. "Gethsemane in the Tradition of the Passion." *NTS* 16 (1970), 231–51.
Bartsch, Hans-Werner. "Die Bedeutung des Sterbens Jesu nach den Synoptikern." *TZ* 20 (1964), 87–102.
————. "Der Schluss des Markus-Evangeliums. Ein überlieferungsgeschichtliches Problem." *TZ* 27 (1971), 241–54.
Benoit, Pierre. "Jesus devant le Sanhedrin." *Angelicum* 20 (1943), 143–65.
Berger, Klaus. "Die königlichen Messiastraditionen des Neuen Testaments." *NTS* 20 (1973), 1–44.
Bickermann, Elias. "Das Leere Grab." *ZNW* 23 (1924), 281–92.
Birdsall, J. Neville. "*To hrēma hos eipen autō ho Iēsous* Mk XIV. 72." *Nov Test* 2 (1958), 272–75.
Black, Matthew. "The 'Son of Man' Passion Sayings in the Gospel Tradition." *ZNW* 60 (1969), 1–8.
Bligh, Philip H. "A Note on *Huios Theou* in Mark 15, 39." *ExpT* 81 (1968), 51–53.

Bode, Edward L. *The First Easter Morning.* AnBib 45. Rome: Pontifical Biblical Institute, 1970.

————. "A Liturgical Sitz im Leben for the Gospel Tradition of the Women's Easter Visit to the Tomb of Jesus." *CBQ* 32 (1970), 237–42.

Boman, Thorleif. "Der Gebetskampf Jesu." *NTS* 10 (1964), 261–73.

————. "Das Letzte Wort Jesu." *ST* 17 (1963), 103–19.

Boobyer, George Henry. "Galilee and Galileans in St. Mark's Gospel." *BJRL* 35 (1953), 334–48.

Borgen, Peder. "John and the Synoptics in the Passion Narrative." *NTS* 5 (1959), 246–59.

Borsch, Frederick H. "Mark XIV, 62 and I Enoch LXII, 5." *NTS* 14 (1968), 565–67.

Boyd, P. W. J. "Peter's Denial Mark XIV.68, Luke XXII.57." *ExpT* 67 (1956), 341.

Brändle, Max. "Musste das Grab Jesu leer sein?" *Orientierung* 31 (1967), 108–12.

————. "Narratives of the synoptics about the tomb." *TDig* 16 (1967), 22–26.

————. "Die synoptischen Grabeserzählungen." *Orientierung* 31 (1967), 179–84.

Braumann, Georg. "Markus 15, 2–5 und Markus 14, 55–64." *ZNW* 52 (1961), 273–78.

Broer, Ingo. "Zur heutigen Diskussion der Grabesgeschichte." *BiLe* 10 (1969), 40–52.

————. "Das leere Grab—ein Versuch." *LiMö* 42 (1968), 42–51.

————. *Die Urgemeinde und das Grab Jesu.* StANT 31. Munich: Kösel, 1972.

Brown, Raymond E. *The Virginal Conception and Bodily Resurrection of Jesus.* New York: Paulist Press, 1973.

Bucher, Gerard. "Elements for an Analysis of the Gospel Text: The Death of Jesus." *Modern Language Notes* 86 (1971), 835–44.

Buckley, E. R. "The Sources of the Passion Narrative in St. Mark's Gospel." *JTS* 34 (1933), 138–44.

Burkill, T. Alec. "St. Mark's Philosophy of the Passion." *NovTest* 2 (1958), 245–71.

————. "The Trial of Jesus." *VigChr* 12 (1958), 1–18.

Buse, S. Ivor. "St. John and the Marcan Passion Narrative." *NTS* 3 (1958), 215–19.

Cangh, J. M. van. "La Galilée dans l'évangile de Marc: un lieu théologique?" *RB* 79 (1972), 59–76.

Conzelmann, Hans. "Historie und Theologie in den synoptischen Passionsgeschichten." *Zur Bedeutung des Todes Jesu.* Edited by Fritz Viering. Gütersloh: Gerd Mohn, 1967. Reprinted in the author's collected essays

Theologie als Schriftauslegung. Munich: Kaiser, 1974. ET: *Interpr* 24 (1970), 178–97.

Cribbs, F. Lamar. "A Study of the Contacts that Exist between St. Luke and St. John." *SBL Seminar Papers*, 1973. II, 1–93.

Crossan, John Dominic. "Mark and the Relatives of Jesus." *NovTest* 15 (1973), 81–113.

———. "Redaction and Citation in Mark 11:9–10, 17 and 14:27." *SBL Proceedings*, 1972. I, 17–61.

Danker, Frederick W. "The Demonic Secret in Mark: A Reexamination of the Cry of Dereliction (15, 34)." *ZNW* 61 (1970), 48–69.

———. "The Literary Unity of Mark 14, 1–25." *JBL* 85 (1966), 467–72.

Delorme, Jean. "Résurrection et tombeau de Jésus: Marc 16:1–8 dans la tradition évangélique." *Lectio divina* 50 (1969), 105–51.

Dewar, Francis. "Chapter 13 and the Passion Narrative in St. Mark." *Theology* 64 (1961), 99–107.

Dhanis, Édouard. "L'ensevelissement de Jésus et la visite au tombeau dans l'évangile de saint Marc (Mc. XV, 40—XVI, 8)." *Greg* 39 (1958), 367–410.

Dibelius, Martin. "Gethsemane." Translated by Morton S. Enslin, *The Crozer Quarterly* 12 (1935), 254–65; German ed. in *Botschaft und Geschichte.* Vol. I, Tübingen: J. C. B. Mohr (Paul Siebeck), 1953.

Dockx, S. "Le récit du repas pascal Marc 14, 17–26." *Bib* 46 (1965), 445–53.

Dodd, Charles Harold. "The Appearances of the Risen Christ: An Essay in Form-Criticism of the Gospels." *Studies in the Gospels: Essays in Memory of R. H. Lightfoot.* Edited by Dennis Eric Nineham. Oxford: Blackwell, 1955. Reprinted in the author's collected essays *More New Testament Studies.* Grand Rapids, Mich.: Eerdmans, 1968.

Dupont, Jacques. "Il n'en sera pas laissé pierre sur pierre." *Bib* 52 (1971), 301–20.

———. "Ressuscité 'Le Troisième Jour.'" *Bib* 40 (1959), 742–61.

Dvořáček, Jan Amos. "Vom Leiden Gottes, Markus 15, 29–34." *CV* 14 (1971), 231–52.

Elliott, James Keith. "The Text and Language of the Endings to Mark's Gospel." *TZ* 27 (1971), 255–62.

Evans, Christopher Francis. "'I Will Go Before You into Galilee.'" *JTS* 5 (1954), 3–18.

———. *Resurrection and the New Testament.* SBT 2d ser 12. Naperville, Ill.: Allenson, 1970.

Farmer, William R. *The Last Twelve Verses of Mark.* NTSMS 25. Cambridge: Cambridge University Press, 1974.

Fitzmyer, Joseph A. "The Contribution of Qumran Aramaic to the Study of the New Testament." *NTS* 20 (1974), 382–407.

Fuller, Reginald H. *The Formation of the Resurrection Narratives.* New York: Macmillan, 1971.

Gaechter, Paul. "Die Engelerscheinungen in den Auferstehungsberichten." *ZKT* 89 (1967), 191–202.

Gaston, Lloyd. "The Theology of the Temple." *Oikonomia—Heilsgeschichte als Thema der Theologie* (O. Cullmann Festschrift). Edited by F. Christ. Hamburg-Bergstedt, 1967.

Gese, Hartmut. "Psalm 22 und das Neue Testament: Der älteste Bericht vom Tode Jesu und die Entstehung des Herrenmahles." *ZTK* 65 (1968), 1–22.

Ghiberti, Guiseppe. "Bibliografia sull'Esegesi Dei Raconti Pasquali e sul Problema della Risurrezione de Gesú." *ScuolC* 97 (1969), 68*–84*.

———. "Discussione sul Sepolcro Vuoto." *RBiblt* 17 (1969), 392–419.

Glasson, T. Francis. "The Reply to Caiaphas (Mark XIV.62)." *NTS* 7 (1961), 88–93.

Gnilka, Joachim. "'Mein Gott, mein Gott, warum hast du mich verlassen?' (Mk 15, 34 Par)." *BZ* NF 3 (1959), 294–97.

———. "Die Verhandlungen vor dem Synhedrium und vor Pilatus nach Markus 14, 53—15, 5." *EKKNT* 2 (1970), 5–21.

Goguel, Maurice. "Did Peter Deny His Lord? A Conjecture." *HTR* 25 (1932), 1–27.

Güttgemanns, Erhardt. "Linguistische Analyse von Mk 16, 1–8." *LingBibl* 11–12 (1972), 13–53.

Gutwenger, Engelbert. "Zur Geschichtlichkeit der Auferstehung Jesu." *ZKT* 88 (1966), 257–82.

Guy, Harold A. "Son of God in Mk 15,39." *ExpT* 81 (1970), 151.

Hamilton, Neill Q. "Resurrection Tradition and the Composition of Mark." *JBL* 84 (1965), 415–21.

Harner, Philip B. "Qualitative Anarthrous Predicate Nouns: Mark 15:39 and John 1:1." *JBL* 92 (1973), 75–87.

Hartmann, Gert. "Die Vorlage der Osterberichte in Joh 20." *ZNW* 55 (1964), 197–220.

Horst, P. W. van der. "Can a Book End with *gar*? A Note on Mark XVI.8." *JTS* NF 23 (1972), 121–24.

Iersel, Bas van. "Besuch am Grabe." *Schrift* 7 (1970), 15–17.

Jeremias, Joachim. "Die Drei-Tage-Worte der Evangelien." *Tradition und Glaube. Festgabe für K. G. Kuhn.* Göttingen, 1972.

———. "Die Salbungsgeschichte Mc 14,3–9." *ZNW* 35 (1936), 75–82.

Johnson, Benjamin Arlen. "Empty Tomb Tradition in the Gospel of Peter." *HTR* 59 (1966), 447–48.

Johnson, Sherman E. "The Davidic-Royal Motif in the Gospels." *JBL* 87 (1968), 136–50.

Juel, Donald H. "The Messiah and the Temple: A Study of Jesus' Trial Before the Sanhedrin in the Gospel of Mark." Ph.D. dissertation, Yale University, 1973.

Kee, Howard Clark. "Scripture References and Allusions in Mark 11–16." *SBL Seminar Papers*, 1971. II, 475–502.

Kelber, Werner H. "Mark 14:32–42: Gethsemane." *ZNW* 63 (1972), 166–87.

Kenny, A. "The Transfiguration and the Agony in the Garden." *CBQ* 19 (1957), 444–52.

Kingdon, H. P. "Messiahship and the Crucifixion." *SE* 3, *TU* 88 (1964), 67–86.

Klein, Günter. "Die Verleugnung des Petrus." *ZTK* 58 (1961), 258–328. Reprinted, with postscript, in the author's collected essays *Rekonstruktion und Interpretation*. Munich: Kaiser, 1969.

Klinger, J. "Zagubiona egzegeza dwóch wierszy z Ewangelii Marka 14,51–52." *RocTChAT* 8 (1966), 126–49.

Knox, John. "A Note on Mark 14,51–52." *The Joy of Study*. Edited by Sherman E. Johnson. New York: Macmillan, 1951.

Kosmala, Hans. "The Time of the Cock-Crow." *ASTI* 2 (1963), 118–20.

Kuby, Alfred. "Zur Konzeption des Markus-Evangeliums." *ZNW* 49 (1958), 52–64.

Kuhn, Karl Georg. "Jesus in Gethsemane." *EvT* 12 (1952), 260–85.

Lee, G. M. "Mark 14,72: *epibalōn eklaien*." *Bib* 53 (1972), 411–12.

Légasse, S. "Jésus devant le Sanhédrin. Recherche sur les traditions évangéliques." *RTL* 5 (1974), 170–97.

Lescow, Theodor. "Jesus in Gethsemane." *EvT* 26 (1966), 141–59.

Linnemann, Eta. "Die Verleugnung des Petrus." *ZTK* 63 (1966), 1–32.

———. "Der (wiedergefundene) Markusschluss." *ZTK* 66 (1969), 255–87.

Linton, Olof. "The Trial of Jesus and the Interpretation of Psalm CX." *NTS* 7 (1961), 258–63.

Lövestam, Evald. "Die Frage des Hohenpriesters." *Svensk exegetisk Årsbok* 26 (1961), 93–107.

Lofthouse, W. F. "The Cry of Dereliction." *ExpT* 53 (1942), 188–92.

Lohse, Eduard. *History of the Suffering and Death of Jesus Christ*. Translated by Martin O. Dietrich. Philadelphia: Fortress Press, 1967.

Luz, Ulrich. "Das Geheimnismotiv und die Markinische Christologie." *ZNW* 56 (1965), 9–30.

Luzarraga, J. "Retraducción semítica de *ephobounto* en Mc 16,8." *Bib* 50 (1969), 497–510.

Maccoby, H. Z. "Jesus and Barabbas." *NTS* 16 (1970), 55–60.

Mahoney, A. "A new look at 'The Third Hour' of Mk 15,25." *CBQ* 28 (1966), 292–99.

Mánek, Jindřich. "The Apostle Paul and the Empty Tomb." *NovTest* 2 (1958), 276–80.

Martini, Carlo M. *Il Problema Storico della Risurrezione negli Studi Recenti*. AnGreg 104. Rome: Gregorian University Press, 1959.

Masson, Ch. "Le Reniement de Pierre." *RHPhilRel* 37 (1957), 24–35.

Maurer, Christian. "Knecht Gottes und Sohn Gottes im Passionsbericht des Markusevangeliums." *ZTK* 50 (1953), 1–38.

McArthur, Harvey K. "Mark XIV.62." *NTS* 4 (1958), 156–58.

———. " 'On the Third Day.' " *NTS* 18 (1972), 81–86.

McIndoe, J. H. "The Young Man at the Tomb." *ExpT* 80 (1969), 125.

Meye, Robert P. "Mark 16,8–The Ending of Mark's Gospel." *BR* 14 (1969), 33–43.

———. "Mark's Special Easter Emphasis. About Christ's Resurrection Promise." *ChrTo* 15 (1971), 584–86.

Mohn, Werner. "Gethsemane (Mk 14,32–42)." *ZNW* 64 (1973), 194–208.

Mussner, Franz. "Die Wiederkunft des Menschensohnes nach Markus 13, 24–27 und 14, 61–62." *BiKi* 16 (1961), 105–107.

Nardoni, Enrique. "Por una comunidad libre. La última cena según Mc 14,22–25 y el éxodo." *RBib* 33 (1971), 27–42.

Nauck, Wolfgang. "Die Bedeutung des leeren Grabes für den Glauben an den Auferstandenen." *ZNW* 47 (1956), 243–67.

Neirynck, Frans. "Les Femmes au Tombeau: Étude de la Rédaction Matthéenne (Matt XXVIII:1–10)." *NTS* 15 (1969), 168–90.

Odenkirchen, P. C. " 'Praecedam vos in Galilaeam' (Mc 14,28 par)." *VD* 46 (1968), 193–223.

O'Neill, J. C. "The Silence of Jesus." *NTS* 15 (1969), 153–67.

Ottley, R. R. "*ephobounto gar* Mark XVI 8." *JTS* 27 (1926), 407–409.

Peddinghaus, C. D. "Die Entstehung der Leidensgeschichte." Dissertation, Heidelberg, 1965.

Perrin, Norman. *A Modern Pilgrimage in New Testament Christology.* Philadelphia: Fortress Press, 1974.

Pesch, Rudolf. "Die Verleugnung des Petrus: Eine Studie zu Mk 14, 54, 66–72 (und Mk 14, 26–31)." *Neues Testament und Kirche: Für Rudolf Schnackenburg.* Edited by Joachim Gnilka. Freiburg i. Br./Basel/Vienna: Herder, 1974.

Poniatowski, Z. "Analiza statystyczna ewangelicznego opisu Pasji Jezusa (The Passion Narrative in the Gospel. A Statistical Analysis)." *Studia religioznawcze* 2 (1970), 71–79.

Reedy, Charles J. "Mk 8:31–11:10 and the Gospel Ending." *CBQ* 34 (1972), 188–97.

Reumann, John. "Psalm 22 at the Cross: Lament and Thanksgiving for Jesus Christ." *Interpr* 28 (1974), 39–58.

Riddle, Donald W. "The Martyr Motif in the Gospel According to Mark." *JR* 4 (1924), 397–410.

Rose, A. "L'influence des psaumes sur les annonces et les récits de la Passion et de la Resurrection dans les Évangiles." *OrBibLov* 4 (1962), 297–356.

Ruppert, Lothar. *Jesus als der leidende Gerechte? Der Weg Jesu im Lichte eines alt- und zwischentestamentlichen Motivs.* Stuttgarter Bibelstudien 59 (Stuttgart: Katholisches Bibelwerk, 1972).

———. *Der leidende Gerechte. Eine motivgeschichtliche Untersuchung zum Alten Testament und Zwischentestamentlichen Judentum.* Forschung zur Bibel 5. Würzburg: Echter Verlag, 1972.

———. *Der leidende Gerechte und seine Feinde. Eine Wortfelduntersuchung.* Forschung zur Bibel 6. Würzburg: Echter Verlag, 1973.

Sahlin, Harald. "Zum Verständnis von drei Stellen des Markus-Evangeliums (Mc 4,26–29; 7,18f.; 15,34)." *Bib* 33 (1952), 53–66.

Schelkle, Karl Hermann. *Die Passion Jesu in der Verkündigung des Neuen Testaments.* Heidelberg: F. H. Kerle, 1949.

Schenk, Wolfgang. "Die gnostisierende Deutung des Todes Jesu und ihre kritische Interpretation durch den Evangelisten Markus." *Gnosis und Neues Testament.* Edited by Karl-Wolfgang Tröger. Gütersloh: Gerd Mohn, 1973.

Schenke, Ludger. *Auferstehungsverkündigung und leeres Grab.* Stuttgarter Bibelstudien 33. 2d ed. Stuttgart: Katholisches Bibelwerk, 1969.

———. *Der gekreuzigte Christus.* Stuttgarter Bibelstudien 69. Stuttgart: Katholisches Bibelwerk, 1974.

Schille, Gottfried. "Das Leiden des Herren. Die evangelische Passionstradition und ihr 'Sitz im Leben,'" *ZTK* 52 (1955), 161–205.

———. *Offen für alle Menschen. Redaktionsgeschichtliche Beobachtungen zur Theologie des Markus-Evangeliums.* Stuttgart: Calwer Verlag, 1974.

Schmithals, Walter. "Der Markusschluss, die Verklärungsgeschichte und die Aussendung der Zwölf." *ZTK* 69 (1972), 379–411.

Schneider, Gerhard. "Gab es eine vorsynoptische Szene 'Jesus vor dem Sanhedrium'?" *NovTest* 12 (1970), 22–39.

———. "Jesus vor dem Sanhedrium." *BiLe* 11 (1970), 1–15.

———. *Die Passion Jesu nach den drei ältesten Evangelien.* Munich: Kösel, 1973.

———. "Das Problem einer vorkanonischen Passionserzählung." *BZ* NF 16 (1972), 222–44.

———. "Die Verhaftung Jesu. Traditionsgeschichte von Mk 14, 43–52." *ZNW* 63 (1972), 188–209.

Schrage, Wolfgang. "Das Verständnis des Todes Jesu Christi im Neuen Testament." *Das Kreuz Jesu Christi als Grund des Heils.* Gütersloh: Gerd Mohn, 1967.

Schreiber, Johannes. "Die Christologie des Markusevangeliums." *ZTK* 58 (1961), 154–83.

———. *Die Markuspassion. Wege zur Erforschung der Leidensgeschichte Jesu.* Hamburg: Furche-Verlag, 1969.

———. *Theologie des Vertrauens. Eine redaktionsgeschichtliche Untersuchung des Markusevangeliums.* Hamburg: Furche-Verlag, 1967.

Schubert, Kurt. "Kritik der Bibelkritik. Dargestellt an Hand des Markusberichtes vom Verhör Jesu vor dem Synedrion." *WoWa* 28 (1972), 421–34.

Schweizer, Eduard. "Zur Frage des Messiasgeheimnisses bei Markus." *ZNW* 56 (1965), 1–8.

Scroggs, Robin, ed., W. Kelber, A. Kolenkow, R. Scroggs. "Reflections on the Question: Was There a Pre-Markan Passion Narrative?" *SBL Seminar Papers,* 1971. II, 503–66.

Scroggs, Robin and Groff, Kent I. "Baptism in Mark: Dying and Rising with Christ." *JBL* 92 (1973), 531–48.

Sidersky, D. "La parole suprême de Jésus." *RHR* 103 (1931), 151–54.

Sloyan, Gerard S. *Jesus on Trial. The Development of the Passion Narratives and Their Historical and Ecumenical Implications.* Philadelphia: Fortress Press, 1973.

Smith, M. A. "The Influence of the Liturgies on the New Testament Text of the Last Supper Narratives." *SE 5, TU* 103 (1968), 207–18.

Smith, Robert H. "New and Old in Mark 16,1–8." *CTM* 43 (1972), 518–27.

Snyder, Graydon F. "John 13:16 and the Anti-Petrinism of the Johannine Tradition." *BR* 16 (1971), 5–15.

Stein, Robert H. "A Short Note on Mark XIV.28 and XVI.7." *NTS* 20 (1974), 445–52.

Storch, Rainer. " 'Was soll diese Verschwendung?' Bemerkungen zur Auslegungsgeschichte von Mk 14,4f." *Der Ruf Jesu und die Antwort der Gemeinde. Festschrift für J. Jeremias.* Edited by E. Lohse. Göttingen: Vandenhoeck & Ruprecht, 1970.

Taylor, Vincent. "The Origin of the Markan Passion-Sayings." *NTS* 1 (1955), 159–67.

Temple, S. "The Two Traditions of the Last Supper, Betrayal and Arrest." *NTS* 7 (1961), 77–85.

Trompf, Garry W. "The First Resurrection Appearance and the Ending of Mark's Gospel." *NTS* 18 (1972), 308–30.

Tyson, Joseph B. "The Blindness of the Disciples in Mark." *JBL* 80 (1961), 261–68.

Vanhoye, Albert. "La fuite du jeune homme nu (Mc 14,51–52)." *Bib* 52 (1971), 401–406.

———. "Les récits de la Passion dans les évangiles synoptiques." *Assemblées du Seigneur* 19 (1971), 38–67.

———. "Structure et théologie des récits de la Passion dans les évangiles synoptiques." *NRT* 89 (1967), 135–63.

Vielhauer, Philipp. "Erwägungen zur Christologie des Markusevangeliums." *Aufsätze zum Neuen Testament.* Munich: Kaiser, 1965.

Viering, Fritz, ed. *Zur Bedeutung des Todes Jesu.* 2d ed. Gütersloh: Gerd Mohn, 1967.

Waetjen, Herman C. "The Ending of Mark and the Gospel's Shift in Eschatology." *ASTI* 4 (1965), 114–31.

Weeden, Theodore J. "The Conflict between Mark and His Opponents over Kingdom Theology." *SBL Seminar Papers*, 1973. II, 203–41.

Wilcox, Max. "The Denial-Sequence in Mark XIV.26–31, 66–72." *NTS* 17 (1971), 426–36.

Winter, Paul. "The Marcan Account of Jesus' Trial by the Sanhedrin." *JTS* NS 14 (1963), 94–102.

———. "Marginal Notes on the Trial of Jesus." *ZNW* 50 (1959), 14–33, 221–51.

———. "Markus 14,53b.55–64—Ein Gebilde des Evangelisten." *ZNW* 53 (1962), 260–63.

See also in the front matter of this book the "Key Books and Articles" listed under "Abbreviations."

Indexes

INDEX OF SCRIPTURE REFERENCES

INDEX OF AUTHORS